Advance praise for *One Step Ahead*

"Hedge funds are being punished, and private equity is getting abuse, for things they did not do – merely because the politicians do not understand them. *One Step Ahead* explains in simple language what hedge funds and private equity are all about – and why they should be left alone to manage wealth and create wider prosperity."

Eamonn Butler – Director, Adam Smith Institute

"This is a book for people looking for deep understanding and careful analysis, rather than empty sloganeering – and yet it will be immediately accessible to the average reader, which is a remarkable accomplishment."

Robert VerBruggen – *National Review*

"Bringing shadow banking out of the shadows, *One Step Ahead* sheds light on alternative invest-ment funds and their role in the economy. Spangler, who understands the nuts and bolts of hedge funds and private equity in the US and European contexts, gives the general public knowledge, which is power, to grasp their role in our economic future. The lines that distin-guish one alternative investment fund from another are anything but bright. *One Step Ahead* identifies some growing trends among hedge funds and private equity funds and the regulatory hurdles ahead for such funds due to new legislation, and outlines why we should care."

Noreen Clancy – RAND Corporation

"Like a series of exceptional *New Yorker* articles, *One Step Ahead* provides a detailed and engaging insider's view of the seemingly-secret world of alternatives from every perspective - birth to death, rumor and myth to simple truths, and whys and wherefores. Practitioners and investors alike should get their hands on this book ASAP."

Karyn Polak – Chief Counsel, PNC Financial Services

"*One Step Ahead* is an excellent insight into the structure and workings of the 'pointy end of capitalism', the hedge fund and private equity industry. From a true insider, *One Step Ahead* introduces us to the main players, the rules under which they play, and the politics of how those rules come about. Written in a very readable and accessible style, this book should be read by anyone wanting to learn more about this important and politically contentious sector."

Professor Julia Black – London School of Economics

"Timothy Spangler, with *One Step Ahead*, has presented a long-overdue synthesis of the economic, legal and political issues surrounding the world of hedge funds and private equity. Spangler fills a gap in the literature and provides the right balance of technical detail and high-altitude perspective needed by investors, lawyers, and policy-makers looking for the big picture in this field."

Thomas Grant – University of Cambridge

"A lucid, inside account of how hedge and private equity funds work and their economic and social utility, with wider reflections upon the context of the political economy. A demystifying read for the intelligent layman."

Dr. Iris H. Chiu – University College London

"When so much of the debate around our financial system is clouded in misunderstanding, it is refreshing to read such an engaging and accessible account as *One Step Ahead*. By setting out the facts clearly and cleanly, Timothy Spangler goes beyond the jargon and the headlines to give readers an accurate portrayal of the role of private equity and hedge funds in modern capitalism."

Mark Florman – Chief Executive Officer, British Private Equity and Venture Capital Association

"*One Step Ahead* expertly combines an insider's understanding of behind-closed-doors industry dynamics with an everyman's ability to tell the story in a way that a Main Street reader will understand and appreciate. By focusing on the 'pointy end' of modern capitalism, Spangler tells a tale that is relevant and educational to us all."

Robert Diamond – Fernbrook Partners

"*One Step Ahead* opens up the opaque world of hedge and private equity funds with precision in an accessible way for the non-specialist. Complex technical issues are conveyed concisely but never over-simplified ... A fascinating read and some surprising, sometimes shocking, conclusions."

Giles Adu – Managing Partner, Brook Street Partners

"Finally a book that sheds a knowledgeable light on the private equity and hedge fund worlds. Long demonized by the media, Timothy Spangler has humanized these often secretive industry sectors all the while revealing just how essential they are for nursing sick companies back to health and bringing rationality to markets."

John Tamny – Forbes Opinions and RealClearMarkets.com

"The ravages of the financial crisis, and the bruising Presidential campaign in 2012 for which it served as backdrop, have catapulted the alternative investments industry into the public consciousness. Spangler provides a comprehensive account of the issues surrounding the industry, invaluable to anyone wanting to cut through the political point scoring and amorphous resentment that have characterized the debate to date."

Solomon Teague – Financial Journalist

"*One Step Ahead* gives a clear, practical and realistic insight into the private equity industry today, in contrast to the pre-conceptions, clichés and 'sound-bites' about private equity that have been sensationalized in the popular press ... this book provides an important voice in seeking to balance the political debate where the industry itself has struggled to do so."

Aristide Stavropoulos – Ridgeway Capital LLP

"Timothy Spangler has written a masterful and comprehensive overview of hedge funds and private equity pre- and post-crisis. Very well written and accessible, *One Step Ahead* is required reading for anyone wanting to understand the challenges and limitations of regulation and enforcement."

Alistair Macnaughton – Chief Legal Officer, Mulvaney Capital Management Limited

ONE STEP AHEAD

Private Equity and Hedge Funds After the Global Financial Crisis

Timothy Spangler

ONEWORLD

A Oneworld Book

Published by Oneworld Publications 2013

Copyright © Timothy Spangler 2013

The moral right of Timothy Spangler to be identified as the
Author of this work has been asserted by him
in accordance with the Copyright,
Designs and Patents Act 1988

ISBN 978-1-78074-295-3
eISBN 978-1-78074-296-0

Typeset by Cenveo Publisher Services, India
Cover design by vaguelymemorable.com
Printed and bound in Great Britain by CPI Group (UK) Ltd, Croydon, CR0 4YY

Oneworld Publications
10 Bloomsbury Street
London
WC1B 3SR
England

Stay up to date with the latest books,
special offers, and exclusive content from
Oneworld with our monthly newsletter

Sign up on our website
www.oneworld-publications.com

For my wife, who only after a few years of marriage realized the important difference between a hedge fund lawyer and a hedge fund manager, and for any young women of marriageable age today who consider this distinction significant.

Contents

CONTENTS

ONE STEP
AHEAD

Prologue

As a result of the global financial crisis, much ill feeling remains toward Wall Street, the investment banks and those individuals who profit from short-term movements in the financial markets. As the crisis drags on into 2013, more questions are being raised about how the modern financial system actually works. Identifying "who does what" when it comes to complex derivative securities or the takeover of well-established, brand name companies by faceless financiers seems much more difficult today than a generation ago.

Over the last decade, private equity and hedge funds have entered the mainstream public consciousness after many years of profitably operating in the arcane shadows of the economy. Although originally developed in the United States, these funds quickly expanded across the Atlantic to establish a base of operation in London. As they became more and more successful, their techniques, tools and structures rapidly spread to financial centers around the world.

The financial meltdown that commenced in earnest during the autumn of 2008 soon led many observers, commentators and regulators to question more closely what it is that private equity and hedge funds actually do. Many of the concerns that were identified, though, require a deeper understanding of the structure and operation of these funds in order to properly evaluate them. Without this broader context, effective criticism simply isn't possible.

In a single weekend in October 2011, however, protesters inspired by the Occupy Wall Street movement held demonstrations in over 900 cities around the world. Their goal was to draw attention to corporate greed and massive cuts in government spending. Images of these protests filled television screens and social media websites for the weeks that followed.

Unfortunately, the lingering financial crisis is about more than just greed. This is why it has been so difficult to understand precisely what is broken and how it can actually be fixed. But talking about greed and making signs about greed and chanting slogans about greed is much easier and much more compelling than actually trying to understand the complex web of linkages between monetary policy and asset values, or how best to oversee the diverse operations of cross-border financial conglomerates, let alone how nimble, entrepreneurial financial firms such as private equity and hedge funds are able to earn the eye-watering profits that they do.

Marching behind a banner that says, "We demand the forgiveness of all debts," has a certain rhetorical conciseness, even if it is an utterly impossible and unattainable goal.

After two years of Tea Party protests in the United States that tapped into popular anger at excessive government borrowing and spending that appeared fatally out of control, the Occupy movement demonstrated that popular anger could also be marshalled by the Left to attack Wall Street and the global financial infrastructure, even if only for a limited period of time.

While the thrust of the Occupy movement was to attempt a critique of the economic superstructure within which we live, the focus of the earlier Tea Party movement was to voice concern over a government that has grown morbidly obese and ineffective on high taxes and incompetent bureaucrats unable to adequately address the mounting problems that the country faces.

These two points are not mutually exclusive.

Americans and Britons were notably quiet in the initial months after the financial crisis first made itself known in autumn 2008.

Despite the near collapse of many parts of the international financial system, and unprecedented levels of governmental intervention into Western economies, for many the events on Wall Street and in the City of London were far removed from their day-to-day lives. It took until 2010 for the Tea Party to gain sufficient momentum in the United States to break through into the public consciousness and until 2011 for the Occupy movement to enter the public stage.

Millions of people are angry, and many millions more are simply frustrated. At the beginning of 2012, it was estimated that over 20 percent of US residential mortgages were under water and almost 15 percent of Americans used food stamp benefits. Statistics in Britain and other European countries were equally bleak. As their attentions turns to out-of-touch governments and moneyed elite that they find hard to understand, Americans and Britons and millions of others are beginning to ask questions about a new generation of independent money managers who have established themselves as key players in the financial markets over the past four decades.

Walk down Fifth Avenue or Knightsbridge in 2013 and it is eminently clear that some people, at least, are still doing very well despite the economic upheaval. As a result, the focus on private equity and hedge funds continues to intensify. Unfortunately, many people still lack a deeper and more nuanced understanding of what these funds really do, and why.

A general public that no longer trusts business and finance will have tremendous difficulties relating to the sponsors and managers of private equity and hedge funds. These individuals operate in niche areas of finance that intersect with traditional investment banking and commercial banking firms, but their mandates differ significantly from stockbrokers, securities underwriters, mergers and acquisition (M&A) advisers and mortgage lenders.

The role of investment advisers and fund managers has been an established part of the world of finance for centuries. In that regard, private equity and hedge funds are clearly not unprecedented. They are not a recent phenomenon. Those with money have long recognized that the fact they amassed significant sums in the past is no guarantee that they have the knowledge and acumen to invest it wisely and effectively in the future. As a result, talented individuals have long established themselves as trusted advisers who can assist in selecting the best use for these pools of capital which can provide for lucrative investment returns while at the same time seeking to maintain some level of security for the capital.

In fact, since the end of World War II, retail investment funds have replaced direct stock market investments as the most important way in which "Mom and Pop" investors access the securities markets. Known as "mutual funds" in the United States, "unit trusts" in the United Kingdom and "UCITS funds" in Europe, these retail funds now comprise an important part of many families' retirement savings.

In the simplest terms, private equity and hedge funds can be seen as different species of this same genus of "investment funds." Unlike retail funds, however, these funds are limited by law to sophisticated, non-retail investors. Uncle Edgar in Topeka and Aunt Edna in Balham are prohibited by their respective governments from putting their savings in these vehicles because the risk is deemed to be too high. These funds are, therefore, strictly off limits.

The sustained success of private equity and hedge funds in the last two decades, however, has led to more and more coverage of their investment activities in the mainstream press. As a result, more and more questions are now being asked about what they do, how they do it and why they have been largely free from direct regulation in the past.

Despite the passage of five years, we are still coming to terms with the events of 2008, and few consensuses exist on either their causes or their long-term effects. Given the increased prominence of private equity and hedge funds recently, it is wholly unsurprising that critics are now turning their attention to these "alternative" investment funds. Too often, however, the drive to further regulate these funds and limit their potential scope of operation is occurring in a vacuum devoid of detailed knowledge of their structure and evolution.

The first thing that strikes you now when you re-read the "Declaration" issued in autumn 2011 by the Occupy protestors assembled in Zuccotti Park in downtown Manhattan is how little of it actually relates to Wall Street. Many of the "demands" inserted into the manifesto drafted by the various grassroots organizations behind the protests have no relation to how Wall Street functions, or to the issues that have arisen since the Credit Crunch led America (and much of the developed world) into this Great Recession.

Following the age-old agitprop dictum that no good popular uprising should go to waste, it seems that a variety of other concerns, such as student loans, public employee pensions, animal rights and genetically modified food, were the principal concerns of many well-intentioned Occupiers. The complexities and intricacies of Wall Street and the City of London were largely ignored, except for a few cursory statements about bank bailouts and excessive compensation that were stapled on to their wish list.

The initial choice of venue – the financial district in Manhattan – gave the protestors a chance to air their long-standing grievances in a location imbued with deep significance. But frustratingly little of what was said, sung, chanted and painted on signs was actually directed at the way the global financial systems currently operate and how these practices could be improved. Few men and women who work on Wall Street or in the City of London would make the claim that modern financial markets have achieved some variant of divine perfection. These markets exist as a result of human endeavors and, as a result, they are subject to human frailties and flaws. There is always room for improvements.

The possibility that a generation of students and young people would remember for the rest of their lives the personal misery and frustration that has arisen in the last five years due to the near-collapse of our financial markets is actually very encouraging. As citizens and savers, we each have a responsibility to ourselves, our families and our country to have an opinion on the current state of our financial system and its regulation – even when the details of credit default swaps and high yield bonds lead to fits of sudden-onset narcolepsy!

Ultimately, though, an attempt at a direct and informed critique of the operation of the global financial system generally, and the role of private equity and hedge funds specifically, was frustratingly absent from the Occupy demonstrations.

The process of connecting savers with borrowers, and providers of capital with users of capital, requires intermediation. This need for intermediares creates a need for savings banks, stock brokers, brokerage firms, mutual funds and investment banks. Otherwise, it would be impossible to put Uncle Edgar's or Aunt Edna's pension contributions into the hands of the corporate treasurers of either Apple or Facebook, or the public coffers of various local, state and federal agencies who fund their operations with regular bond issuances.

Without such intermediaries, Uncle Edgar's or Aunt Edna's money would remain in an old coffee tin, where it would slowly lose its buying power when faced with the steady erosion of inflation. Simple laws of financial thermodynamics are at work all around us. Money at rest loses value over time. Money in motion provides the possibility of gains in excess of inflation, but also the risk of potential losses.

What we call "Wall Street" is a significant component of this intermediation infrastructure. Unless we move away from a monetized economy, and opt in favor of bartering on a scale never seen before, then the intermediaries must remain. The question then becomes what to do with these intermediaries, and the risks they pose to the rest of us.

The financial markets require regulation. Thousands of government employees around the world have as their direct responsibility the policing of banks, stockbrokers, hedge fund managers and pension trustees in their countries. The adoption in the United States of the Dodd-Frank Wall Street Reform and Consumer Protection Act (known as "Dodd-Frank") in 2010 and the ongoing restructuring of the financial regulatory regime in the United Kingdom demonstrate the belief that more needed to be done to keep regulation up to date in a rapidly evolving industry. Today, however, it remains unclear what the net effect of these numerous changes and "improvements" will actually be.

There will always be valid criticism that can be made about any industry, and Wall Street is certainly no exception. To the extent that the demonstrators in Zuccotti Park would have coalesced around a few convincing, compelling themes directly relevant to improving the financial infrastructure and ensuring that Wall Street is successful at spurring economic growth for the United States and its citizens (as well as in other developed and developing countries around the world), then they could very well have had a meaningful and lasting impact.

Since the Occupiers' demands remained frustratingly vague and ambiguous, distracted by an amorphous assault on rhetorical bogeymen and unable to propose clear and specific criticisms, then it was always highly unlikely that they would have anything like the impact that they desired and deserved.

Just "wanting change" is never enough.

The Occupy movement, however, was simply the most public display of concern and hatred that remains widespread to this day.

For example, in the autumn of 2011, a group of students at Yale University turned up at a recruitment event for the leading Wall Street investment bank, Morgan Stanley, which was being held near their campus. They were not dressed in blue power suits, tastefully complemented by a Hermes tie or a single string of

Mikimoto pearls. Instead, their purpose was to protest alleged Wall Street improprieties, and to encourage their fellow students to seek employment opportunities elsewhere. Despite the protesters' sincere and heartfelt pleas, the eager job applicants who assembled in New Haven that evening were simply following in the footsteps of countless prior Yale alumni who did exceedingly well on Wall Street, including, among others, Stephen Schwarzman, the founder of private equity titan Blackstone Group.

Emotions were so high at this time that some critics even went so far as to compare these recruitment events, which brought leading investment banks and financial firms to leading universities, to on-campus recruitment during the Vietnam War by the American military, in the form of Reserve Officers' Training Corps programs. The willingness to make such comparisons demonstrates how dramatically perceptions of the financial industry have changed since the global financial crisis began. Indifference and ignorance has for many been replaced by suspicion and anger. Around the same time, at Stanford University, an online campaign entitled "Stop the Brain Drain" sought to convince students that they should say no to the "dark side" of lucrative careers in high finance.

If Wall Street (and the private equity and hedge funds that have evolved in recent years) in fact depends on human capital as much as financial capital, as many of its champions have claimed over the years, then a lack of the best and brightest young men and women could eventually suck the oxygen out of the financial markets.

But where else would these talented, numerate and highly competitive graduates actually go?

It is easy to talk about the contest between "Wall Street" and "Main Street." It is a simple analogy and like most simple analogies, it can be very compelling.

When we witness a catastrophic event, such as the collapse of Lehman Brothers in September 2008 at the virtual epicenter of the global financial crisis, there is a deep-seated instinct to see those events as occurring in a completely different system of rules, concepts and language than what applies in your own neighborhood to a family desperately trying to refinance their home or a small business owner attempting to fund expansion at a time when his or her competitors are gobbling up market share.

But they are related in an intricate and insoluble way.

It is an oversimplification to say that Wall Street must exist for the purpose of serving Main Street. The problems that Main Street faces could be solved locally, without recourse to the financial markets that Wall Street and other financial centers orchestrate. Investors, savers, borrowers and issuers turn to these financial centers because they are in search of returns that are higher, or financings that are less expensive, than they can obtain in their own local communities.

Operating as a middleman, investment banks earn lucrative profits by matchmaking investors with potential investments. As more money is funnelled into the financial markets, there are more opportunities to trade in these investments and earn further profits based on which way the market moves over the short, medium and long term. Private equity and hedge funds are formed to identify and profit from precisely these opportunities.

After the early, and most spectacular, failures produced by the global financial crisis began to recede in our memories, the public conversation eventually returned to the concept of "fairness." In particular, more and more of the debate seemed to focus on a perceived lack of fairness in the context of excessive pay being earned by those operating at the highest rung of the financial services industries. Politicians on the Left, for example, have never been especially reluctant to play the fairness card when in search of further tax revenue, and the tax increase brokered in the closing days of 2012 between President Barack Obama and the US Congress was driven primarily by this desire for a "fairer" allocation of tax burden.

The great linguistic contribution of the Occupy movement – and perhaps its only lasting contribution – was mainstreaming the propaganda terms "the 1 percent" and "the 99 percent." On both sides of the Atlantic, as economies today remain fragile and unemployment stubbornly high, identifying with the 99 percent has resonated with many earners and savers who are having difficulty navigating the new financial landscape.

Eyes are increasingly turning to the so-called 1 percent. What is the proper role of the ultra-wealthy in addressing these issues? What should we expect from the private equity and hedge fund professionals who earn large sums of money from their investment acumen?

Interestingly, simply being wealthy does not appear to be enough to earn someone the negative sentiment that is directed at the 1 percent by the Occupiers and their sympathizers. It is curious how the bright lights of media coverage that follow around a lottery winner do not invoke the vitriol and judgmental language that a large Wall Street bonus does. This is particularly true if one gives any thought to the shockingly low payout rates of lotteries and how they disproportionately prey on the wallets of the working poor.

Is it right that money won by sheer luck from gambling should be considered morally superior to money that was earned through work? What is it about the manner in which the 1 percent are commonly believed to have acquired their fortune that is giving these critics so much concern?

It is increasingly difficult to find someone who is agnostic about private equity and hedge funds.

Many in the financial industry champion these investment vehicles as a means to deliver absolute returns, regardless of which way the market is moving on any given day, while providing other market participants with much needed liquidity.

Critics, however, have become louder and louder in recent years. A number of hedge fund blow-ups have raised concerns over the consequences of speculation on the "real economy." Names of now-defunct firms such as Long-Term Capital Management and Amaranth Advisors have become bywords for the possible systemic risks that we could face if a hedge fund is big enough and its bets are wrong enough. With the presidential campaign of Mitt Romney in 2012, private equity was examined under the microscope like never before. Both Republicans and Democrats used stump speeches and debating platforms as a means to attack private equity funds and their managers as job-destroyers who profit from the infliction of widespread financial misery.

Private equity and hedge funds operate within the financial markets alongside the large institutions that populate Wall Street and the City of London. However, their entrepreneurial nature distinguishes them in a number of very important respects from investment banks, stockbrokers and other firms of intermediaries. Private equity and hedge funds are *not* middlemen. They actually buy and sell financial assets rather than simply facilitating transactions by other market participants. They take risks in a way that traditional intermediares avoid (at least intentionally).

Even though these funds seek to make profits regardless of how the markets are moving on any given day, they are still impacted, directly and indirectly, by the same sentiments that affect economic life on Main Street. The accumulation of millions of individual decisions to buy this product instead of that product, or to hire one service over another service, necessarily shifts the value of financial instruments over time. As private equity and hedge funds back one company or industry over others, they are open to the possibility of stratospheric profit and catastrophic loss. In recent years, it has become clear that the same fund can suffer such profits and losses in quick succession, as one set of decisions goes very well, but another set of decisions goes quite poorly.

Many experts and commentators feel that a healthy, vibrant Wall Street is essential to a robust economy. Few private equity firms and hedge fund managers would disagree.

In April 2012, President Obama signed into law the acronym-friendly Jump-start Our Business Start-ups Act (or "JOBS Act" for short). Intended to undo many of the impediments to initial public offerings IPOs that were the unforeseen consequences of the Sarbanes-Oxley Act, originally passed in 2002, the JOBS Act seeks to significantly revamp the way in which private capital is raised in the United States. The intended beneficiaries of this liberalization are so-called "emerging growth companies," whose IPOs and resulting jobs and economic growth federal lawmakers want to expedite.

However, private investment vehicles, such as hedge funds, private equity funds, venture capital funds and mezzanine funds, also benefit from the JOBS Act. These funds are now able to more easily obtain money from "accredited investors," who include those individuals who earn more than $200,000 per year or have more than $1,000,000 in net worth, excluding their family home.

Until now, it has been necessary for anyone approaching prospective investors in the United States to purchase privately-placed securities to have a substantial pre-existing relationship in place in order to actually discuss a particular investment opportunity with them or provide them with marketing materials. Post-JOBS Act, anyone can be approached as long as it is determined before they invest that the individual in question is actually an accredited investor.

What could this mean in practice for private equity and hedge funds seeking more capital from new sources?

Perhaps full-page advertisements in a widely circulated daily newspaper, or *GQ* magazine, or *Sports Illustrated*? Maybe commercials during the Super Bowl, or during the sombre Sunday morning talk shows, such as "Face the Nation" or "Meet the Press"? What about mass mailings to everyone in the state who bought a Mercedes-Benz or a Rolex watch last year? All of the above are now fair game!

As private equity and hedge funds continue to enter mainstream life in the United States, the United Kingdom and around the world, it becomes more and more important for all of us to have a clear understanding of what it is that they really do, who benefits from their successes and who is at risk from their losses. These funds and the firms that manage them are too important to ignore or to explain away with simplistic and shallow rhetoric.

In the following pages, the story of how private equity and hedge funds operate in the modern economy will be laid out, together with insights into how they are structured, staffed and sold to investors.

These funds have been with us for several decades and can be seen to have evolved naturally to provide services much in demand from institutional and other sophisticated investors. However, it has only been in the last few years that these funds – and their often highly remunerated managers – have broken into wider public attention.

As a result, there are still many misconceptions and biases about them that fill the mainstream media. Only by stripping these inaccuracies away can we fashion a useful and compelling portrait of these financial entrepreneurs. Once we have done this, we can then start to form a view on what is the best approach for integrating these funds into our financial, economic and political lives.

But first, an aesthetic question is now in order. What do poets, those unelected legislators of the world, think about private equity and hedge funds?

Fortunately, we do not have to rummage through countless Quatro-size pages of free verse and labored sonnets to find this answer. Instead, we can look to a scandal that recently enveloped a leading British literary prize, and subsequently reached newspapers and media reports around the world.

In 2011, to great media fanfare, two well-known poets, Alice Oswald and John Kinsella, withdrew their names from consideration for the Poetry Book Society's prestigious T.S. Elliot Prize. The reason? The prize that year was sponsored by Aurum Funds, a hedge fund, which donated money when the Society lost its public grant due to cuts in the British budget that were a consequence of austerity measures.

As you would expect from a poet, Kinsella was not at a loss for words. When asked why he withdrew his name from consideration, he pithily referred to hedge funds as the "very pointy end of capitalism."

The JOBS Act is opening the door for more wealthy, experienced investors in the United States to put their money to work with private equity and hedge funds at capitalism's "very pointy end." These new investors join the hundreds of thousands of investors around the world who have begun allocating money to these alternative funds in recent years. Some of these investors will be rewarded, others may lose significant sums, but that pointy end of capitalism is a necessary component that allows the rest of the economy to operate effectively and efficiently.

There is no need either to demonize or romanticize private equity and hedge funds. Capitalism's pointy end is where they must operate in order to uncover those lucrative returns for their investors.

Post-JOBS Act, President Obama and the US Congress are placing responsibility for these investment decisions squarely in the hands of interested investors. As a result, prospective investors in private equity and hedge funds must dedicate the necessary time and attention before they invest in order to ensure that they do not end up sticking this "pointy end" into their own eye.

It is to this "pointy end," therefore, that we now turn.

PART ONE

WHAT WE TALK ABOUT WHEN WE TALK ABOUT PRIVATE EQUITY AND HEDGE FUNDS

1: THE POINTY END OF CAPITALISM

A Short Introduction to Private Equity and Hedge Funds Without Charts or Graphs

Hedge funds, private equity funds and other kinds of investment vehicles help to dispose risk and add liquidity.
Timothy F. Geithner, President of the Federal Reserve Bank of New York, October 18, 2005

You've seen very, very dramatic enforcement actions already by the enforcement authorities across the US government, and I'm sure you're going to see more to come. You should stay tuned for that.
Timothy F. Geithner, US Secretary of Treasury, October 14, 2011

Perhaps no single building in the world is as much a monument to the rise of private equity and hedge funds as 9 West 57th Street in New York.

Home to private equity giants (KKR & Co. LP and Apollo Global Management LLC), rising stars (Silver Lake Partners) and start-ups (Lightyear Capital and Sycamore Ventures), as well as leading hedge fund managers (Och-Ziff Capital Management Group LLC), this office tower provides an enviable home to many of the most successful practitioners of alternative investing, or at least those willing to pay $200 a square foot for the privilege.

Owned by real estate tycoon Sheldon Solow, and identifiable at some distance at street level by the iconic red "9" located in front of the building, the office tower block has an impressive history. So high-profile is the building and its tenants that when a power outage occurred and the elevators failed, *The New York Times* quickly reported about "private equity deal makers" who were "forced to hoof it up as many as twenty flights of stairs – twenty flights!"

On a cool autumn afternoon, midtown Manhattan looks and feels significantly different from the historic home of American financial capitalism that is located further south in the downtown area surrounding Wall Street. Just a short walk from Park Avenue and the traditional homes of New York's aristocracy, the tenants of 9 West 57th Street clearly don't need to be in New York. Many of them could just as easily be operating from offices in Greenwich, Connecticut or a designer loft in Tribeca. They could be staring at Bloomberg screens or reviewing portfolio company spreadsheets on a yacht floating just off a picturesque beach in the Seychelles or at their ski chalet in Corchaval.

Unlike the older parts of the financial industry that grew up adjacent to, or in ready walking distance from, a stock exchange or a central bank, private equity and hedge funds have found their footing and taken their rightful place in the current financial hierarchy at a time when technology has freed them from both physical locations and the need for "safety in numbers." Perhaps that is part of the reason why a growing number of people in positions of influence and power have begun to express concerns about these new financial entrepreneurs. Perhaps their short histories and small, discreet offices, which seem slightly out of place when compared with their ability to influence events in the financial markets, cause a certain amount of unease.

When you are standing in front of a building housing a bulge-bracket investment bank, such as Merrill Lynch, Morgan Stanley or Goldman Sachs, or a financial powerhouse, such as Citibank, JP Morgan, UBS or Deutsche Bank, you know very clearly whose headquarters you are loitering in front of, with a double skinny latte in your hand. Regardless of whether you happen to be in New York, London, Frankfurt, Tokyo or Hong Kong, these firms are very keen to let you know, in no uncertain terms, "Here we are!"

The indifference of private equity and hedge fund firms to public acknowledgement and popularity, at least until very recently, is strikingly different. In the face of this aloofness, in part driven by regulatory restrictions and the exclusively non-retail nature of their investors, these funds must now answer mounting questions about who they are and what it is that they actually do.

To begin at the beginning, a fund is an answer to a question.

This question will typically involve how to connect people with talent, but insufficient money, with people with money, but insufficient talent, in order to allow the former to make investments on behalf of the latter. Simple enough. Whether the fund in question is a mutual fund for retail investors, a retirement fund for employees of a particular company or government department, a film fund looking to finance a slate of motion pictures, or a real estate fund planning to buy apartment buildings for university students, the same basic commercial logic applies. And it applies to private equity and hedge funds just as well.

In an ideal world, each investor who desired the services of a particular investment adviser would have enough money to entice this adviser to take his or her money and manage it subject to individually negotiated parameters, customized to fit the investor's particular needs. The investment objective and remuneration for such an account would be determined based on the requirements of both parties. This, however, is not an ideal world.

Many investors, unfortunately, lack the sums of money required to meet typical account size minimums set by established and proven investment advisers, which can start at $25 million. Funds, therefore, are created as a means to aggregate these individual sums of money into a single pool, which can be managed efficiently and effectively. Each investor in the fund is entitled to a portion of the proceeds from the fund in proportion to the amount of money they initially contributed, less any expenses and fees provided to the fund manager.

Through a fund, the professional services of an investment adviser can be provided to a large number of prospective clients, so long as all agree that they are pursuing similar investment objectives. In order to provide these services, an intermediary vehicle is placed between an investment manager, on the one hand, and a group of potentially disparate participants, on the otherhand. The vehicle serves both as a means of pooling the investors' money and as a single client for the investment adviser.

The use of funds provides access for the individuals and institutions with smaller sums to invest to investment advisers who would not otherwise be commercially motivated to take them on as clients. Additionally, these vehicles provide investment advisers with administrative efficiencies where multiple clients wish to retain the firm to provide substantially similar services.

It is probably worthwhile making a few observations about the modern private equity and hedge fund industries before going into too much more detail about how these funds are structured and operated. Because of their private nature, there are no generally accessible central repositories for information on these funds. This has historically made rigorous analysis about the size, number and activities of private equity and hedge funds more difficult to conduct, at least when compared to the wealth of publicly reported information available on banks, insurance companies, brokerage houses and other financial firms. As a result, for those eager to uncover a little more information about these funds and their managers, the best sources of data are often either trade associations or private commercial firms who have been able to accumulate enough information upon which to make reasonable estimates.

In the case of private equity funds, it is estimated that close to $3 trillion dollars are invested in these funds, with just over 60 percent of new funds launched by managers based in the United States (50 percent) and the United Kingdom (11 percent). In the case of hedge funds, it is estimated that there are approximately 6,800 hedge funds in existence, managing over $2 trillion in assets. The majority of hedge fund managers are based in the United

States, with the United Kingdom being the next largest country. Estimates for 2013 show continued growth for both asset classes.

Clearly these are significant industries, which have grown up quickly in the last few decades. Perhaps most surprising is the relatively small amount of independent research and academic work that has been attempted on these funds, at least until very recently. One might be forgiven for expecting that these industries would have been the focus of extensive research and analysis by leading experts and research universities around the world. In reality, academics have shown surprisingly little interest in uncovering the truth behind the rumors and accusations and public relations banter that surround private equity and hedge funds. As a result, the debate has largely been left to partisans.

Are private equity and hedge funds "mysterious" and "controversial"? Are they "inherently evil?"

Periodically, stories bubble up in the mainstream press that paint these funds in a poor light. Unfortunately, both critics and champions of alternative funds attempt to reduce complex financial transactions into simple language. In doing so, important details are inevitably lost and the search for meaningful insights is thwarted.

A quick perusal of recent newspaper headlines makes it clear that hedge funds are squarely on the radar of a wider cross section of society than ever before. They present hedge funds as an opportunity ("Good at Chess? A Hedge Fund May Want to Hire You" or "Pitching the Hedge Fund Masters") or a threat ("Big British Hedge Fund Takes Aim at the States"), as a potential force for good ("Hedge Fund Chief Takes Major Role in Philanthropy") or a potential force for evil ("Hedge Fund Manager Gets 60 Years for Fraud"), or simply as an odd source of humor and diversion ("Hedge Fund Hippies").

But what does an actual, real life hedge fund really do?

Hedge funds have been described as "mutual funds on steroids." This is not an entirely unhelpful first impression. If mutual funds take risks on what stocks will go up and currency exchange rates will go down, hedge funds take very, very big risks. Unsurprisingly, the individuals taking these risks are celebrated and admired when their bets pay off. The roll call of great hedge fund managers includes many names that are becoming more familiar to casual readers of mainstream newspapers and magazines: Arthur Samberg, Paul Tudor Jones, Philip Falcone, Steven Cohen and Paul Singer.

Are hedge fund managers really the smartest people around? This is an alluring, but obviously quite futile, question. Regardless of whether they are or aren't, they are still human. They are capable of making mistakes, and many do. Interestingly, like professional athletes, often the heights reached early in a career will not be seen again as the years go by.

Each year, many new hedge funds are launched in the hope of attaining the success and recognition of the giants in the industry. In 2012, for example, new start-up hedge funds came to market focusing on a diverse range of investment strategies, including FMG Mongolia Fund (emerging markets), Context BH Partners LP (equity long/short), Citizen Entertainment Fund Ltd (fixed income), Ancora Merger Arbitrage Fund LP (merger arbitrage) and 36 South Black Eyrar Fund (volatility trading). There are now even firms which are dedicated solely to identifying new managers and backing them in their early days with significant early investments. Known as "seeders," firms such as IMQubator and Reservoir Capital have had great success at picking the next generation of star hedge fund managers. Notably, IMQubator is ultimately backed by APG, the Dutch pension fund, a significant institutional investor.

In addition to single-strategy hedge funds that may invest in Japanese equities or high-yield bonds of technology companies, there are also funds whose sole purpose is to invest in other funds. Known as funds of funds, firms such as Grosvenor Capital Management, Lyxor Asset Management, K2 Advisors, Pacific Alternative Asset Management Company and Financial Risk Management have received billions of dollars from investors in order to assemble diversified portfolios of underlying hedge funds.

Their clients simply need to write a single check to gain access to a collection of funds selected and overseen by their teams of experts. Taking the first step toward including hedge funds in your multibillion investment portfolio couldn't be easier for the institutional investor with the courage and wherewithal to embrace alternative investments. Or so it would seem at first.

The actual term "hedge fund" is notoriously difficult to define with any precision.

In part, this is due to the derogatory manner in which the phrase is now often used. At its broadest, "hedge fund" can refer to all unregulated investment vehicles not otherwise categorizable as "private equity funds" or "real estate funds." An overly narrow definition might settle on those funds that engage in highly leveraged trading strategies which utilize short selling or complex derivatives. Neither approach is particularly helpful for the informed layperson eager to learn more about their motivations and activities.

It would be more useful, perhaps, to simply describe certain of their key features and establish a working definition from there. Hedge funds constitute private pools of capital, with investors meeting certain net worth or sophistication requirements. Unregulated by the US Securities and Exchange Commission (SEC), the UK Financial Conduct Authority (FCA) or other relevant regulators, hedge funds are not subject to the limitations and restrictions imposed on their public fund brethren, such as retail mutual funds in the United States or authorized unit trusts in the United Kingdom.

Hedge funds generally invest in publically listed securities and derivative instruments based on such securities. The strategies followed by these funds can be categorized in a number of ways. One possible set of groupings would include: "long/short," which combines long positions with short sales; "event driven," which seeks to identify the likelihood of certain corporate transactions; "relative value," which seeks to exploit pricing discrepancies that arise between securities; and "tactical trading," which identifies and follows macro-economic and other trends in various markets. Importantly, new strategies are being conceived of every day, as bright young men and women discover unique trading opportunities that arise from the day's headlines.

A few generalizations can also be made about the economics of a hedge fund. It is common for these funds to charge a performance fee, based on the success they have pursuing their investment strategy, in addition to an asset-based management fee, based on the amount of money provided by investors. Also, the capacity constraints imposed by certain investment strategies mean a limit may exist on how much capital can be employed by a particular hedge fund without negatively impacting its returns and, thereby, the lucrative performance fee accruing to the fund manager.

Structurally, hedge funds may be set up either onshore (i.e. in the market in which the investors are located) or offshore (i.e. in a different market). They make use of either tax transparent entities, such as limited partnerships, or tax exempt entities, such as companies established in jurisdictions where broad tax derogations are possible. The most common offshore jurisdictions are no doubt the Cayman Islands, located in the warm waters of the Caribbean. Hedge funds are typically open-ended. This means that they issue and redeem units or shares directly with investors on a regular basis, based on the net asset value of the units or shares on a particular day. The mutual funds and unit trusts sold to Uncle Edgar and Aunt Edna are also open-ended, allowing retail investors to move money in and out when needed. By contrast, the units or shares of closed-ended funds (such as a private equity fund) are not eligible for interim liquidity. As a result, they must either be held until liquidation or traded from investor to investor in secondary transactions.

Currently (and for the foreseeable future) the primary investor market for hedge funds is the United States, consisting of US tax-exempt investors, such as public and private pension funds and university endowments, and US high net worth investors. However, the significant growth in United Kingdom and European-based fund managers over the past fifteen years has meant that structuring hedge funds has become an increasingly multi-national endeavor.

Alfred Winslow Jones is widely acknowledged as having established the first hedge fund in 1949. Unlike the Abner Doubleday myth that shrouds the origin of baseball, the American national pastime, there are actually reliable contemporaneous reports of Jones's investment venture and how he sought to differentiate himself from the other money managers plying their trade in the United States in those early, post-War years. Over the intervening decades, the universe of hedge funds has expanded far beyond the relatively straightforward long/short equity strategy Jones pursued. Now the term "hedge fund" is casually used to encompass any strategy that seeks to generate positive returns irrespective of rises and falls in the securities markets.

A frustrating feature of hedge funds for many would-be investors is the lack of transparency with regard to a fund's actual holdings. Investors rarely receive position-level information about a fund's portfolio. Fund managers are very concerned that this information could be used by third parties to trade against their fund and harm its performance over time. Often, the profits captured by hedge funds can be based on small price differentials that could evaporate before they have fully completed their trading.

A growing trend in the market, however, is for hedge fund managers to provide significant institutional investors and funds of funds with limited, but meaningful, information about the fund's holdings. This information can be provided in an aggregated manner, by sector, geography or currency, rather than a complete listing of each stock, bond or derivative held. In this way, concerns about "trading against" the fund can be addressed, while still providing useful metrics to concerned investors about their risk exposure. This tiering of transparency is steadily becoming a feature of market practice, as individual investors remain willing to accept significantly lower disclosure as the price for access to hedge funds.

Institutional investors, on the other hand, have fiduciary duties that they owe to their ultimate beneficiaries. These duties require them to seek and obtain increased transparency in order to allow them to fulfill their own legal obligations. An institutional investor who fails to take adequate steps to oversee the managers with whom they entrust their money could find themselves facing costly (and embarrassing) litigation from their beneficiaries, whose interests they were charged with protecting.

Perhaps unfairly, hedge funds are often associated in the mainstream press and in popular imagination with fraud and other criminal activities. Little is reported about most funds most of the time, but when a significant loss occurs, or rumors of fraud begin to circulate, the financial pages regularly fill up with scandalous stories. As a result, it's easy to envision the managers of many of these funds as pantomime villains, who are simply waiting for their chance to rob their helpless investors blind when the right opportunities arise.

In fact, the actual cases of such frauds have been relatively few, both in absolute and relative numbers. Even where no criminal malfeasance occurs, however, investors in hedge funds can suffer catastrophic losses where comprehensive risk management systems are lacking and unforeseen market developments expose weaknesses in the construction of the portfolio and its risk exposure. The global financial crisis provided us with many examples of these.

As a result, the most successful investors will always be actively considering and re-considering which funds to invest in and how much money to entrust with each one. Investor preferences and prejudices have a surprisingly large impact on which managers survive and thrive and which managers eventually withdraw from the market. The preferences and prejudices of investors have been a significant driver in determining the shape and scope of today's hedge fund industry. In order to fully understand the nature and operation of these funds, a full understanding of the motivation of these investors must be developed. Absent that, the concerned layperson is only evaluating half the picture.

Since the global financial crisis, it has been particularly hard to be a small hedge fund.

Many of those brave investors who eventually re-entered the market after the dramatic events of 2008–09, when over 1,000 hedge funds closed and many more reneged on their promise to give investors their money back, still shy away from all but the largest hedge funds. Those intrepid souls who are now willing to write checks seem inclined to write checks so large that many funds just starting out are unable to accept them without throwing their portfolios, and their investor demographics, well out of whack. In addition, many cautious investors take comfort (whether deserved or not) in the belief that larger managers must have withstood the test of time in order to reach their current size, and therefore are somehow less risky. Experience, however, often teaches otherwise.

But regulatory developments, and the insatiable human desire for success and monetary rewards, have meant that more new hedge funds continue to launch each year. For example, as the Volker Rule, a highly controversial provision of the Dodd-Frank Wall Street Reform and Consumer Protection Act (the Dodd-Frank Act), forces banks in the United States to disgorge their proprietary trading desks, and the hot shot quants and superstar traders who staff them, there are growing numbers of start-up hedge funds opening their doors and looking for anchor tenant investors. Interestingly, studies have regularly indicated that many fund managers (like athletes) do best in their early years. As a result, a perverse effect of the preference for larger established fund managers with audited five-year track records is that investors who categorically exclude new managers from their allocations could potentially be significantly limiting their returns.

If there is indeed some measure of added risk in backing a start-up fund, how can an interested investor make sure that they are being adequately compensated for taking that additional risk?

For an investor willing to make a substantial investment in a new fund at its initial launch, it is not uncommon for that investor to receive an ownership interest, and a profit participation, in the fund manager. To the extent that the fund is a roaring success, this anchor tenant investment could significantly increase the investor's overall return by adding a share of the manager's lucrative performance fee to the investment performance of its own money at work in the fund. This seed investment recognizes the value added to the manager's nascent business by the validation provided by an established, respected institution entrusting money with the new team on day one. Such value is real and measurable and on the table for the right prospective investor.

Understanding what hedge funds actually do requires a more-than-casual familiarity with the large investment banking teams that are these funds' entry point into the global markets – that is, prime brokers. Trading securities on the scale and with the frequency of the most successful hedge funds takes more than a few Bloomberg screens and an online brokerage account. Prime brokers are central to the operation and ultimate success of most hedge funds, especially those that want to sell short or to magnify their bets with borrowed money.

In many ways, there would not be hedge funds if it weren't for the bulge-bracket investment banks such as Goldman Sachs, JP Morgan, Bank of America Merrill Lynch and Credit Suisse that provide them with these prime brokerage services.

What does a prime broker actually do? In addition to execution and custody services, a prime broker provides hedge funds with the ability to borrow stocks and bonds (known as "securities lending") and to borrow money to buy stocks and bonds (known as "margin financing"). The prime broker stands as an intermediary between hedge funds and two important sets of counterparties – on the one hand, pension funds and other institutional investors with shares to lend (for the ultimate purpose of short selling); and on the other hand, commercial banks with money available for margin loans.

Short selling is so closely associated with hedge funds that perhaps a few words of explanation are warranted. When selling a security "short," the underlying bet being made is relatively straightforward. By engaging in short selling, an investor is betting that the price of a security will fall. In a properly functioning market, prices rise and fall regularly and freely. As a result, shorting can be seen as a way of ensuring that price bubbles burst before they distort the market and end up causing catastrophic losses to innocent (and not-so-innocent) bystanders. Although the effect of short sellers on a particular company can be very painful to the management and shareholders of the target under siege, many experts believe that the contribution to overall market efficiency outweighs the short-term pain that short selling inflicts.

In addition to lending either securities or cash, prime brokers also offer a number of concierge services to their top hedge fund clients. "Capital introduction," for example, is provided by dedicated teams within a prime broker to assist new funds in identifying new potential investors. In practice, however, the results of these matchmaking services can be highly varied. At the very least, these services can expedite the fundraising process for strategies and individual principals currently favored by the market. Although in recent years prime brokers have expanded their services to include risk management and capital introduction, securities and cash financing remains their core (and most profitable) services.

The differences between borrowing cash and borrowing securities are significant to a hedge fund, and worth expanding on in more detail. While lending cash is a commodity service with a transparent cost structure, lending securities is not. As a result, spreads (and ultimately the profit to the bank) can vary widely.

Lending often requires collateral, and prime brokerage is no exception. Prime brokers typically operate on a fully collateralized basis. As a result, the assets of a hedge fund are held by the prime broker in its role as custodian. Those assets are, therefore, available when needed at a moment's notice as collateral, at which time they are quickly transferred to the prime broker's own account. This allows a prime broker, with custody of a hedge fund's portfolio, to provide higher leveraging amounts to these borrowers than they would otherwise receive from traditional bank loans.

A very important distinction needs to be made at this juncture. Collateralization is different from leverage, a topic that will come up again and again in the following chapters. Leverage refers to the use of borrowed money. Using borrowed money to buy stocks and bonds has traditionally been referred to as "margin finance." Like with the purchase of residential real estate, a buyer will have some, but not all, of the purchase price and will look to a lender to supply the balance.

The margin terms made available by the prime broker to the hedge fund will determine the maximum leverage (or borrowings) available. Often, funds may find themselves in the position of being offered more margin at a given point in time than they want. Hedge fund managers must familiarize themselves fully with a prime broker's margin rules as well as how those rules are developed and implemented over time, in order to ensure that unexpected movements in the market do not have unforeseen effects on a fund's portfolio.

Selecting the right prime broker is always a very important decision for a hedge fund manager, regardless of whether they are a new start-up or a multi-billion dollar fund closed to further investments. The factors typically considered by hedge funds in choosing a prime broker include price, access to hard-to-borrow securities, creditworthiness and access to term lending. In practice, many prospective investors do take comfort (whether rightly or wrongly) in the selection of a particular prime broker by a new hedge fund manager. This is due to the level of due diligence perceived to be involved in a leading financial institution agreeing to have a particular fund as a counterparty.

Typically, a detailed understanding of the individuals behind the fund manager, the structure of the management operations and the investment process to be followed by the fund is developed by the prime broker before a hedge fund is taken on as a client. However, because of its position as an over-collateralized creditor, the prime broker's view of risk differs quite significantly from an investor's view of risk.

Just like hedge funds, private equity funds have steadily gained in prominence over recent years. Flipping through leading newspapers also reveals that these funds are subject to a range of different and often contradictory perceptions. Private equity funds are either conquering the world ("Private Equity Goes International" or "Private Equity's Love Affair with China") or on the verge of seeing their best days behind them ("Defending Private Equity from a Flawed Picture"). They may be wrestling with divisive internal conflicts ("A Clash Between Venture Capital and Private Equity") or benefiting from a broad consensus among leading practitioners ("Private Equity Titans Find Common Ground").

Private equity funds differ in many important respects from hedge funds, even though they share several common traits in terms of their structure and operation. Private equity funds are unregulated investment vehicles formed to facilitate investments in listed and unlisted shares and other securities. Such investments may also include public companies that, after acquisition by the fund, will be "taken private" and delisted. Traditionally, these funds have focused on capital appreciation rather than current income. Accordingly, they are usually established as closed-end funds where an investor's money may be locked up for between ten to fourteen years.

A number of different strategies to access investment opportunities in public and private companies can be grouped under the heading of "private equity." These strategies may be categorized under three broad headings. First, venture capital funds invest in young, entrepreneurial companies, frequently focusing on new technologies. Second, buyout funds purchase significant positions in mature businesses, often with significant amounts of borrowed money, with a specified exit period. Third, special situations funds are active in a broad array of debt instruments and other investments in distressed or rapidly changing companies.

Once a decision is reached by an investor to allocate money to private equity, there are a number of different options available. The investor could identify and invest directly in particular target companies, assuming he or she has access to potential transactions and the time and expertise to negotiate and oversee. Alternatively, the investor could invest in a private equity fund, which would allow him or her access to investment professionals with demonstrated abilities and past success, together with the benefits of increased diversification across a number of investments. Finally, the investor could allocate to a fund of funds, which would make available to him or her a portfolio of different private equity funds across strategies and vintage years, many of which he or she would not have been able to invest in directly.

Two key features of private equity funds easily distinguish them from hedge funds. First, an initial "commitment" is made at the launch of the fund to provide up to a certain amount of capital to the fund whenever required, rather than fully investing a sum of money on the first day. Second, the fund has a fixed life, ranging from seven to ten years, with all investments having been made during the defined life being realized on or before the termination date.

These features derive from the types of investments targeted by private equity funds – typically, illiquid stakes in unlisted companies. For example, private equity funds require a commitment from investors of up to ten years, which may be subject to further extensions. Upon launch, only a fraction of the investor's capital commitment will be payable, with the balance drawdown as and when investments are identified. The investment period may range from three to five years with a distinctive drop in performance in the fund's early years (known as the "J curve" or the "hockey stick") due to the small amount of invested capital and the effect of organizational expenses and management fees until investments begin to be realized.

Although private equity funds have, until very recently, provided fairly consistent rates of return, they have certain pronounced disadvantages to many investors. These include irregular capital calls, difficulties in forecasting the distribution of cash proceedings and highly illiquid investments by the fund that can be difficult to value. Private equity funds clearly do not suit every investment portfolio. As a result, typically only the largest institutional investors around the world have allocated their money to these funds.

In most other ways, however, the similarities of private equity and hedge funds far outnumber the differences. They are typically established as unregulated collective investment schemes and have surprisingly similar asset-based and performance-based remuneration. These structural similarities will be discussed and dissected in the following chapter.

Before commencing any rigorous analysis of the private equity industry, it is important to maintain a proper sense of scale when talking about the size of these firms and the funds they manage. A private equity firm managing, say, $4 billion can be referred to as "mid-sized," even though they may have high-profile institutional investors, such as the California Public Employees' Retirement System (CalPERS) and Harvard University, participating in their fund. The "big guys" in the industry are firms such as Henry Kravis's KKR & Co, Stephen Schwarzman's Blackstone Group, David Rubenstein's Carlyle Group, Leon Black's Apollo Global Management or David Bonderman's TPG Group, who have several times more in investor capital to put to work in each fund they raise.

For example, in 2011, when sentiment was still only turning back in favor of private equity, the largest fund to successfully launch was Lexington Capital Partners VII, which closed on $7 billion. Importantly, the Lexington fund is a "secondaries" fund, which focuses on buying the limited partnership interests of other ("primary") funds from disaffected investors seeking liquidity. Other significant funds that launched in 2011 included the

Swedish-based EQT VI (€4.75 billion), Oaktree Capital Management's OCM European Principal Opportunities Fund III (€3 billion), Summit Partners Growth Equity Fund VIII ($2.7 billion) and Australia's Archer Capital Fund V (AUS $1.5 billion).

Today, some of the larger firms that sponsor and manage private equity funds are now publicly traded on the New York Stock Exchange or Nasdaq Stock Market, such as Blackstone, KKR, Carlyle and Apollo. Although their funds remain limited to only large sophisticated investors, these listings allow any retail investor to log-on to their online brokerage account and buy into these private equity giants, should the whim ever arise. Due to the public disclosure requirements that listed companies must fulfill, more technical information is available about these firms today than many of their competitors. As a result, private equity is steadily becoming less and less "private" with the passage of time. In addition, the passage of Dodd-Frank in the United States led to many private equity firms being registered with, and supervised by, the SEC, although the information required for disclosure is still significantly less than for public companies.

With all these billions of dollars of investors' money sloshing around, what sort of companies do private equity funds buy? They run the gamut of industry sectors and can vary from small companies looking to expand, to large companies in need of restructuring. These funds can either be generalist in their investment approach or have very specific geographic or industry sectors that they target. It is difficult today to identify a geographic area or an industry segment that has managed to avoid the attention and affection of private equity funds sniffing out big returns.

By way of example, TPG (formerly known as Texas Pacific Group) has held stakes in Caesars Entertainment, J Crew, the Neiman Marcus upscale department stores, IMS Health and Spanish-language network Univision. Carlyle Group, which in 2012 had $150 billion in assets and almost 100 different funds operating across private equity, venture capital and real estate, has invested in communications companies CommScope and Syniverse, as well as Florida-based Bank United. Blackstone portfolio companies have included SunGard (a software company) and Leica Camera. Apollo has owned SiriusXM Radio and Lyondell Bassell (a plastics and chemical company).

These acquisitions, and the thousands like them, have meant that growing numbers of men and women in the United States, the United Kingdom, across Europe and around the world now work for companies owned by private equity funds. These companies are being operated and managed (and often restructured and refinanced) in such a manner as to deliver outsized returns to the investors in the fund.

What does this mean to the man or woman on the street who might be worried about the impact of private equity on his or her life and livelihood?

In a bold move to better explain the private equity business model to the general public, the industry reached out to the "Schoolhouse Rock" generation of middle-aged men and women who grew up in the United States watching those toe-tapping, easily-hummable Saturday morning cartoons by producing their own animated defense of their business practices. In May 2012, the Private Equity Growth Capital Council released its own cartoon video on YouTube that walked viewers briskly through the inner workings of leveraged buyouts. Although not as memorable as "Conjunction Junction," and lacking the emotional arc of "Verb, That's What's Happening," the trade association's first attempt at animation conveyed several important talking points about the way private equity functioned to work with companies in need of capital and expertise in a succinct and understandable manner.

Questions remained in many laypersons' minds about how private equity fits into the larger economy, but the trade association earned kudos for at least attempting to tell the story of private equity from the perspective of its most sincere practitioners.

As noted above, private equity is becoming less and less "private." Public scrutiny and negative publicity is now a feature of daily life for much of the industry. In 2012, Colin Blaydon of the Tuck School of Business at Dartmouth College pointedly observed that "[t]he industry has done a terrible job of explaining what it does, and now has this bright spotlight being shown on it that no one ever anticipated."

This transition has been difficult for the industry, which historically was not inclined to sing its own praises or engage proactively with the press or with the government. Until the formation of the Private Equity Growth Capital Association in 2007, the US private equity industry had not engaged in coordinated lobbying efforts in Washington DC. By contrast, the British Venture Capital Association (BVCA), which represents both venture capital firms and buyout firms, was first founded over twenty-five years ago and the European Venture Capital Association (EVCA) has been operating since 1983. Interestingly, the membership in the National Venture Capital Association in the United States has traditionally been limited solely to venture firms.

Much of what gets reported about private equity can be very negative. The actual facts, however, on closer examination tend to be much more ambivalent and banal. Academic studies have shown that private equity neither destroys nor creates significant numbers of jobs over time. In addition, private equity-backed businesses do not appear to go under at any higher rate than similarly situated businesses. Not many catchy sound bites there for either side unfortunately.

Much of the academic research that has been done in recent years demonstrates that private equity does create real value in the portfolio companies in which it invests, as well as giving investors the possibility of high returns. Studies from academics at Harvard Business School, Columbia Business School, University of Chicago, University of Virginia in the United States, the University of Oxford in the United Kingdom, as well as professional firms such as Ernst and Young and Cambridge Associates repeatedly provide back-up for the basic claims made by private equity's champions.

According to R. Glenn Hubbard, dean of Columbia Business School, "Private equity firms have an impact on productivity. That doesn't mean that people don't lose their jobs. But the question of whether private equity adds value? It's settled among economists."

On occasion, a positive story about private equity firms can break through in the mainstream media. In an April 2012 issue of *Bloomberg BusinessWeek*, the mid-sized private equity firm Monomoy Capital Partners was featured in a cover story that sang the praises of their focus on eliminating waste and inefficiencies in their portfolio companies in order to significantly increase their earnings. Contrary to the widespread image of private equity as making money by slashing employee ranks and performing financial acrobatics with balance sheets, Monomoy are portrayed as constructively engaged in increasing the efficiency and effectiveness of the companies in which they invest.

Often, however, partisan political sentiment comes into play, and attacks on private equity can be a proxy for larger philosophical arguments about economic policy. For example, in June 2012, Moody's Investors Services issued an interesting report that compared private equity owners to other owners when times start going bad for their companies. Counter to public opinion, more jobs are saved under the watch of private equity firms. Regardless, a campaign ad for President Barack Obama's re-election labeled Republican challenger Mitt Romney as "outsourcer-in-chief." This was in addition to the old stump-speech favorite that Romney was a remorseless job-destroyer. The ad focused pointedly on Bain Capital companies that relocated jobs to China and India. This aggressive "politicization" of private equity that became a feature of the 2012 US presidential election is a very important trend that will be discussed in detail in a later chapter.

Importantly, despite efforts to categorize different types of funds into discrete groups, there is a significant amount of overlap. Private equity and venture capital, for example, are similar in many ways. Both represent financial investors growing and professionalizing private companies for either a sale on to a strategic investor or an IPO that will put the company into public ownership. "Venture capital" is usually used to refer to investments in young, high-growth companies at an early stage of their development. Intellectual property may be crucial to the companies' success. "Private equity" typically refers to more mature companies, which may either be listed or unlisted at the time of investment. If listed, the company will first be delisted and taken private in order to allow either its capital structure or its operations (or both) to be comprehensively restructured.

Private equity often focuses on situations where public investors lack the ability or resources to address the challenges facing a company. These can include building new businesses from inception, restructuring companies to better face the future or consolidating participants in mature industry to drive profitability. From the perspective of an investee company, private equity can be a very expensive source of capital. As a result, the companies that take money from private equity funds generally are ones that are facing significant challenges in the current market. Better (and cheaper) options simply aren't available to a manufacturer who is facing relentless competition from overseas firms, or a chain of department stores that haven't been able to keep pace with internet shopping.

For example, one high-profile acquisition in 2013 involved the purchase of the Twinkies business from the bankrupt Hostess by Apollo Global Management and Metropoulos & Company, two successful private equity firms. The failure of Hostess, due to intractable labor concerns, caused a fear that the much-loved snack cakes produced for many years might vanish from store shelves. Where the management of Hostess failed, the investment professionals within Apollo and Metropoulos feel confident that they can succeed.

In both private equity and venture capital funds, any investment bought must ultimately be sold. The point of these funds is not to own a company for decades and decades, come what may. At the most opportune moment, and not more than several years after being acquired, each company must be sold to a willing buyer at a significant profit in order to return to investors their original capital, together with sufficient profit to provide for the carried interest to become payable. The ultimate exit strategy is, therefore, a crucial element of any investment decision.

Although as a general rule private equity and hedge funds each pursue different investment objectives, there is potential for overlaps. At certain times, these different funds can find themselves actually competing against each other for the same prospective investments.

In 2011, for example, a new technology bubble was starting to build. Unsurprisingly, some hedge funds eventually decided against simply waiting for allocations in the next hot IPO. Instead, they began to put money into start-up companies while they were still private. As a result, they found themselves in direct conflict with established venture capital houses whose sweet spot is providing expansion capital to young businesses in the hope of either taking them public or selling them to an established industry leader. Unlike venture capitalists, hedge fund managers are not typically known for their patient, long-term perspective, or their hand-holding bedside manner, should a start-up company run into some challenges along the way!

Another example of competition can be seen with so-called "vulture funds." These are funds that invest in distressed, or undervalued, assets. They can follow any of a number of particular investment strategies, which often differ significantly as to the liquidity of their investments and the turnover of their portfolio. As a result, these funds can be established as either open-ended hedge funds or closed-ended private equity funds. In fact, they may even be structured as highly customized vehicles exhibiting some characteristics of each approach.

Of the two possible approaches for structuring a distressed fund, two key factors of the hedge fund structure are worth noting. First, performance fees in a hedge fund are earned on both realized and unrealized gains, so the need to harvest investment inherent in a private equity fund structure is absent. Second, as an open-ended fund, new investors can come into the hedge fund on a regular basis and existing investors can similarly redeem themselves out, so the hedge fund can continue indefinitely. On the other hand, a private equity fund structure may be more appropriate where the fund acquires large positions within a single company, exerting some level of influence on the company or its restructuring process, or where the valuation of the investments it acquires will be problematic. This is a good example of where decisions as to a fund's structure (discussed in more detail in the following chapter) can determine the types of investors or investments that a fund will pursue.

Due to the manner in which alternative investment funds have evolved over the last few decades, private equity funds are typically described using different nomenclature from hedge funds. Similarly, onshore funds are often described using different terms and concepts from offshore funds. However, the similarities between these funds far outweigh the differences. In addition, structural approaches once common in one category of funds are now finding uses among other categories. Finally, investors and regulators, such as the SEC and the FCA, are increasingly viewing alternative investment funds as a single broad category of investment vehicles.

Understanding the points of commonality between these funds, therefore, has become imperative. As a result, the approach taken here will be to use terminology that is "asset class neutral" to the fullest extent possible. Clearly, certain circumstances will arise where it is essential to discuss particular aspects of a fund, its structure or its operation in a specific context. In many circumstances, however, the following terms and concepts will be used regardless of the fund's structure or investment strategy.

The term "alternative investment fund" will occasionally be used to refer to both private equity and hedge funds, as well as other similar private funds offered exclusively to non-retail investors. These other funds could include venture capital funds, distressed debt funds, mezzanine funds, as well as a variety of others.

The "fund" is the legal vehicle in which one or more investors place their money in exchange for an ownership interest in that vehicle. The money provided will be aggregated and managed to the greatest extent possible as a single pool, irrespective of the identity (or subsequent views, doubts or reconsiderations) of the investors. Although funds may be structured on other bases, almost all funds are established as blind pools. As a result, once an investor has invested or committed his or her money, the fund manager will have an almost completely unfettered discretion over what to buy and what to sell, as well as, in many instances, when and on what terms an investor can be given back his or her money.

The "fund manager" is the party responsible for the operation of the fund and the selection of investments. Where investments will be held for a considerable time, the fund manager may become highly involved in the oversight of particular investments. Where investments are not liquid, the manner and timing of realization will be of critical importance to the fund manager's success.

The "investors" are the persons participating in the fund. The form of their interest in the fund will be dictated largely by the fund's choice of legal entity. An investor's interest may take the form of a partnership interest, in the case of a limited partnership, or shares, in the case of a company.

Hopefully, this simplified terminology will serve to clarify many of the similarities that exist among the thousands and thousands of private equity and hedge funds now operating around the world, as well as the hundreds of new funds being formed each year. It is important for a layperson keen to understand the actual structure and operation of these funds to be able to identify and track their key elements, without being distracted or discouraged by jargon.

Despite their reputation as being unregulated, many legal and regulatory issues in fact arise in the structuring and operation of alternative investment funds, including the interaction between the fund vehicle and the investment firm acting as the fund manager.

Generally, the individuals and investment firms who launch alternative investment funds will attempt to minimize the extent of their regulation. In the United States, exemptions will be secured under the Securities Act of 1933 (the Securities Act), the Securities Exchange Act of 1934 (the Exchange Act) and the Investment Company Act of 1940 (the Investment Company Act). These exemptions are provided by the government to address circumstances where regulation has been deemed unnecessary. This can be, for example, because of the sophistication of the individuals involved or because of the limited scope of activities conducted. In the case of alternative investment funds and their managers, the regulatory regimes in both the United States and the United Kingdom focus on regulation and oversight of the fund manager as an authorized firm, and not on the structure and operation of the fund itself. This distinction has been questioned recently, particularly in the months immediately following September 2008. Today, the wisdom of this approach is still an open question in some quarters.

As a result of "opting out" of the regulation imposed on public funds marketed to retail investors, such as Uncle Edgar and Aunt Edna, the extent to which private equity and hedge funds provide for investor protection concerns varies greatly from structure to structure. Proactive steps, therefore, must be taken to ensure that investors fully understand the current status and prospects of their fund, and that they are empowered to intervene effectively should the need arise.

Balancing risk and reward in a commercial relationship is always challenging. In the context of investing, the risks can be particularly complex and interconnected. Alternative investment funds seek to generate high returns against a background of external factors over which they have little direct influence, including market volatility, counterparty risks, liquidity crises and political uncertainty.

Where funds are not registered for public distribution to retail investors (as is the case of private equity and hedge funds), the non-retail investors who elect to participate in them are left to negotiate any limitations and protections with the fund and the talented men and women who seek to manage their money. Much of the legal and regulatory regime that surrounds these funds is based on the assumption that these negotiations are effective. Unfortunately, during the global financial crisis awkward questions arose about the real effectiveness of these negotiations.

When prospective investors are contemplating an investment in a particular fund, their analysis will primarily (if not exclusively) focus on the skill and abilities of the fund manager. The assembled wisdom and experience of other fund service providers and participants will be an overwhelmingly secondary concern, if it is even expressly considered at all. Similarly, each investor will expect only limited circumstances where management of the fund can be materially changed by action of the other investors. Instead of control, the governance issues that arise in private equity and hedge funds are focused around the need for the fund manager to be held accountable to fund participants as they exercise their broad discretionary authority.

The legal vehicles which predominantly serve as private equity and hedge funds have established their prime position not due to any inherent advantage or benefits to be found in their internal governance structures. In general, both limited partnerships and offshore companies offer tremendous flexibility for fund managers to significantly limit the influence and oversight of participants, while facilitating the ability of managers to exercise control.

The typical choice between either doing nothing, attempting to suspend the manager or terminating the fund is often too stark to address any situation other than the most dire and catastrophic. Simple problems can often be better solved by simple solutions than with extreme solutions. Where investors have recourse only to extreme solutions, fund managers may feel immune to investor sentiment when making important decisions for the fund.

Importantly, even where the funds they manage are unregulated, investment managers that are regulated by the SEC or the FCA owe regulatory duties arising under the Investment Advisers Act of 1940 (Investment Advisers Act) in the United States and the Financial Services and Markets Act 2000 (the FSMA) and EU legislation in the United Kingdom.

In the case of public investment funds, such as retail mutual funds, comprehensive product-level regulations have been adopted to ensure that risks associated with conflicts of interest, lack of transparency and mismanagement, as well as portfolio risk, are adequately addressed. In the case of private equity and hedge funds, the participants are expected to rely on their own ability to negotiate adequate levels of protection to address those risks. If they fail to negotiate effectively, they will be left exposed and with limited (or no) recourse.

As a consequence of limiting the extent to which alternative investment funds may be marketed and establishing particular status or size requirement in participants (e.g. sophisticated investors), the presumption of the SEC or the FCA will be that such investors have adequate negotiating leverage to address any concerns over the operation and governance of these funds that they may have. The reach of regulators in the area of alternative investment funds, therefore, is limited and, more importantly, often only indirect.

Through both rules of direct application to fund managers and the indirect influence that can be exerted on regulated firms through the adoption and promotion of "best practices" on a voluntary basis, financial regulators can significantly impact the day-to-day operation of private equity and hedge funds. However, such influences can be exercised by such regulators only within the natural limitations that exist due to their limited resources and competing agendas and the needs that exist across the entire financial landscape.

One thing that quickly becomes apparent when examining the numerous regulatory reforms that are currently being attempted on both sides of the Atlantic in recent years is that the attitude of regulators has changed significantly during the global financial crisis. Although many critics have attempted to draw the government's attention to issues raised by the rapid growth of private equity and hedge funds over the past two decades, the unravelling of national and international markets in the autumn of 2008 meant that government officials had an opportunity to reconsider their positions. And many of them did.

To take one such senior figure as an example, the passage of a few years would appear to have led to a significant rethink in Timothy Geithner's views on the subject of alternative investment funds, or perhaps it was simply a change in his job title. On October 18, 2005, Geithner provided the standard, enlightened view on these funds, while serving as President of the Federal Reserve Bank of New York. "Hedge funds, private equity funds and other kinds of investment vehicles help to dispose risk and add liquidity." Six years later, on October 14, 2011, when he was serving as US Treasury Secretary, Geithner greeted the prosecution of several hedge fund managers for various trading infractions in a much more confrontational tone. "You've seen very, very dramatic enforcement actions already by the enforcement authorities across the US government, and I'm sure you're going to see more to come. You should stay tuned for that."

Of course, to be completely fair, no champion of alternative funds, no matter how enthusiastic, would ever go so far as to support insider trading or illegal market abuse. Consistent enforcement of the "rules of the game" ultimately benefits all market participants. However, the change in tone is still quite significant. In a small way, Geithner's drift reflects a larger shift among many in government from a more neutral stance of private equity and hedge funds to a more suspicious view. In light of this heightened focus, alternative investment funds and their managers have had to adapt to the new world around them.

Private equity and hedge funds have evolved to fill particular needs in the financial markets. Those needs center on enabling experienced and sophisticated investors to access talented investment professionals, while ensuring that retail investors retain the protection of detailed rules and regulations designed to prevent fraud and to promote transparency. The quality of investment advice, whether provided directly to a client or indirectly through a fund, is very important both to the financial markets generally as well as to each individual who benefits or suffers as a result.

Of course, there is a necessary element of market risk here: every bad outcome suffered by an alternative investment fund is not necessarily proof of incompetence or malfeasance. Similarly, not every superlative return generated by a fund is proof of excellence or fair dealings. Nonetheless, investors must take steps to better protect themselves from the many types of "management risk" that they face, including the malfeasance and negligence of the fund managers themselves.

The historic status of private equity and hedge funds as (largely) unregulated arrangements is based on the explicit assumption that their participants have adequate knowledge and negotiating leverage to protect their interests. The occurrence from time to time of investor protection failures in these funds, however, raises the awkward question of whether this assumption is correct in all cases.

As commercial ventures, these funds – and the individuals who establish and manage them – are seeking to generate profits through their investment activities. In this regard, they are similar to other businesses that raise capital from investors and seek to generate profits from, for example, building and selling a better widget than their competitors. However, profiting from the mispricing of risk in multiple-currency financial derivatives, or from the fact that a particular supermarket chain is undervalued, is harder for people outside the enclaves of Wall Street or the City of London to understand. Difficulties that everyday citizens (and voters) have with evaluating the merits of the most well-known financial services firms are multiplied when the challenge is to form a judgment on the long-term value provided by unknown, entrepreneurial firms who engage in financial transactions that are far removed from their own everyday lives.

The following chapters will attempt to address several of the key issues that arise when trying to establish a more complete and detailed understanding of private equity and hedge funds. By giving greater context to what these funds really are and what they seek to accomplish, a more accurate judgment can be made about whether these funds are being effective and delivering on their promises to their investors, as well as whether the overall financial markets and economy actually do benefit from their activities, like their champions claim.

2: BUILDING THE BETTER FUND

Understanding the Structure and Operation of Alternative Investment Funds

[O]rganizing as a limited partnership affords to the hedge fund manager overwhelming flexibility in managing its internal affairs and carrying out its investment strategy.
Houman B. Shadab, New York Law School

What distinguishes limited partnership law in the venture capital context is not so much the limitations it imposes on the parties to a venture capital limited partnership contract, but rather the broad freedom it gives the parties to craft an agreement that allocates duties and risks in a way that satisfies both investors and venture capitalists.
David Rosenberg of the Zicklin School of Business at Baruch College

Does the world need any more private equity and hedge funds? At least for some investors, the answer is a clear and unqualified "yes."

In 2011, a particularly difficult year by historical standards, over 1,100 new hedge funds and over 600 new private equity funds were set up. Some were launched by established fund managers with trackrecords for successful investing. Others were formed by start-ups seeking to demonstrate their investment talent on a global stage. One way to better understand what private equity and hedge funds do is to learn a little more how they are actually created and operated. Form often follows function, but in many instances the former drives the latter.

Investment funds – whether retail mutual funds designed for the nest-eggs of Uncle Edgar and Aunt Edna or the more exclusive private equity and hedge funds aimed at sophisticated institutional investors – enable the collectivization of investment management relationships through the use of an intermediary vehicle. Over the last three hundred years, as investment funds have been established in different countries to pursue different investment opportunities, one recurring theme is that the intermediation of a fund vehicle between the prospective clients and the investment manager is a "necessary evil" that the clients must endure when they lack the money individually to retain the investment adviser directly. The fund vehicle must simultaneously appeal to the would-be fund manager, to induce it to provide its services, and to the prospective fund investors, to induce them to entrust their money to it.

In a simple bilateral arrangement, a client could negotiate "bespoke" terms with a prospective investment manager and would retain the responsibility for overseeing the ongoing fulfillment of those terms. By contrast, an investment fund provides "off the shelf" terms to prospective participants, many of whom may have relatively small percentage positions in the ultimate fund, although the sums of money they provide will often be very significant to them.

Despite well-established "market forms" for many types of private equity and hedge funds, each fund is structured to address a series of unique requirements. These requirements derive from the tax treatment of the participants and the underlying investments, the regulatory status of the fund manager and the types of underlying investments being made.

First and foremost, the tax consequence of the entity being used as an investment fund must be thoroughly examined. Unless the intermediary vehicle is broadly "tax neutral" for the proposed investors, they will be very reluctant to participate. Investors generally want to be in essentially the same tax position as if they were to make the investments directly. Unlike retail mutual funds, which benefit from explicit tax code provisions that provide for their beneficial treatment, private equity and hedge funds must address the tax issues structurally by selection of an appropriate legal vehicle and the inclusion of necessary provisions in the legal documentation.

Historically, limited partnerships, which are tax-transparent in most jurisdictions, and companies established in offshore jurisdictions (such as the Cayman Islands), which are effectively tax exempt, have served as alternative investment funds. Importantly, neither partnerships nor offshore companies were originally developed specifically for the purpose of serving as a fund vehicle. Their use as such has been driven by the need for tax efficiency, rather than any genuine affinity for the history and governance structures of these vehicles.

The structure of alternative investment funds has also been driven by the need to comply with financial regulatory rules, while simultaneously addressing a series of interrelated tax issues arising from various pieces of anti-avoidance legislation adopted over the years. Private equity and hedge funds must sail between this "Scylla and Charybdis" in order to deliver to the parties an effective structural framework for their agreed commercial arrangements.

As a result, after forty years of accelerating growth, alternative investment funds look and operate as they do largely in response to the financial regulation and tax requirements imposed on them by onshore governments, such as the United States and the United Kingdom. This may come as a surprise to many laypersons just beginning their examination of private equity and hedge funds.

The influence of onshore governments on private equity and hedge fund structures should not be downplayed. Onshore tax authorities (such as the US Internal Revenue Service and the UK HM Revenue and Customs) establish the basis on which certain vehicles will be taxed and others left untaxed. Onshore financial regulators (such as the SEC and the FCA) determine who must be authorized and who may be sold securities and what sorts of investment activities are forbidden.

Generalizing about private equity and hedge funds can be very difficult at times. They vary greatly in size and complexity from small entrepreneurial start-up funds to complex global structures with billions of dollars in assets. They differ in terms of the securities and instruments in which they invest, the strategies that they pursue, the legal form in which they are structured and the types of investors from whom they seek contributions. Regardless, sufficient structural similarities exist between the different types of alternative investment funds that a broad description can be given of how they are established and operated.

An alternative investment fund will consist of one or more vehicles in which the investors have received interests, units or shares in exchange for their capital contributions. The particular structure of a fund will be based on decisions made regarding a number of different parameters, including, for example, the types of investments that will be made; the types and domiciles of investors; the legal vehicle chosen for the fund; the domicile of the fund; and the domicile of the managers. As discussed above, onshore partnerships and offshore corporations remain the most common fund vehicles for private equity and hedge funds, despite the significant growth and evolution of these funds in the past few decades.

Alternative investment funds are also unique in that they are externally managed. In other words, they are established and operated by individuals and firms whose financial interests, and primary duties of loyalties, lie outside of, and apart from, the legal entity they have just formed. Funds are therefore unlike ordinary businesses established as traditional operating companies, which possess executive and non-executive directors, as well as officers and employees. The fund manager is a counterparty to, and in many ways at arms-length from, the fund. The impact of the potential conflict of interests between fund and fund manager sits behind, and casts a shadow over, all aspects of day-to-day relations between the various parties.

Several key legal documents are prepared in the course of organizing and launching a new private equity or hedge fund.

Any of the thrill and raw emotion involved in the original drafting of these thick and wordy legal documents, so essential to effectively establish a fund, is largely lost on any unlucky reader tasked with reviewing them.

An offering memorandum is provided to prospective investors to explain the structure and goal of the fund. The offering memorandum is a disclosure document, which outlines key information about what the fund can and cannot do. Although alternative investment funds can be structured to avoid many requirements otherwise imposed by financial regulators on retail mutual funds, the application of far-reaching anti-fraud rules, which prohibit material misstatements or omissions in connection with the sale of securities, means that most well-drafted offering memoranda will contain detailed and extensive disclosure for prospective investors.

Constitutional documents of the fund are also prepared in order to bring the fund into legal existence. The type of legal entity used as a fund vehicle will dictate the form of the fund's constituent documents. Whether a limited partnership agreement or memorandum and articles of association, similar issues are addressed. These include the grant of authority to the fund manager to invest the assets of the fund; the calculation of the performance allocation and management fee; the process by which fund interests are issued, valued and redeemed; and the allocation of initial and ongoing expenses as between the fund and the fund manager.

Subscription applications must be completed and returned by each prospective investor and the relevant fund vehicle. These documents, full of blanks to fill in and boxes to check, will vary in length based on the type of investors sought and the jurisdictions in which they are located. Importantly, the subscription application, completed and signed by the investor, is the principal means by which a fund manager can obtain from each investor the necessary representations, warranties and indemnities required to protect the fund manager and bind the investor going forward.

An investment management agreement will also be negotiated between the fund manager and one or more fund vehicles. This crucial document, establishing the terms of engagement of the fund manager, will be relevant in determining the scope of the duties owed to the alternative investment fund as client. Generally, a power of attorney is granted enabling the manager to buy and sell investments on behalf of the fund.

All of this documentation is crafted in order to allow the fund manager to use his or her unique talents and abilities to invest the fund's money. But what can the fund manager actually invest in?

When funds are structured as blind pools, investors necessarily rely on the fund manager to identify successful investments without retaining for themselves a veto over whether or not to participate in a particular investment. Although a fund manager's discretion may be quite broad, limits are typically agreed by reference to detailed investment restrictions contained in the offering memorandum. These restrictions can include diversification and concentration limits on the fund, which impose discipline on the fund manager providing confidence to the investors that the investments will be of a type, size, and sector as previously agreed. In a typical blind pool fund, the investors will find their protection against style drift in the scope and detail of the investment restrictions.

Each alternative investment fund has an investment policy which determines the type of assets in which it may invest. An investment policy may be defined in terms of asset classes; types of instruments; market sectors; or geographic region. The investment objective of a fund may be included directly within the constituent documentation or incorporated by reference from the offering documentation. Investment objectives provide investors with the comfort that they require prior to committing money, while simultaneously giving the fund manager the flexibility to pursue investment opportunities in a rapidly changing environment.

In periods where particular investment strategies are in high demand, investors may obtain fewer contractual constraints on the investment activities of highly sought-after fund managers. When particular funds are out of fashion, investors may have the ability to negotiate more comprehensive and exacting investment restrictions. The forces of supply and demand are regularly on display in the world of private equity and hedge funds. However, the link between elaborate concentration and diversification limits and higher investment return has yet to be clearly demonstrated.

Partnerships are frequently used in the structuring of alternative investment funds. They are often established under the laws of Delaware or England or an offshore jurisdiction such as the Cayman Islands or Bermuda. The ability of limited partnerships to serve as effective fund vehicles has been recognized by a number of academics. Houman B. Shadab of the New York Law School has noted that "organizing as a limited partnership affords to the hedge fund manager overwhelming flexibility in managing its internal affairs and carrying out its investment strategy." David Rosenberg of the Zicklin School of Business at Baruch College also observed that "the limited partnership under Delaware law is uniquely suited to create ... incentives and satisfy the needs of all parties (including passive investors and venture capitalists) involved with venture capital funds."

The benefits of partnerships are many. Most importantly, they provide for flow-through tax treatment. In effect, the vehicle is disregarded for tax purposes and each partner is treated as if he or she owned a pro rata share of assets and income directly. Other benefits include flexible remuneration arrangements for general partners and flexible internal governance and control. Rosenberg also pointed out in the context of venture capital funds that "[w]hat distinguishes limited partnership law in the venture capital context is not so much the limitations it imposes on the parties to a venture capital limited partnership contract, but rather the broad freedom it gives the parties to craft an agreement that allocates duties and risks in a way that satisfies both investors and venture capitalists." The same can be said of other varieties of private equity funds, as well as of hedge funds.

The affairs of the partners are governed by the partnership agreement, which is negotiated by the general and limited partners

40

(or rather, their hard-working and diligent lawyers). At the heart of any limited partnership is the fundamental distinction that is made between the two different categories of partner: general partners, who control the management of the partnership and have unlimited liability for the debts of the partnership; and limited partners, who are passive investors and whose liability to the partnership is limited to their capital contributions. Importantly, limited partners may be deemed to be general partners, and lose the benefit of their limited liability, if they participate in the management of the partnership. Where this line is ultimately drawn varies significantly from jurisdiction to jurisdiction. Crossing this line can lead to potentially catastrophic outcomes for the wayward limited partner.

The partnership agreement constitutes the partnership and establishes the parameters of the relationships among the limited partners and between the limited partners and the general partner. These agreements can vary widely in their level of detail and breadth of subject matter, depending on the number of investors, any special needs or requirements of particular investors, and the complexity of the commercial arrangements involving the general partner and its remuneration. Once all the relevant terms are negotiated and addressed, these documents can exceed over 100 pages in length. Interestingly, negotiations over the language in the partnership agreement tend to focus on either the compensation system that incentivizes the general partner or the covenants restricting the general partner's activities. Many of the remaining provisions often receive only cursory attention from prospective investors.

The Cayman Islands are lovely. Located in the Caribbean between Cuba and Jamaica, this collection of tropical islands enjoys a wonderful climate, great sailing and diving, and is home to only about 50,000 people. More importantly, perhaps, registered companies in Cayman significantly outnumber its population.

Cayman's great achievement over the past fifty years was to establish itself as a leading financial center. By some estimates, it is the fifth largest in the world. As a result, Caymanians enjoy the highest standard of living in the Caribbean, in addition to being able to live tax free. The Cayman government derives its revenues solely from fees and indirect taxes on the many legal entities and businesses based there.

In addition to banks and insurance companies, many hedge funds are formed using Cayman companies. Private equity funds also now make use of Cayman partnerships and companies as needed. This high level of activity by the Caymanians has, on occasion, drawn criticisms from those in a position of power and influence elsewhere. For example, President Barack Obama went out of his way to single out Cayman as a tax haven in a speech he gave in May 2009. Unsurprisingly, Caymanians, and the alternative investment industry and its investors, were not amused.

Comparisons can readily be made between Cayman and the US state of Delaware, which has established itself over the last 100 years as the jurisdiction of choice for establishing companies and other business organizations in the United States. Opponents of offshore finance would stress that there are a number of important differences between the two, including no doubt the quality of diving in Delaware Bay.

Regardless, in recent years, the Cayman Islands have established themselves as one of the most popular jurisdictions for the establishment of funds. One of the most popular approaches is to establish limited companies that issue shares to investors. Their constitutional documents will generally consist of their memorandum of association and articles of association, which deal with matters related to the internal workings of the company and authorize the directors to transact the business of the company.

Just as in Delaware or England, the directors of a Cayman Islands company are responsible for the management of the company. They exercise all the power of the company, absent explicit restrictions in the memorandum and articles. All companies, as artificially created legal persons, must act through their agents. The board of directors acts as agents of the shareholders to manage the company in accordance with the memorandum and articles of association and the provisions of applicable laws. Since private equity and hedge funds are typically externally managed and lack executive officers and employees, such agents will predominantly be the directors themselves.

Ultimately, much of the Cayman Islands' success in attracting both fund managers and investors to use their vehicles as funds is derived from the confidence that Cayman laws and government officials inspire. Of course, just as confidence can be built over time, it can also be lost.

Unfortunately, in December 2012, the stability and predictability of the Cayman Islands was given a slight knock when the country's Premier, McKeeva Bush, was arrested on charges of misuse of a government credit card and importing explosive materials without proper permits. In the months that followed, the Cayman Islands continued to successfully launch private equity and hedge funds of various shapes and sizes. However, competition between offshore jurisdictions is higher than ever.

If not the Cayman Islands, what about Bermuda or the Bahamas? Prefer a time zone more favorable to Europeans? What about the Channel Islands (Jersey or Guernsey), or perhaps the Isle of Man? Today, there are many choices available, each with its own particular advantages and incentives.

What makes private funds, such as a hedge fund or a private equity fund, "private"? The answer is a series of affirmative decisions taken by the proposed fund's sponsors, and explicitly agreed to by prospective investors, to operate within designated exemptions to securities laws and financial regulations.

As discussed earlier, private equity and hedge funds must be operated in such a way as to remain in compliance with detailed financial regulations that govern who is allowed to invest in them. Marketing restrictions determine who is, and who is not, permitted to participate in an alternative investment fund. The principal effect of these restrictions, in both the United States and the United Kingdom, is to exclude retail investors. Uncle Edgar's and Aunt Edna's money should not be going into these vehicles. As a result of limiting these funds to non-retail investors and deciding as an explicit policy choice not to subject it to product-level regulation like public investment funds, the government explicitly places primary responsibility for the investment decision on the prospective investor.

Marketing restrictions operate in conjunction with tax rules to determine the structure and operation of alternative investment funds, but to countervailing effect. On the one hand, the financial regulatory regime attempts to exclude retail investors who may not have the knowledge or experience required to negotiate adequate protections from participating in private investments. On the other hand, in order to prevent these vehicles from being instruments of tax avoidance, the taxing authorities – such as the US Internal Revenue Service or the UK HM Revenue and Customs – often impose ownership restrictions or require management and control of these vehicles to be conducted in such a way as to limit the influence that these investors can exert on a day-to-day basis.

In the United States, exemptions must be secured under a number of federal statutes that govern the securities industry. These include both the Investment Company Act, for the fund vehicle itself, and the Securities Act, for the marketing of the fund's interests. Absent an exemption, most private equity and hedge funds would be required to register with the SEC as a retail mutual fund under the Investment Company Act and become subject to a number of constraints incompatible with many investment strategies pursued by alternative investment funds. Private equity and hedge funds typically make use of the exemptions provided by Section 3(c)(1) and Section 3(c)(7) of the Investment Company Act and forgo registration, and the substantive restrictions that this entails.

Section 3(c)(1) is the older of the two exclusions from the definition of "investment company." The requirements are twofold: the interests in the fund must be privately placed to investors; and the fund must not have in excess of 100 investors. Section 3(c)(7) instead focuses on the status of investors in the fund, rather than their number. The requirements are also twofold: as with Section 3(c)(1), the interests in the fund must be privately placed to investors; and the fund may only have as investors those who are either "qualified purchasers" or "knowledgeable employees" of the fund manager.

When marketing an alternative investment fund to US investors, it is also necessary to ensure that each offer and sale of interests in the fund is exempt from registration under the Securities Act. Whether constituted as a limited partnership or a company, the interests of a fund will fall within the definition of a "security." Absent a suitable exemption, the offer and sale of such interest will require registration with the SEC. Alternative investment funds generally avoid the registration requirements by relying on the exemption provided by Section 4(2) of the Securities Act, which covers transactions by an issuer not involving any public offer, and the safe harbor rules adopted by the SEC as part of Regulation D.

Traditionally, there was a prohibition in the United States that meant that no general solicitation or general advertising could occur. This led to the exemption being lost if, for example, advertisements or articles were published in a newspaper or magazine, or interviews or notices were broadcast on television or radio. However, in April 2012, President Obama caught many by surprise by signing into law the controversial JOBS Act, undoing with a flourish of the pen decades of law and practice that limited the publicity that could surround a private placement of securities. Private equity and hedge funds are among the beneficiaries of this liberation.

Regardless of the marketing free-for-all that is now possible, other restrictions on private placements remain intact for now. Importantly, a fundamental concept within Regulation D is the "accredited investor," which includes an individual earning more than $200,000 per year (or $300,000 jointly with their spouse) or has net assets of $1,000,000, excluding their principal residence. Underlying the "accredited investor" definition is the belief that sophisticated investors have the resources and financial expertise required to obtain and evaluate the information necessary to make their investment decisions. In short, they can "fend for themselves." A similar belief serves as the rationale behind the categories of exceptions that operate in the United Kingdom and across Europe.

There are a number of different exemptions under the US securities laws for wealthy individuals, of which "accredited investor" is the most familiar. As Vijay Sekhon, a Senior Counsel with the SEC's Office of General Counsel, has observed, "The federal securities laws are littered with exemptions for wealthy investors. The rationale underlying these exemptions is that wealthy investors can fend for themselves because they either possess sufficient financial sophistication to make informed decisions or can acquire the services of advisers who possess such sophistication."

Some critics have argued that the fact that so many sophisticated investors fell victim to Bernard Madoff's infamous Ponzi scheme is compelling evidence that, in fact, such investors are either unable or unwilling to protect themselves. Among Madoff's victims were celebrities and hedge fund managers, as well as sizeable pension funds and charities. If this is correct, continuing to provide a private placement exception to enable marketing of investments to these people would ultimately be a mistake.

Based on the misery that resulted from the Madoff fraud, will legislators and regulators be willing to reexamine the premises underlying the current approach that sophisticated investors should be left to fend for themselves?

Given the significant increase in income and wealth since the original adoption of the accredited investor standard, the SEC has begun to slowly question the uniform ability of every member of this group to have the means to "fend for themselves." Ultimately, as part of Dodd-Frank, the net worth test for individuals to qualify as accredited investors was amended to exclude a natural person's primary resource from such calculations. The SEC is further mandated to periodically review the numeric threshold set for accredited investors every few years.

However, the "accredited investors" standard in the United States is for all intents and purposes sacrosanct in federal securities law. The adoption of the Dodd-Frank amendments to the existing US financial regulatory regime represents an attempt by Congress to address some, but not all, of the concerns identified by critics of the policies that led to the recent global financial crisis.

Curiously, within less than two years of adopting the Dodd-Frank reforms, a bipartisan consensus, led by President Obama, substantially liberalized government oversight by passing the JOBS Act. The net effect of this legislative schizophrenia remains to be seen, but private equity and hedge funds quickly geared up to take advantage of the increased marketing opportunities.

Once it is known who can invest in a fund (and more importantly, who wants to invest in this particular fund), it will be necessary to draft the commercial terms of the fund documentation in such a way as to reflect the method by which money will actually flow back and forth between the parties. For example, investors will want to know how and when they will get their money back before they initially write their checks. Private equity and hedge funds differ in their answer to this question.

Typically, funds choose to operate as either open-ended or close-ended funds. Open-ended funds allow for periodic subscription and redemption by investors throughout the life of the fund. As a result, the fund itself may have no pre-set termination date and the investment horizon will vary from one investor to another. Hedge funds are often established on an open-ended basis. Closed-ended funds do not allow for such periodic liquidity at the request of investors. Commonly seen in private equity and real estate funds, closed-ended structures allow these funds to take investors' committed capital during the early years of a fund's life and only return proceeds to investors when the underlying investments are realized. In part, a fund being closed-ended or open-ended will be driven by the liquidity of the underlying investment, and whether it is viable to realize partial stakes from time to time to fund redemption requests.

Some closed-ended funds are listed on stock exchanges, which facilitate the regular trading of the interests, enabling willing sellers to transact with willing buyers. Like any market price, however, the price at which a closed-ended fund is sold will reflect the sentiments of the market, which may either overvalue or undervalue any security. Importantly, once an investor has sold his or her interest, the underlying assets of the fund remain unchanged. Where a liquid secondary market has not been established for a closed-ended fund, investors must instead rely on the fund manager to return some or all of the capital of the fund, together with any profits, either at predetermined dates or at the fund manager's own discretion. A limited life may be required by investors to assure them that their capital (with any profits) will be returned to them at a predetermined time (e.g. seven years).

The appeal of an open-ended fund is significant. We like the idea that we can take our money back whenever we want. Our bank accounts operate in essence on an open-ended basis. If a need for cash arises, we can go to our bank (either in person or electronically) and simply request that some portion of our account is converted into cash. This simplicity on the surface, however, hides a number of important practical issues.

By providing investors with the ability to receive a return of net asset value for their interests, an open-ended fund removes the necessity of the investor to identify a buyer and negotiate a price, or wait until the fund manager decides it is time to return money. Further, it allows investors with different time horizons to participate in the same fund, confident in the knowledge that they can obtain liquidity when most suitable to their own internal requirements. The fund, however, faces the prospect of significant changes in the amount of its capital in situations where redemptions on a particular date exceed new subscriptions. Investments may need to be sold to fund redemption requests. As a result, funds either investing in illiquid assets or pursuing longer term investment strategies may find open-endedness incompatible with their objectives.

In an open-ended fund, the frequency with which a fund manager will be willing to accept further investments may be the same or different from the frequency with which it will be willing to provide an investor with his or her money back. Both decisions will be driven in part by the nature and liquidity of the underlying assets and the perceived ability to identify new investments and to realize existing investments.

Where the assets are highly liquid and actively traded, subscriptions and redemptions may be possible with great regularity. Otherwise, interim liquidity may be highly restricted. In either case, redemptions may be subject to initial lock-in periods, fees charged on redemptions or limits on the amounts that may be redeemed at one time.

Whenever further subscriptions or redemptions are permitted, it will be necessary to recalculate the fund's net asset value. These calculations entail determining the current value of each of the fund's investments and allocating profits and losses to each investor.

However, periodic redemptions can, at times, pose risks to non-redeeming investors, particularly in volatile markets. Returning to the example of a bank discussed above, a run on a bank (as graphically portrayed in the Christmas television stalwart, *It's a Wonderful Life*) demonstrates the effects of massive withdrawals in a short period of time. Funds are equally susceptible when they are open-ended. To prevent the occurrence of a "downward spiral" in a fund's net asset value caused by redemptions being made in a falling market, some funds impose a "gate" system to limit the ability of investors to take more than a predetermined percentage of the fund's assets out on any one dealing date.

As a result, a holding in such funds tends to be subject to potential illiquidity at precisely the time when an investor may most want his or her money back. Without such limitations, however, non-redeeming investors face the prospect of being left with a share in a rump of assets disproportionately undervalued, since in practice the most highly valued assets would be the easiest for a fund manager to sell at short notice to meet pending redemption requests.

Gate provisions differ significantly from fund to fund, with different thresholds and notice periods applying to different classes of investors. Often, such funds will limit withdrawals to 10–20 percent of their assets. Where a threshold is met, investors in a particular class can participate up to the threshold pro rata. The balance of their redemption request is then postponed to the next dealing day.

In late 2008 and early 2009, the gate provisions of many hedge funds on both sides of the Atlantic were put to the test. As funds began to record significant losses because of rapid collapses in asset values, fund managers took advantage of these provisions to limit investor withdrawals for several months. Eventually, as cash-strapped investors sought liquidity from any source they could find, the so-called "ATM effect" became evident. Investors soon started pulling money from whatever fund would permit redemptions, regardless of how healthy that particular fund happened to be. A number of well-known fund managers, such as DE Shaw, Farallon Capital Management, Fortress Investment Group, RAB Capital and Centaurus Capital, were reported in the press at this time as having enforced gate restrictions.

There is actually such a thing as "too much money" in alternative investment funds, although many laypersons might be surprised to hear it.

There are actually sound commercial reasons to impose limits on the overall size of the fund. The amount of money raised for a private equity or hedge fund will be driven by the number and size of potential investment opportunities that the fund intends to pursue. In part, this will be a function of both the fund's investment strategy and the size of the team that the fund manager has assembled. Money raised above this "capacity constraint" will often be hard to deploy in the specific investment objective agreed with investors. As a result, the risks are that the fund experiences a style drift into other areas of investing, or earns a lower investment return because the money is ultimately invested in less appealing sectors or styles.

Particularly in private equity funds, it is increasingly common for fund documents to include "hard caps" that limit the ability of a fund manager to raise more than an agreed amount. Further, limits may be placed on the fund manager to prevent reusing or "recycling" the proceeds from one investment to fund further investments. Interestingly, the trend over recent years toward "mega funds" in the private equity space (i.e. funds in excess of $10 billion) appears to be reaching its natural limit, with a number of fund managers offering investors in large buyout funds the opportunity to decrease their capital commitments in the face of decreasing investment opportunities and limited access to debt financing.

In the case of hedge funds, limits on fund size typically take the form of "soft caps" which are imposed and lifted at the sole discretion of the fund manager. The purpose of these caps is to ensure that money is only accepted into the fund if the portfolio manager knows that he or she can effectively use it without negatively impacting performance.

For example, in June 2011, the GLG European Alpha Alternative UCITS Fund, a long/short market neutral fund, announced that it would soft close after reaching the $1 billion, while a few months later, in December 2011, Taylor Woods, a commodities-focused hedge fund, also announced a soft close at $1 billion. More recently, in June 2012, the Hong Kong-based Segantii Capital announced that its Asian hedge fund would soft close after tripling its assets to reach $680 million.

One important distinction between hedge funds and private equity funds can be seen in the manner in which an investor pays his or her money into the fund. As investors in a private equity fund typically contribute their capital to the fund over time, upon receipt from the general partner of a drawdown notice (unlike in a hedge fund where the entire cash sum is typically contributed on "day one"), a number of features of that particular fund structure deserve special consideration.

Drawdown structures directly affect how private equity funds must operate. Under this approach, limited partners commit to provide a certain amount of capital to the fund at launch, but this amount is only called for in instalments by the fund manager where a suitable investment is identified. Where investments are illiquid and to be held for a considerable time before their realization, a drawdown structure allows a fund manager to avoid having excess cash on hand. This uninvested cash could negatively impact the fund's returns.

In practice, when the fund manager needs money from investors either to acquire a new investment or to pay expenses, drawdown notices are sent to investors that require that some or all of the capital that they are obliged to provide must be paid within a prescribed period. A limited partner would usually have ten days to provide the fund with the money requested or be subject to potentially quite serious consequences. Failure to comply with the notice by an investor would prevent a fund from being able to complete a proposed investment.

The drawdown feature of a private equity fund has a significant impact on performance. Simply put, drawdowns minimize the holding period of investors' capital by the fund. Performance of the fund, as reported by the fund manager, is intrinsically linked to the period of time that the money was invested. Uninvested capital will be a drag on the real performance of the fund, and the actual return earned by an investor. It is imperative that, while maintaining sufficient liquid assets to comply with the drawdown notices as and when received, investors invest their uninvested capital commitments in such a manner as to maximize their overall returns.

Because of the limited life of their funds, private equity fund sponsors typically launch a new fund every few years, raising further commitments from investors for additional investments, once their existing funds are substantially invested. Both the ability to identify suitable investments and to realize them by trade sale or IPO will drive whether a private equity fund will run to its full term or be wound down earlier. Extensions to the life of the fund may be necessary in order to ensure the most successful realizations. These are typically provided for further one-year periods, subject to a final "drop dead" date.

The investment period of a private equity fund will often last between four to six years. At the end of this period, any undrawn capital commitments of a limited partner will fall away and not be subject to drawdowns by the general partner, except to pay for expenses or, in limited circumstances, to fund follow-on investments in companies already in the fund's portfolio.

An investor's capital commitment to a private equity fund typically lasts until the end of the prescribed investment period, which will be the first few years of a fund's life. Commitments not drawn down during this period will be waived by the fund, except for a certain amount which will be available for further investment in current fund assets.

As a general rule, once capital has been drawn by a private equity fund and invested, when that investment is realized, the proceeds must be returned to the investors. Typically, this is the only liquidity option that investors in a closed-end drawdown structure possess. Exceptions may be made for investments that are realized in a very short time (e.g. one year), which are often known as "bridge investments." By contrast, proceeds from realized investments in hedge funds are immediately used to purchase new investments.

The limited partnership agreements of private equity funds almost universally impose stringent penalties on investors who default. For example, a defaulting investor may see his or her interest in the fund forfeited or sold to other investors or third parties. Such provisions are not frequently invoked, but rather serve as the backdrop against which investor liquidity difficulties or disputes with fund managers may be resolved.

When things go bad between a fund manager and the investors in a fund, it is not a pretty picture!

Often potential disputes between a limited partner and a general partner will involve threats from both sides that invoke these default provisions. A belief that the general partner has breached a duty owed to the partners may be actioned by one or more limited partners indicating that they will not comply with any further drawdown requests until the alleged breach is resolved.

Negotiations which follow between the parties will seek to avoid the need to invoke the default provisions by resolving the underlying issues. Some limited partners will be concerned about the risk to their limited liability should they become involved in the management of the partnership. Also, a fund manager may choose not to exercise their full scope of rights. Rather than risk open disputes, and the possibility of litigation, many fund managers prefer to simply reduce capital commitments voluntarily. This can provide for a solution across the entire fund, rather than haphazardly on an investor-by-investor basis.

Behind every fund – regardless of whether it is a private equity or a hedge fund – is a fund manager.

It makes little sense to discuss the past performance of XYZ Bolivian Mining Opportunity Fund without a thorough analysis and evaluation of its fund manager, XYZ Capital Partners LLC. If a fund is a puppet, created from partnerships, offshore companies and contracts instead of wood, felt and cloth, then the fund manager is the puppeteer. It is the talent of particular portfolio managers that drives the spectacularly high returns which investors eagerly seek. It is on the basis of the perceived skills, experience and track record of the fund manager that investors typically decide to entrust their savings in a particular fund.

The legal structures and regulatory hurdles described above simply prescribe the space in which these funds may operate. Ultimately, though, it is the investment decisions actually made by the fund manager that dictate a particular fund's trajectory in the financial markets.

Accordingly, our attention now turns to the men and women who establish and run private equity and hedge funds.

3: WHO WAS THAT MASKED MAN?

A Brief Discussion of Fund Managers and Sponsors

By many measures, we are one of the largest and most diversified asset managers in the world. We've been a first mover, with teams on the ground in almost all the major emerging markets today.
Daniel D'Aniello, Carlyle Capital

Private equity firms should not seek public listings. Suddenly they have two masters: the public markets and their limited partners.
George Sudarskis, former chief investment officer at the Abu Dhabi Investment Authority

Few sixtieth birthday parties have had such lingering impact for the guest-of-honor (or an entire industry) as the extravagant celebration thrown on February 14, 2007 for Stephen Schwarzman, co-founder of Blackrock Group.

Blackrock, which Schwarzman established with his former Lehman Brothers boss and Washington insider Peter G. Peterson, was just a few months away from making its debut on the New York Stock Exchange at an eye-watering valuation of over $30 billion. As the global financial crisis began to make itself known, this valuation would cascade steadily downwards. On this day, however, Schwarzman was Wall Street's "Man of the Moment." Performers at the birthday party included Rod Stewart, Patti LaBelle and comedian Martin Short. His photo would eventually grace the cover of the March 5 edition of *Fortune* magazine, a few weeks before the paperwork for the Blackstone IPO was filed with the SEC in Washington DC.

Unfortunately, not everyone was uniformly enthusiastic about Schwarzman's impending windfall.

Soon after details of the amount of money Schwarzman was due to make in the IPO became public in June, Senators Max Baucus and Chuck Grassley, along with Congressman Charles Rangel, launched proposals to suspend the beneficial tax treatments that firms such as Blackstone enjoyed. In the highly politicized game of who-gets-taxed-and-how-much, private equity's time of hiding in the shadows was by this time well and truly over. Questions over how much tax these businesses could (and should) pay would circle the industry incessantly for the years that followed. Even today, threats to impose additional taxes on carried interest are trotted out at regular intervals as a way of reminding private equity that they are not forgotten by their opponents in Washington.

Of course, it wasn't too long after this historic IPO that Wall Street, the City of London and financial centers around the world began shuddering under the accumulating weight of subprime mortgage defaults. The correction that was expected, and inevitable, was finally beginning. Unfortunately, the scope and duration of this "credit crunch" was far beyond what recent experience would have predicted. It soon became evident that something very, very painful was happening.

The unravelling of the global financial markets had begun.

A surprisingly wide cross-section of individuals and organizations establish and manage private equity and hedge funds.

Leading investment professionals often leave the security and comfort of successful merchant banks, investment management firms and other financial institutions in pursuit of the increased investment flexibility and higher rewards that can be gained from independence and entrepreneurship. In 2010, for example, two former Credit Suisse traders, George Taylor and Trevor Woods, formed the hedge fund management firm Taylor Woods, based in Greenwich, Connecticut, and launched a commodities-focused fund. In 2012, Frank Dominick of Morgan Stanley and Charles Woo of Lehman Brothers joined Hong Kong-based Ardon Maroon Fund Management to launch an Asian fund focused on mergers and acquisitions. No one likes seeing perfectly good talent walk out the door, though. Increasingly, traditional fund management firms have also entered the frame, either by establishing their own range of alternative investment funds or by joint venturing with independent firms.

But who are these men and women who decide to leave the security of large firms and set up on their own?

It would be a careless mistake to simply categorize hedge fund managers and private equity professionals as just the same as anyone else working on Wall Street or in the City of London. There are significant differences between an investment banker or a stock broker on the one hand, and the men and women who establish and run alternative investment firms. These distinctions stem from the structure and operation of private equity and hedge funds, and need to be recognized in order to understand how these firms operate both internally and in the financial markets as a whole.

Private equity and hedge funds tend to be entrepreneurial businesses that are established as new and independent ventures. The process of launching a new fund is a complicated and risky process, as is the start of any new business. Whenever individuals trade certainty for uncertainty, there will be a lot of concerns, fears and doubts. All must be addressed. This process will inevitably draw out a number of issues concerning the future structure and operation of the fund management firm, as well as the proposed fund, including allocation of economic rewards (such as carried interest or performance fees) among team members; succession issues for senior team members; and documenting and calculating track records.

The same issues that drive fund structuring – pass-through taxation and limited liability – are also of importance when structuring the new fund management business. To the extent feasible, individuals providing the investment advice through the fund manager will seek to escape double taxation of their incentive allocations and to receive as beneficial a treatment of these payments as possible. Equally, these individuals will want to ensure that they are protected from any claims against the fund manager, whether from the fund itself or from other third party creditors.

A key distinction between alternative investment funds and much of the rest of Wall Street is the relationship between a fund and its fund manager. This relationship is an important one that is easily misunderstood or misconstrued. Therefore, it is important that these arrangements are laid out unambiguously to ensure that the roles and responsibilities of each individual involved are clearly demarcated.

Decisions regarding the purchase and sale of investments are made by the fund manager. However, it is not the fund manager's money that is being invested. Fund managers do not typically enter transactions as a principal, but rather as an agent on behalf of the fund. This distinction is crucial and its importance cannot be overstated. The fund itself is the principal and subject to any and all duties or obligations involved in the transaction.

If the fund manager says "buy," then the fund must buy. If the fund manager says "sell," then the fund must sell. The risk is wholly on the fund. As a result, the fund manager is able to significantly limit its own risk exposure. Simply losing money for a client is not enough, by itself, to see a lawsuit succeed against an investment manager.

This arms-length portrayal of the relationship between a fund and a fund manager, however, is an over-simplification. One or more vehicles established and owned by the fund manager often participate in the fund structure in order to provide investment advice, execute resulting investment decisions and receive fees from the investors for such services.

A fund manager may act as a general partner to a fund formed as a limited partnership or may simply enter into a bilateral investment management agreement with the fund formed as a company to provide advice in return for fees. The precise role will be determined by the ultimate fund structure designed for the investors. In many fund structures, therefore, there may be a number of legal entities, all owned by the fund manager, playing similar or overlapping roles. The need for multiple management entities in the fund structure is often driven by either particular tax concerns relating to the characteristics of the remuneration being received; the commercial relationships between the promoters of the fund and the ultimate portfolio managers; or the regulatory status (or lack thereof) of the management company.

Although the fund and the fund manager are separate vehicles, subject to separate ownership structures, the line between them can easily be blurred. Blurring can result from either an investor's ownership of an equity stake in the fund manager or the fund manager's ownership of an investment interest in the fund. Any attempt to critique the operation of these funds must bear in mind the potential for multiple roles, and the risks that they bring.

For example, as discussed earlier, a significant investor that provides a cornerstone investment in a new fund may request an equity participation in the fund manager as well, in order to capture a portion of the franchise value that its investment has created. This participation recognizes the value brought to the fund manager as a result of this "concept validating" investment. In this regard, the investment of a well-respected investor (such as, for example, a CalPERS or a Kuwait Investment Authority) can be seen as functionally equivalent to a celebrity endorsement. The terms of the participation are highly negotiable and can include rights to only the initial fund in which the investment was made or to all funds launched by the fund manager. Either approach may be counterbalanced by time limits or earn-out provisions.

Regardless of how the participation is structured, to the extent that one or more particular investors have both an interest in the fund and a stake in the fund manager, the governance issues facing the remaining investors can become very complicated very quickly.

As a result of this dual role, investors who also have a stake in the fund manager may be less willing to ensure that the fund manager is subject to adequate oversight and accountability in all areas.

Often, a fund manager will also invest in the fund, alongside the fund investors. This demonstrates the faith that the fund manager has in his or her ability to make investment decisions. In these cases, the fund manager is simply putting its money where its mouth is.

As a result, any direct investment that the fund manager has in the fund will be in addition to its receipt of management fees and performance fees, which are discussed in more detail in the following chapter. This investment may consist of interests in the same vehicle as the investors or in another vehicle which co-invests in parallel with the main fund. Historically, for funds set up in the United States as partnerships, tax rules once required a 1 percent investment by the general partner in order to receive partnership tax treatment. Although no longer applicable, the 1 percent investment standard has lingered in some corners of the alternative investment market.

Private equity and hedge funds have not lacked for colorful characters. These industries have thrived over the last several decades under the leadership of highly individualistic men. Unsurprisingly, their lives reflect the idiosyncrasy and individuality that first drove them to turn their back on the paved road to success on Wall Street and instead choose to set out on their own.

Warren Hellman, who passed away in 2011, was the founder of San Francisco-based private equity firm Hellman and Friedman. He was also a devout student and promoter of banjo picking and bluegrass music, who frequently wore cowboy shirts. Not the image that most laypersons would have of someone who had demonstrated immense prowess at the highest level of corporate finance! Hellman regularly toured with his own bluegrass band, the Wronglers, and his three-day bluegrass festival, known as Hardly Strictly Bluegrass, draws 750,000 music lovers.

Unfortunately, 2011 also saw the passing of Theodore Forstmann, founder of Forstmann Little and a passionate philanthropist. Fans of the gossip pages might recall his name from the brief period when he dated Diana, Princess of Wales. Forstmann was both strong-willed and strong. While at Yale, he played ice hockey. Private equity owes its fundamental economic structure to Forstmann. He created the "carried interest" model of private equity in the late 1970s. As a dealmaker, his skills were renowned, especially his spectacular turnaround of Gulfstream. His passing generated compelling recollections from his colleagues and competitors, as well as from senior Washington figures.

He also had the honor of coining the term "barbarians at the gate" in the late 1980s as a description of the surge during this time in leveraged buyouts. That phrase would develop a life of its own, as questions were inevitably raised about the short-term and long-term effects of these buyouts.

Forstmann's philanthropy focused on children, both in the United States and internationally. He even went so far as to sign Warren Buffett's "Giving Pledge," thereby promising to give half of his fortune to charity. Although unmarried and without children, he became the guardian of two boys he met at a South African orphanage in the late 1990s.

David Bonderman, who would go on to form Texas Pacific Group, now TPG, started his professional life as a civil rights and bankruptcy lawyer after graduating from Harvard Law School. He gave up the law to work with financier Robert Bass in Texas, before setting up his own shop with James Coulter. Bonderman's birthday parties over the years would not be overshadowed by his rivals at other private equity firms. Musical entertainment might feature the Rolling Stones and former Beatle Paul McCartney, for example.

Some might be surprised to learn that even the giants in the private equity industry pride themselves on their senses of humor.

The co-founders of Carlyle went to great lengths in the days before Christmas 2011 to demonstrate just that point. In their three minute "Holiday Founders' Video," David Rubinstein, William Conway and Daniel D'Aniello took the time to show investors what their lives might have been like if they hadn't formed Carlyle two decades ago. By suggesting that they would have, respectively, run a lemonade stand, been an operator in a call center or worked at the counter of a Dunkin Donuts, the trio made clear to viewers that they didn't take themselves too seriously.

No less than Stephen Schwarzman of Blackstone put his own comedic talents to the test in a more long-form format during his speech at the 2011 Alfred E. Smith Memorial Foundation Dinner. He managed to include light-hearted references to his famous birthday party as well as a number of well-crafted zingers directed at several of the great and the good in the audience.

So how does someone become a hedge fund manager or a private equity professional? What makes a young boy or girl decide that when they grow up they want to work for an alternative investment firm?

The individuals who work for (and succeed at) these entrepreneurial firms are both products of the traditional financial service firms and in many important ways reactions to those traditions and stereotypes. Often, the same things that motivate investment bankers or stockbrokers or bond traders also motivate a hedge fund manager or a private equity professional. This might include compensation, prestige or just the raw pleasure of being demonstrated again and again to be correct. But the differences in self-perception are very important, and in many ways they have shaped these industries and made them culturally distinct. For example, transaction-based compensation causes a banker to focus on getting the next deal done. Focusing on performance over time rather than deal volume is a feature of performance fees and carried interests.

These individuals are quite different from others on Wall Street, but perhaps most importantly, they are in short supply.

In the case of hedge funds, one of the most difficult tasks for a start-up, or rapidly growing, firm is recruitment. Hiring the right people can be particularly difficult when the founders would much rather sit in front of a Bloomberg screen and test out new investment ideas than sift through stacks of resumes and interview large numbers of applicants. Not to worry, though – Wall Street's largest investment banks are here to help!

As discussed earlier, prime brokerage teams at leading bulge-bracket firms, such as Goldman Sachs and Morgan Stanley have added "talent introduction" to the long list of services that they offer to their more lucrative hedge fund clients. By placing senior professionals into a hedge fund, the banks hope to reap the benefits of those relationships for years to come. Of course, the potential for conflicts of interest abound. The risk that an aggrieved fund manager may claim that a prime broker has "poached" a key employee from them to place at a more lucrative fund client is ever present.

Banks active in talent introduction are keen to claim, however, that what they actually do is function simply as a clearing house for potential applicants and nothing more. They do not see themselves as "head hunters" luring otherwise happy employees away from their current jobs.

By some estimates, hedge funds amount to as much as 35 percent of the brokerage commissions paid to the leading investment banks, so winning and maintaining trade relationships with these funds is an important source of profits for many banks since the financial crisis began. Creating extensive databases of industry personnel and skill sets is a simple way to maintain close ties with key decision-makers. And unlike headhunters, the prime brokers do not demand recruitment fees of 25 percent of the first year's compensation package. Instead, they provide these services for free, simply in the hope of earning future commissions.

Free is a good price. In fact, it is a very good price.

Regulators, however, soon began to focus on the risks of conflicts here. William Galvin, the head of Massachusetts's financial regulator, has said, "It's the type of relationship investors should know about, or simply shouldn't exist." Galvin sent an enquiry letter in October 2011 to leading US prime brokers, including Bank of America, Deutsche Bank, Goldman Sachs, Morgan Stanley and UBS, requesting a list of those hedge funds for which they made employment referrals. One particularly thorny issue is whether funds need to provide disclosure to the investors when their manager uses recruitment referrals from a prime broker in order to highlight potential situations where brokerage commissions paid from fund assets are being directed to one bank over another.

Part of the mythology that has grown up around hedge funds in recent years includes the contention that the men and women who manage these funds are actually "the smartest people in the room." Their advantage over other market participants arguably stems from their intellectual advantages. Of course, the collapse of Long-Term Capital Management has led many investors and commentators to take any overly simplistic claims of mental superiority with at least a grain of salt. However, hedge fund infatuation with Nobel Prize winners still continues today. In November 2011, Thomas Sargent, a recent co-winner of a Nobel Prize in economic science, was hired as a consultant by the Hutchin Hill multi-strategy hedge fund. With $1.5 billion in assets, Hutchin Hill will use Sargent's expertise in macro-economics to attempt to earn higher returns for their investors. Sargent's day job is as a professor at New York University.

A unique view of hedge fund managers letting their hair down, and their own highly revealing self-image at a time when their wider role in global finance was first being generally acknowledged, was a display on the grounds of Knebworth House in Hertfordshire, England in June 2006. The festivities were known as "Hedgestock." What was in effect an industry conference dressed up in Woodstock nostalgia and featuring a live concert by the Who quickly gained international notoriety. Photos of hedge fund traders and marketers wearing bell-bottom jeans and tie-dyed shirts were published by news outlets around the world. High-end watchmakers and car manufacturers had their luxury goods on display, as attendees drank expensive champagne while wearing love beads.

Despite the negative backlash that resulted, Hedgestock demonstrated how differently many hedge fund managers view themselves from the more traditional and straight-laced sections of Wall Street and the City of London. And like most industry conferences, the official program, no matter how boring or flamboyant, was simply an excuse for groups of people with money to be in the same location for a few days as people who are asking for money in order to match would-be investors with willing managers.

As a sign of how well the industry has done since 2008, rumors were circulating in November 2012 that a new Hedgestock might actually be held again, sometime in the near future. The band Mumford & Sons was even mentioned as a possible headlining musical act. Interestingly, band member Winston Marshall is the son of hedge fund titan Paul Marshall.

Many of the points made above can be translated over to private equity easily, although there are at the date of publication no rumors circulating of plans for a "PrivateEquityStock" or a "GladstonPrivateEquity." Displays such as that are probably uniquely for the hedge fund community.

Regardless, as private equity has grown in recent years, their need to recruit investment professionals has also increased. At present, many private equity firms focus on relatively young men and women in their early twenties, who are finishing their first jobs on Wall Street with the bulge-bracket investment banks. The competition for entry-level positions is fierce. It has been estimated that over one thousand junior analysts in New York compete each year for only fifty slots.

The lure? Money, of course. Carried interest represents the gold standard of compensation in the financial world, in part, of course, due to its beneficial capital gains treatment, which will be examined in more detail in the following chapter.

As a result, talent of all sorts can be lured away from their current homes by the promise of private equity riches. When Blackrock needed a general counsel, Stephen Schwarzman went straight to a top partner at a top Manhattan law firm. John Finley, a twenty-year veteran of the prestigious firm, Simpson Thacher & Bartlett, left behind private practice law firm life for the role as Blackstone's first chief legal officer. According to SEC filings, Finley took home over $7 million during his first year. Finley's fellow Simpson Thacher alumni, David Sorkin, has a similar role, and similar compensation at the rival private equity house, KKR.

Notably, despite the significant growth of private equity and hedge funds in recent years and the frequent references to the industries being meritocracies, fund professionals remain overwhelmingly male, and overwhelmingly white. In a survey of US hedge funds conducted by consulting firm Rothstein Kass in April 2012, 6 percent of responding firms indicated that they were owned or managed by women, while 10 percent said they were owned or managed by minorities. In 2011, a worldwide survey conducted by research firm Preqin revealed that approximately 9 percent of senior private equity professionals were women.

As alternative investment firms continue to attract the attention of the mainstream media, their managers will need to be increasingly mindful of how closely their ranks, including eventually their most senior ranks, reflect the countries in which they operate and the constituencies of the investors who provide them with the much-needed capital that they invest.

As mentioned above, the relationship between a fund and its fund manager is an agency relationship. It is important to bear in mind at all times that the fund, as principal, delegates decision-making power to the fund manager, an agent.

In the case of investment funds, the agent is often itself a legal entity (such as a corporation) with its own matrix of agency relationships. If a human being walks into a room and claims to be acting on behalf of the fund, it will be necessary to work through the various levels of agency in order to determine how that claim to authority was developed.

Most importantly, the fund's agent (the fund manager) will have a distinct advantage in its transactions with its principal (the fund). Why? Due to its more substantive existence. A fund manager will typically possess its own professional and administrative staff, which the fund will lack. A fund manager would also possess infrastructure, such as permanent office space and informational technology resources, which the fund will lack. Finally, in almost all cases, the fund manager will both pre-exist and ultimately survive the fund.

As a result, the principal will both be very dependent on its agent, and also potentially face significant procedural impediments and inefficiencies in conducting the corporate actions necessary to oversee and monitor the agent. This is at the very heart of the dilemma in all funds. Since decision-making resides with the fund manager, who takes investment decisions on his or her own initiative, the question inevitably becomes to what extent control over the decision-making process can reside with fund participants.

In other words, to what extent can these investors have a voice in connection with such decisions, either before or after they are made? How can investors in a fund successfully oversee the fund manager's activities and ensure that they are not victims of fraud, malfeasance or negligence?

When we talk about investment managers and their clients, generally, and these particular questions, specifically, we must inevitably use the "F word" – that is, "fiduciary."

The relationship between an investment manager and his or her client differs in many important ways from the relationships between most other participants in the financial markets. Where many counterparties to a financial contract will have only an obligation to perform their contractual duties (e.g. delivering of a security, exchange of payments), an investment manager will owe to his or her client both a common law duty of care, and also a set of fiduciary duties. The nature of this relationship is similar in many respects to the relationship that lawyers, accountants and doctors have with their clients, where an element of trust and dependence sits at the core of the interactions.

In the investment management agreement, for example, the client will typically confer on the investment manager the discretion to buy and sell the client's assets at such prices and in such amounts as the investment manager will determine to be in the best interests of the client. This discretion can serve as the basis for the relationship of "trust and confidence" required of a fiduciary. This fiduciary duty provides a means to protect a client against conflicts of interest on the part of the investment manager. In the context of today's complex web of financial regulation, this fiduciary duty also exists alongside a growing array of regulatory measures addressing conflict management in the modern financial services firm.

However, the bitter reality for some unlucky investors will often be that the fund manager who broke the law ultimately turns out to be "judgment proof." This means that despite the merits of the case to a court of law, the guilty party has few assets available to fulfill successful damages actions against them. Also, the plethora of various fund management entities and multiple fund vehicles that can be involved in fund structures of substantial size raises the legitimate question of who fund participants can look to for recourse when fraud, malfeasance or negligence is uncovered. In many cases, by this time often it can be too late.

Fortunately, however, there are a number of fund managers who have done well enough over the years to ensure that they will not be "judgment proof." For them, the more perplexing question is what to do with all the money they have earned over the years.

The "Robber Baron" era of the late nineteenth century did, at least, produce a number of significant charitable and cultural organizations, such as museums, libraries and other artistic venues that have survived to the present day. Huge amounts of wealth were accumulated by industrialists and financiers during these gilded decades, but an effort was made by at least some individuals to make a display of sharing that money with the wider population.

Today, critics have begun to pose an awkward question. Where are the similar contributions of the current generation of private equity and hedge fund magnates? Where are their foundling hospitals? Where is their Metropolitan Museum of Art?

Although several high-profile hedge fund managers and private equity professionals have joined the boards, and become patrons, of established charitable organizations, there is little evidence to date that they have made anything approaching the contribution to contemporary public life as, for example, a Rockefeller or a Carnegie. Has this introversion and insularity contributed to the negative public opinion that the hedge fund and private equity fund industries have been wrestling with in recent years?

Of course, some hedge funds have attempted to make a good name for themselves through their philanthropic activities. For example, James Simmons, founder of Renaissance Technologies, a highly successful hedge fund, made a $150 million donation in 2011 to Stony Brook University in New York. Simmons had once served as chairman of the Stony Brook mathematics department, before he left the halls of academia in 1978 to become a "quantitative" investor on Wall Street. His donation was the sixth largest ever given to an American public university. In March 2013, the UK hedge fund manager Brevan Howard donated $30 million to the business school at Imperial College in London to set up a finance research center, which will be named in their honor. Alan Howard, the firm's founder, had studied chemical engineering there when he was younger. Brevan Howard now manage an estimated $39 billion for clients. The best known, and increasingly contro-versial, hedge-fund-manager-turned-philanthropist is George Soros, whose Open Society Foundation operates around the world. In 2011 alone, Open Society gave away approximately $860 million.

On occasion, the founders of the great private equity giants will also reach for the checkbooks and make headline-grabbing philanthropic donations. In 2008, Stephen Schwarzman donated $100 million to the New York Public Library. In 2010, Henry Kravis donated $100 million to Columbia Business School. In 2012, Leon Black donated $48 million to Dartmouth College, where he graduated in 1973, in order to build a visual arts center. Black also enjoys fine art, having paid $47 million at a Christie's auction in 2009 for a Raphael drawing.

However, the place where private equity and hedge fund professionals have had their most high-profile impact on everyday life in the United States has been their acquisition of professional sports teams. To be fair to the Rockefellers and the Carnegies, the value of baseball teams during their day was not sufficiently stratospheric to warrant their attention (or their precious profits). In recent years, though, the successful investment professionals of our modern era have stepped into the national and international spotlight to claim the handful of sporting treasures that make their way onto the market.

Millions of everyday workers and savers who do not follow the machinations of Wall Street's insular investment community have begun to learn more about these funds, and the men and women who run them, when a rumor begins to circulate that one of them is poised to gobble up their local sports team.

For example, the decision of Steven Cohen of SAC Capital in early 2012 to pursue the Los Angeles Dodgers attracted great media attention, following on from the failed attempt earlier by David Einhorn of Greenlight Capital to buy a one-third interest in the New York Mets. The Dodgers were ultimately purchased in 2012 by a group of investors led by Mark Walker, chief executive officer of Guggenheim Partners, after a prolonged bidding process. With a $2 billion price tag, the acquisition set a global record across all sports.

Joshua Harris, a co-founder of Apollo, purchased the Philadelphia 76ers in 2011, together with David Blitzer of Blackstone. One month earlier, Tom Gore, of Los Angeles-based Platinum Equity, bought the Detroit Pistons. Boston has been a trendsetter in this area. The Red Sox are owned by hedge fund superstar John Henry and the Boston Celtics by a group of private equity professionals including many from Mitt Romney's alma mater, Bain Capital.

Interestingly, the skybox in a contemporary sporting facility appears to be the place where hedge fund and private equity titans feel most comfortable putting their accumulating earnings on display. Public perception of these men and women is influenced, accordingly.

It has become commonplace to describe private equity and hedge funds as "unregulated." Much of the mainstream media coverage of these funds reflexively use this label as a key component of any description of these funds and their investment activities. As discussed in the previous chapter, the truth is slightly more nuanced.

A fund manager, however, will typically be registered with and supervised by a financial regulator, such as the SEC or the FCA. As a result, they must ensure that they comply with all the legal and regulatory requirements of the country where they operate, as well as the domiciles of the funds which they advise. In other words, although the fund vehicles themselves are not subject to intensive, product-level regulation like mutual funds and other retail savings products, everything that these funds do with the money they raise is regulated, just like any other participant in the financial markets.

Simply put, the lack of retail investors in an alternative fund does not give them free reign to do anything they want with the money entrusted to them.

An example might be useful. Let's imagine that Sir Richard Branson has decided to enter the weight loss business and, after researching his competitors, starts buying shares in the market leading company in this sector, which happens to be listed on the London Stock Exchange. If a hedge fund or private equity fund were to engage in the same investment strategy, then both the fund and Sir Richard would have to make the same regulatory disclosure filings and be subject to the same rules and regulations with regards to buying and disposing that investment.

It is not the case that simply because the fund is "unregulated" it somehow gets a free pass through *all* restrictions otherwise applicable to its actions. Market participants, whether a sandy-haired former entrepreneur, a bank's proprietary trading desk or a Cayman hedge fund, must all comply with the same rules of the road.

Being unregulated, however, does mean that investors must look out for their own interests and cannot come running to financial regulators if the wheels fall off the fund and they suffer huge losses as a result.

Every fund raises potential tensions between the fund manager and the investors in two areas: conflicts of interest and informational asymmetries regarding the assets of the fund. For funds that are approved for retail distributions, such as mutual funds, detailed rules are imposed to address, among other things, governance mechanisms, the manner in which shares are issued and redeemed, self-dealing, periodic reporting and capital structure. The same concerns exist with regard to private equity and hedge funds. However, the decision is taken by regulators that, due to the nature of the participants, prescribing these matters will not be necessary. Investors in alternative funds are expected to have the knowledge and ability to negotiate with the fund manager those aspects of investor protection that are appropriate in a given circumstance.

Once the policy judgment is made that sophisticated investors should be allowed to invest in innovative investment products, impediments to this arrangement are, therefore, removed and exemptions made available on the marketing and operation of such products by fund managers. However, the issues of conflicts and informational asymmetries remain. They cannot, and do not, magically disappear.

Now, it is the responsibility of these investors to police their managers themselves, not the SEC or the FCA. Unfortunately, the managers often have much more time to make their decisions than the investors have the time to oversee and review those decisions. This dynamic shapes the ongoing relationship between the two parties as well as the source of potential risks that must be addressed by the would-be investor.

How does a fund manager organize its own decision-making? This question is one that a concerned investor will spend a great deal of time reflecting on, whenever questions about the fund manager's fulfillment of its duties arise.

To answer this question, some time must be spent analyzing the structure and operation of the business and organizational structure of the fund manager. Based on the underlying commercial and economic relationships between the founders who establish and run the firm, a fund manager entity can be structured with either elaborate mechanisms for internal governance and dispute resolution or very minimal provisions. In part, this will be driven by the number of principals involved, as well as the complexity of their business plan and commercial arrangements. As the business of a fund manager expands, the principals may need to re-examine the organizational structure they originally adopted at launch to ensure that decisions made then are still suitable today.

For example, where several principals are involved at the launch of the new business, multiple tiers of "partners" may be created to divide out the voting rights and economic rights more finely. A robust decision making process can then be established within the fund manager entity. This can allow for majority or super-majority voting provisions, both among all partners or on a class-by-class basis. Some decisions may even require different levels of approval by different classes.

Unsurprisingly, the allocation of profits is perhaps the most hotly contested point. Approaches to compensation for members and employees of the fund manager can include participation in annual management fees, participation in incentive compensation, and an equity stake in the fund manager itself. Each fund manager will have a different combination of these factors that reflects the history and personal dynamics of their group of senior principals.

For example, either a fixed proportion or variable proportion approach can be taken, or a combination of the two. Participation in management fees and incentive compensation can, therefore, be dealt with in many different ways. It is up to the individuals involved to devise an allocation of rewards that best matches their particular circumstances. As more funds are eventually launched by a fund manager over time, the decisions only get more complicated. Fund managers with more than one fund must also address how much of the profit of any one fund is shared with other partners.

Founding partners of a fund business can also be asked to provide capital either into the fund manager entity or into the fund itself or both. The amount of capital put into a fund represents the so-called "skin in the game" – that is, the amount of money the founders are willing to put at risk next to the investors' money. Different levels of participation may be required of more senior partners, either in line with their profit sharing ratios or based on some other matrix. Investments by the founders into the funds they actually manage may or may not be subject to a lock-up or mandatory buyout provisions, and may or may not be subject to the payment of fees. This will depend on the commercial relationships between the parties and the needs of the fund itself.

Interestingly, the arrangements between the individual principals and the fund manager are generally not within the oversight of fund investors. The argument is that they are a private matter between the individuals involved and do not impact the operation or prospects of the fund in any material ways. One important exception to this is the extent that certain principals may be named as "key persons" for purposes of termination of the fund manager or where principals are asked to provide personal guarantees to support clawback obligations in private equity funds.

"Key persons" provisions provide that if a person identified by the investors at the launch of the fund departs, then there will be particular consequences for the fund, including the possibility of suspending investment activity until a suitable replacement is found. Clawback obligations allow fund investors to be repaid carried interest if subsequent poor performance means that the fund manager is not entitled to it at the end of the fund's life. Both place individual principals squarely within the sights of the fund and its investors.

However, investors are increasingly asking more probing questions about the structure and operation of the fund manager's business. Where the fund manager's investment process is built around a team rather than a single individual, very particular questions may be asked concerning how performance-based remuneration is divided amongst the team. The potential of sudden departures of senior and mid-level professionals can raise concerns about the stability of the fund manager's business.

As alternative investment firms continue to grow over time, more sophisticated questions about management structure and succession inevitably arise. As firms begin to institutionalize, they become less dependent on the presence of a single individual. Then the potential exists for ongoing success in the long term. To facilitate institutionalization, the development of management committees and co-decision staffing can provide opportunities for the rising generation of professionals to participate in the running of the firm, while reinforcing a firm's unique culture.

This raises a very important question that has been vexing fund managers (and fund investors) for the last decade – who will be the next generation of leaders for the giant private equity and hedge fund firms that have grown up over the past few decades?

Without adequate arrangements for succession, these firms face the risk of collapsing, no matter how much success they enjoyed previously. As has often been reported in the financial press, a surprisingly high number of senior private equity leaders are now in their sixties. Given the "birth" of private equity during the 1970s in the United States, this is to be expected. Founders of some of the largest names in private equity, such as Stephen Schwarzman of Blackstone, David Rubinstein of Carlyle, Henry Kravis and George Roberts of KKR, and David Bonderman of TPG, have ably led their firms for decades. Although these men uniformly insist that they have no plans to retire, questions inevitably arise about succession planning.

How deep are the benches at the top private equity houses? Without exception, each of these firms will point to large numbers of senior professionals in their forties and early fifties who have demonstrated many, or perhaps all, of the traits necessary to lead. Also, they will point to the relatively uncontroversial assertion that the challenges of more mature businesses are very different from the challenges of a start-up. As a result, they will insist, leaders in the future will need a very different skill set than the founders' generation.

Occasionally, circumstances will provide natural solutions. At a firm like Apollo, succession discussions are noticeably easier. Two of the three co-founders, Joshua Harris and Marc Rowan, are still in their late forties. As a result, these otherwise divisive decisions have a chance to simply "make themselves." At other shops, unfortunately, founders often maintain a high profile and a tight grip on the reins, clearly intending to be steering their ships for some time to come.

If there is a bigger, more pressing issue than succession, it is probably retention. All of these firms are comprised of highly motivated individuals who want to succeed year in and year out. Unfortunately for everyone, their definition of success expands a little more each year. One practical benefit of keeping succession plans vague may be that this helps put off decisions by other senior personnel to seek their brighter futures elsewhere.

Hedge funds are also wrestling with the issue of succession. Since many funds have obtained tremendous levels of success on the back of a single visionary portfolio manager, the issues of leadership change are even more pronounced than with private equity funds. A typical private equity firm will launch around a small group of founders, but rarely these days around a single individual.

Bruce Kovner, co-founder of Caxton Associates, made headlines in September 2011 when he announced that he was passing the torch to his long-standing chief investment officer, Andrew Law. The same week, Campbell & Company, the forty-year-old hedge fund based in Baltimore, announced that chief executive Terri Becks was retiring and would be replaced by Stephen Rousin, currently serving as company president. In the past, many hedge funds had simply closed up shop when their original mastermind retired, preferring their yacht or ski chalet to the continuing stress and irritation of a trading floor. But there has been encouraging success over the past decade, such as the succession of a six-person management committee at D. E. Shaw after David Shaw's retirement in 2001.

The question ultimately raised by succession is what type of business has actually been built by the founder – an organization with a complete set of skills and talents necessary to survive and thrive on its own, or simply an alter ego for a unique and irreplaceable individual?

Not every employee, or even great employee, can stay at a fund management firm forever. As with any employer, a fund manager must be prepared for the possibility that its employees may depart, with the expected disputes either preceding or following their exit. Employment agreements are therefore prepared in a manner that will protect the fund manager's ongoing business. Such agreements can include a variety of mechanisms to limit the impact of any departure, including whether the employee can use the track record of the fund with which he or she was associated; whether the employee can contact or solicit investors in the fund; what information and data is proprietary and confidential; and how performance remuneration will be determined up to the date of departure.

At least one well-known fund is reported to have gone so far as to include in the subscription documentation of investors an undertaking on their behalf not to invest with former employees without the consent of the fund manager. Of course, the ultimate arbiter of the viability (if not the validity) of such a provision is the investors themselves. If an investor has his or her heart set on following the departing individual to a new firm, it would be a quite over-confident and tone-deaf former employer who attempts to impede this decision!

As the largest alternative investment firms continue to diversify into other financial businesses, they are moving away, at least in part, from their original business proposition.

For example, private equity firms are increasingly broadening their business in an effort to build diversified asset management companies. Blackstone has demonstrated the advantages of this approach through the success of their $40 billion fund of hedge fund business. In 2012, Blackstone earned less from private equity than from its other alternative investment activities.

In June 2012, KKR announced its acquisition of hedge fund manager Prisma Capital Partners, which manages approximately $8 billion in assets. According to KKR co-founder Henry Kravis, "Many institutional investors are seeking more liquid alternative investment products, and we believe that customized hedge fund solutions play a key role in meeting that need. This makes Prisma a good fit for KKR ..." Interestingly, Prisma was originally founded by three Goldman Sachs partners.

As a result, decisions made regarding the structure of a new fund manager at its launch typically envision the possible sale, in whole or in part, of the business at some time in the future. Over recent years, the number of "strategic" investments in fund managers by third parties has steadily increased. Importantly, firms dependent on a single "star" which lack depth and the likelihood of institutional persistence will generally not make for attractive acquisition targets.

As a means of expanding their product offering, large financial institutions frequently acquire existing successful managers of alternative investment funds rather than developing the relevant capabilities organically. Notable examples have included the acquisition of Highbridge Capital by JP Morgan and FrontPoint Partners by Morgan Stanley, although with significantly different results for the acquirer.

Valuing an alternative fund management business is notoriously difficult. An essential aspect of ultimately preparing the business for sale is to demonstrate that the business is viable even upon the departure of one or more key individuals. Any prospective buyer will require a detailed understanding of the business's profitability, together with a comprehensive review of the risk profile of the funds as well as the fund manager itself.

In the past, a commonly held view was that these firms were no more than an alter ego of the particular individuals who formed them. With tremendous uncertainty over the value left to the franchise should one or more of the principals leave, strategic investors were unwilling to pay a multiple on the current management fee and incentive compensation income necessary to acquire an equity stake in a mature business. Over recent years, however, a number of fund managers have grown significantly in size, as well as diversifying across asset classes to increase the breadth of products they offer under the same brand.

Why would a successful manager of private equity or hedge funds look to bring in outside investors, and potentially lose their firm's much vaunted independence?

Despite the apparent contradiction, there can be sound commercial reasons for "selling out." Possible reasons include providing a partial realization of value for the firm's founders, obtaining access to the services of the strategic partner (such as distribution to new investor groups), and obtaining working capital for the further extension of the firm (and its franchise) into new asset classes and new products.

The motivation of the potential buyer is even clearer. As discussed earlier, it has been customary for some time for cornerstone investors in the first fund of a new fund manager to acquire an equity stake in the firm to recapture some of the value brought by their participation. In addition to a participation in fee income from other funds managed by the same firm, cornerstone investors are increasingly looking at these stakes as "venture capital" investments that may in the future, upon a suitable "liquidity event," provide them with further return.

Strategic investors interested in acquiring an alternative fund manager may be either significant institutional investors frequently allocating to this fund manager, or a financial institution looking to develop or diversify its revenue streams. By acquiring a stake in a fund manager, the strategic investor may be seeking improved access to the funds, increased opportunity to participate in co-investments and distribution of the funds to clients of the strategic investments.

In terms of valuation, much thought will go into the analysis of the fund manager's revenue streams and the structure of the funds that generate them. Management fees are relatively straightforward, but incentive compensation can be more complex to forecast over longer periods of time. Since the value of the assets of the funds will drive the amount of incentive compensation a fund manager can expect to earn, the value of the fund's underlying investments becomes of primary importance, especially where they are illiquid and not readily transferable, when valuing a business for sale or investment.

Importantly, no matter how much franchise value a fund manager has acquired as a firm, enormous value will remain in the particular individuals responsible for advising and managing the funds, both present and future. As discussed earlier, many hedge funds were historically seen by the market and investors as the alter ego of the founder, even when the organization has grown significantly in size. For example, hedge fund firms such as Bridgewater, Pershing Square and SAC Capital are closely associated with, respectively, Ray Dalio, William Ackman and Steven Cohen. Demonstrating the institutional strength of any organization founded by a single high-profile individual is a long-term process.

In addition to agreeing to economic participations, the strategic investor will have numerous discussions with the original principals regarding the ongoing control and management of the fund manager. Where a minority interest has been acquired, veto rights might be obtained over certain decisions, such as launching new funds, either generally or in new asset classes of strategies; further investments by other strategic investors; and promotion or dismissal of original principals and retaining future principals.

Frequently, an obligation on the strategic investor to invest in the future funds of the fund managers comes hand-in-hand with the equity stake. These obligations may be either soft or hard, depending on the level of commitment obtained. A soft commitment may be no more than an undertaking to consider future funds that fall within agreed parameters. A hard commitment can be set out as either an absolute or a percentage investment obligation with regard to each new fund.

One reason that alternative investment funds have entered public consciousness in a very big way over recent years has been that a number of large fund managers have decided to sell themselves to the public through IPOs on leading stock exchanges. This is, in effect, another "exit strategy" for firm founders who want to monetize their stakes in the firms that they have built up over the years. Today, listed private equity firms include Apollo, Blackstone, Carlyle and KKR, while US hedge fund firm Fortress is listed in New York, and the UK's Man Group has been listed for many years in London.

Hedge fund giant Oaktree Capital Management announced its plans to list on the New York Stock Exchange in May 2011, having previously traded its shares privately on a proprietary exchange run by Goldman Sachs. Apollo, which listed on the NYSE in March 2011, had also traded privately on the Goldman exchange before going public. Oaktree was founded in 1995 by two former investment professionals from TCW, Howard Marks and Bruce Karsh.

Following on in the weeks after Oaktree Capital's IPO, which performed ambivalently in the markets, Carlyle's IPO in May 2012 was meant to secure its position at the top of the table of leading private equity firms. In the investor roadshows, Carlyle co-founder Daniel D'Aniello made a persuasive case for his firm's future prospects. "By many measures, we are one of the largest and most diversified asset managers in the world. We've been a first mover, with teams on the ground in almost all the major emerging markets today." The public offering featured Wall Street investment banking giants JPMorgan Chase, Citigroup and Credit Suisse as lead underwriters.

When Carlyle rang the bell at the New York Stock Exchange and took its place as a publicly traded company, one measure of the relative standing of the global private equity giants emerged. Based on its first day's closing price, Carlyle was worth almost $7 billion, while KKR was valued at $4 billion and Blackstone at $16 billion. As expected, the prices of these firms would rise and fall, both absolutely and relatively, in the weeks and months to follow, but comparing their relative standing on a particular day is now an easy thing to do.

The verdict on the economic performance of listed private equity firms is still out. Some listed firms have done particularly poorly for their public shareholders. Since listing in 2007, for example, Blackstone fell over 60 percent, while Fortress went down a staggering 80 percent.

Unsurprisingly, listed private equity firms have their critics. George Sudarskis, a former chief investment officer at the Abu Dhabi Investment Authority, noted, "Private equity firms should not seek public listings. Suddenly they have two masters: the public markets and their limited partners."

Although a relatively new phenomenon in the United States, listed alternative money managers have a longer history in the United Kingdom, although often facing similar challenges. Man Group, the London-based publically listed hedge fund manager, had faced a particularly difficult time in recent years. In 2010, Man merged with GLG, another large fund manager based in London, but performance lagged and assets began to flow out. Since it is listed, Man has had to get used to the harsh glare of public shareholder scrutiny. In May 2012, the share price for Man reached an eleven-year low. Other public hedge fund managers, such as Och-Ziff Capital Management and Fortress, have also faced significant drops in share price.

Activity at both the very top and the very bottom of the alternative investment sector bears close and regular scrutiny. To focus exclusively or predominately on one at the expense of the other only results in a skewed perspective.

Despite the steady stream of new funds launched each year, the hedge fund industry is, in fact, highly concentrated. It has been estimated by the SEC that just over 200 US-based hedge funds are actually responsible for 80 percent of all hedge fund assets.

A few of the biggest names in hedge funds, such as Och-Ziff and Paulson & Company, are familiar to regular readers of financial pages and websites. A larger number of funds, though, escape unnoticed by the wider world even though they manage hundreds of millions of dollars. Names like Brenner West Capital Advisors, Jericho Capital, Lakewood Capital Management, Point Lobos Capital, Redmile Group and Route One Partners mean little to the layperson not deeply familiar with the elite and rarified world of money management.

Developments among start-up funds, or among traditional money managers attempting to expand into alternative funds, can often reveal important trends that have broader application. For example, one question that has drawn a great deal of thought and comment recently is, "Where have all the good young hedge funds managers gone?"

This was a quandary that began pressing forward in many investors' minds in late 2011. By January 2012, a concerted push to create a better incubation platform for new fund managers took shape. Deutsche Bank and Financial Risk Management announced a partnership to create their own incubator, as did IMQubator (backed by AP, a large Dutch pension plan) and Synergy Fund Manager. They joined the list of existing seeders, such as Reservoir Capital, Blackstone and Goldman Sachs, who have successfully positioned themselves as partners to select new funds. In exchange for a significant stake in the new fund manager, these seed investors will invest sizeable amounts of money in fledgling funds.

What's in it for them? As noted earlier, hedge fund managers often achieve their highest performance in their earliest years, so bringing new funds to market can be seen as a way of sourcing outsized returns. Interestingly, due to the Volker Rule, which forms part of the Dodd-Frank reforms and bans proprietary trading, a growing pool of proven talent quickly began to look for new places to hang their hats.

However, despite the recent rise of incubation platforms, life for a small, start-up hedge fund today can still be a very tricky business. On the one hand, they tend to pursue innovative investment strategies that can differ significantly from what more established managers are doing. On the other hand, the main drivers of hedge fund growth in the past decade, namely public pension plans and charitable endowments, largely avoid new funds that lack proven track records. When a large institutional investor is allocating money in $100 million increments, they don't want to find out that they are half of the money in a fund. Only a handful of particularly brave public pension funds, such as CalPERS and the Ohio Public Employee Retirement System, regularly invest in new, unproven hedge funds.

In addition, name-brand traditional money managers are also deciding to enter the market and launch hedge funds off their own existing platforms, further squeezing the classic independent start-up funds. Even traditional money managers with long pedigrees are getting into the hedge fund business. For example, Morgan Stanley Investment Management, originally built by investment guru Barton Biggs, announced in January 2011 that it was launching a new $1 billion hedge fund, pithily titled Morgan Stanley Credit Partners, which focused on mezzanine debt.

It remains unclear what long-term impact the Volker Rule will have on the ability of large financial institutions to operate hedge fund and private equity fund businesses. As discussed above, if investment banks are ultimately forced to unwind their businesses in these areas, there will likely be a surge in individuals and teams setting up independently. In addition, these conglomerates will cease to be acquirers of mature hedge fund and private equity firms, taking one potential "exit strategy" for such firms off the table.

American private equity titan Stephen Schwarzman clearly has at least one eye now clearly fixed on the history books.

With great fanfare, Schwarzman announced in April 2013 that he was creating a new scholarship program at Tsinghua University in Beijing, which would bear his name. Comparisons to the British colonial tycoon Cecil John Rhodes, who established the Rhodes Scholars program in 1902 to bring scholars to Oxford University to study, were quickly and easily made.

When Rhodes established his program, Great Britain was the great power of its day. An endowment of $200 million permits approximately two hundred international scholars to pursue two-year programs among the "dreamy spires" of Oxford. By contrast, the $300 million that will fund the foundation of the Schwarzman College at Tsinghua University will bring two hundred students from leading countries around the world to study for one year in the world's next rising power.

The goal of the program, which will launch in 2016, is to promote understanding between China and the rest of the world. Central to this will be the program's ability to influence and mold generations of future leaders. Importantly, Tsinghua is one of China's top universities, which counts Xi Jinping, the current Chinese president, as an alumni.

In addition to the philanthropic and other, more personal, reasons that drive such monumental gifts as this one, the Schwarzman endowment highlights how important China is to leading financiers in the coming decades. As the relationship between the United States and China grows ever more tense, in part due to the complex web of competitive and collaborative situations in which the two large economies increasingly find themselves, the potential for misunderstanding grows.

In addition to providing $100 million himself, Schwarzman secured another $100 million in donations from businesses and financial institutions who have prioritized China in recent years, such as Boeing, BP, Caterpillar, JPMorgan Chase, Bank of America and Credit Suisse. The balance of donations is still to be raised, although given the caliber of early sponsors, it doesn't seem like this will be much of an issue. Schwarzman is clearly building for success. For example, the advisory board which will oversee the program is comprised of a jaw-dropping list of world-renowned former presidents, prime ministers and diplomats.

Notably, Blackstone, the private equity giant whose initial public offering earned Schwarzman over $4 billion, is not involved in the scholarship program. Schwarzman made clear that he was acting in a personal capacity in this regard.

As China's economy continues to grow at a rate that far exceeds what the United States and Europe can generate, China's importance in the world continues to rise each year. Ignoring China, or even just making decisions based on a view of the world that steadily grows more and more outdated, is no longer an option.

The Schwarzman scholarship program recognizes that education is an important and effective way to bring people together and broaden horizons. Experiences that challenge students in new environments can have a lasting impact on those individuals in the decades that follow. In their absence, students may find that their focus remains narrow and their goals unchanged.

Many critics of private equity and Wall Street will bemoan Schwarzman's attempt at securing his historical legacy by donating a small fragment of the large windfall he earned from the IPO of Blackstone to support this eponymous educational endeavor. To them, the benefits purportedly provided by the global financial markets today, which have evolved so rapidly in recent decades, are nebulous at best.

However, Schwarzman's own life hints tellingly at the power of a path not taken. Before he became one of the most successful practitioners of the "dark arts" of leveraged buyouts, he was a student at Yale University who dreamed of studying in England. Turned down first for a Rhodes Scholarship at Oxford and then later denied a fellowship at Cambridge, Schwarzman had little choice but to follow the well-trodden path to Wall Street.

Perhaps had he had the chance to enjoy cycling down Broad Street or punting on the river Cam, the history of modern finance might have been a little different. And perhaps the Schwarzman scholarship program will take more than one would-be hedge fund manager, investment banker or real estate impresario and, by showing them a different view of the world, lead them down another path entirely.

Despite the intervening global financial crisis, which shook markets around the world and drove many families into fore-closure and bankruptcy, the sixtieth birthday party of Leon Black, co founder of Apollo Global Management, in 2011 was just as impressive a celebration as Schwarzman's.

Elton John was the featured entertainment, giving a ninety-minute performance. Guests included an unsurprising mixture of fellow private equity giants, political heavyweights and Hollywood celebrities. Black's former boss at Drexel Burnham Lambert, Michael Milken, joined Goldman Sachs CEO Lloyd Blankfein and Schwarzman himself in rubbing shoulders with New York Senator Charles Schumer and New York City Mayor Michael Bloomberg. Howard Stern even dropped by The party was held at Black's home on Meadow Lane in Southampton, with its breathtaking ocean views.

Despite the events of the past few years, private equity again appeared vibrant and in control of its own destiny. Confidence in the markets again appeared to be building, and a measured optimism was the order of the day. The sustained attack on private equity that would form an integral part of the upcoming US presidential election was still some months away.

However, a sense of history and its cycles was not absent from Black's party. Guests reportedly overhead the Goldman Sachs boss gently joking with Schwarzman, "Your sixtieth got us into the financial crisis. Let's hope this party gets us out of it."

4: SHOW ME THE MONEY

Who Gets Paid What, and Why?

If you can make 20 percent of the profits on other people's money, you are going to make a lot of money if you are good at what you do.
David Rubenstein, Carlyle

How can we ask a student to pay more for college before we ask hedge fund managers to stop paying taxes at a lower rate than their secretaries? It's not fair. It's not right.
President Barack Obama

Just like there may be a 99 percent and a 1 percent, the 1 percent has its own 99 percent and 1 percent.

Although people who work on Wall Street earn high salaries, with big bonus checks often arriving at the end of the year, it is surprisingly not a significant source of the ultra-wealthy. For example, few billionaires can trace their overflowing coffers to time spent working day-to-day on Wall Street. The richest individuals in the world almost invariably have built their fortunes after having started a new, highly successful business, such as Facebook or WalMart. Those in private equity and hedge funds who have crossed the billionaire threshold typically have done so by building a larger firm – such as Blackstone or Soros Capital – that magnifies the efforts and legacy of a single person.

One fringe benefit of the decision in recent years of so many of the leading private equity firms to go public is that now all sorts of interesting tidbits about these businesses and their senior executives are now available to the public courtesy of their regular filings with the SEC. Stories now regularly appear in the mainstream press about "ten-digit paychecks" that a handful of top fund managers have earned in a given year. Clearly, $1 billion is a lot of money on any remuneration scale, but when you generate $5 billion in profits off a $20 billion portfolio of securities, the 20 percent performance fee adds up so very quickly.

Of course, everything is relative. In a world of Russian oligarchs, Middle Eastern oil tycoons and Silicon Valley billionaires, the more modest achievements of men and women working in the private equity and hedge fund industries are clearly of lesser impact on the world around us. But as the models for alternative investment funds have disseminated rapidly in recent years, highly numerate and technologically savvy individuals have been able to set up their firms quickly and easily, and make their money equally quickly, even if not so easily.

It is important nonetheless to bear in mind that while Fortune 500 CEO, investment bankers, movie stars and professional athletes can earn millions of dollars a year, there are a number of hedge fund managers who earn billions each year, and even a few private equity professionals who have racked up a billion dollars over their careers.

As discussed earlier, an annual management fee is charged to the fund based on either the size of its assets or the amount of capital that has been either invested in the fund or is committed to the fund, where money is drawn down from investments periodically. Performance-based remuneration would also be payable on increases in the value of the investments over time. The percentage of gain or profit reallocated to the fund manager will vary from fund to fund, but 20 percent has emerged as a *de facto* standard across a variety of asset classes.

Since a typical private equity or hedge fund will earn a 2 percent annual management fee, paid against the assets in the fund, as well as a 20 percent profit participation, this is often known in the business as "two and twenty." It is unclear where exactly in the Old Testament it actually says, "Thou shalt earn the two and twenty for the investment of other peoples' money in the pursuit of uncorrelated, absolute returns," but these terms are market standard and even apply generally to other types of alternative investment funds.

Importantly, the annual management fee is not a replacement for the fund paying its costs as they occur. Day-to-day expenses of the fund are still its own responsibility. As a result, certain costs associated with identifying and executing the various trans-actions (in the case of a hedge fund, for example, brokerage commissions) will be charged to the fund and its investors as well, rather than being paid by the fund manager.

However, where a fund manager has retained a third party placement agent to facilitate the promotion of the fund, an additional fee may be charged to investors or deducted from the investment proceeds. The widely acknowledged rule in private equity and hedge funds is that the fund manager is responsible for those types of fundraising costs, although other organizational costs of launching the fund would be charged to the fund (and, therefore, ultimately to the investors).

The relationship between investment returns and fund manager compensation is, therefore, very direct and immediate. There is little room for rewarding failure or hiding behind others. Transparency is the rule, and those who can deliver success get rewarded almost immediately.

Doug Lowenstein, president of the Private Equity Growth Capital Council, summed up the key distinction quite nicely in his June 2011 letter to the SEC. He observed that the compensation paid to private equity professionals "are the result of direct and detailed negotiations with sophisticated third-party stakeholders." By contrast, Lowenstein asserted that investment bank bonus arrangements "traditionally have been put into place with no input from shareholders."

Many critics of private equity and hedge funds have had a field day with the apparent disparities between what, for example, a successful hedge fund manager can earn in a year, and the relatively modest amounts taken home by actors, musicians, athletes, lawyers and business leaders. In 2010, for example, the top ten hedge fund managers earned an average of $1.75 billion each. For those inclined to do so, this breaks down into $842,788 for each mythical hour's work.

As noted above, the gateway to these vast sums is the simple fact that hedge funds earn a 20 percent performance fee on the profits they generate for their clients. For example, a manager who receives $500 from a client, and doubles it to $1000, would be entitled to 20 percent of the $500 profit, or $100. The client, of course, now has $900 and is not unhappy with the results by any stretch of the imagination.

Along the way, the hedge fund manager will also charge his or her client a 2 percent per year management fee for the ongoing services he or she provides. However, since this is a fraction of the much larger fees routinely charged to "Mom and Pop" retail investors by mutual funds for the good services they provide, this revenue stream is clearly secondary to generating the large earnings that offend the critics' sympathies so much.

Over $2 trillion is believed to be invested in hedge funds now. This is a strikingly large amount of money. A few basic calculations, however, are instructive at this point. Let's assume, just to put the earnings of hedge fund managers in perspective, that half of that $2 trillion does not generate any profits this year, and that the remaining half generates a 10 percent return. Crude approximations, but the point here is to place the "$842,788 per hour" calculation above into a more meaningful context. Then, the $1 trillion of profitably invested hedge fund money would generate $100 billion in profits.

The clients who provide the money would keep $80 billion, the lion's share by far, and $20 billion would be paid out to the managers who delivered this return. Since the clients only need to pay out these high fees when the funds generate high returns, they are happy and are, no doubt, often clamoring at this time to put even more money to work with these successful men and women overseeing their savings.

Simply put, to say a hedge fund manager – or a private equity professional, for that matter – earned $1 million, $500 million or $2 billion is just another way of saying that his or her clients earned $4 million, $2 billion or $8 billion this year. Unfortunately, the attentions of the critics of alternative investment funds are often strangely absent from the actual clients of these funds.

As David Rubenstein of Carlyle once succinctly remarked, "If you can make 20 percent of the profits on other people's money, you are going to make a lot of money if you are good at what you do." Never have truer words been spoken about the underlying structure and operation of incentives in the financial markets.

Performance-based compensation can be viewed as a call option that permits a fund manager to benefit from a rise in the value of the fund. The purpose is to incentivize managers for absolute returns, rather than simply tracking (and periodically beating) a benchmark index like the S&P 500 or the FTSE 100. However, performance fees and carried interest can also have a potentially negative influence on risk-taking. As overall performance of a fund declines, for example, a particularly greedy fund manager may be motivated in the short term to increase the risk of investments to move his call option back "in-the-money." Steps can be taken, however, to mitigate this risk-taking behavior.

As mentioned above, in both private equity and hedge funds, the fund manager traditionally invests a certain amount of money alongside the investors. This is done in order to ensure the interests of all parties are adequately aligned. Absent a significant investment in the fund by the fund manager, the concern of many prospective investors will be that the operation of the carried interest will be to present the manager with a "heads I win, tails you lose" scenario. The co-investment of the fund manager can occur directly through the fund vehicle itself, which would ensure that it participates equally with every investment made by the limited partners, or the manager may participate in fund investments of its choosing on a case-by-case basis.

Hedge funds and private equity funds differ in how the profit share is ultimately paid out to the successful fund manager. This has important consequences to the recipients. The performance component of a fund manager's remuneration is commonly called a "performance fee" in connection with hedge funds and a "carried interest" in connection with private equity funds. Generally, the structure of a hedge fund's performance fee is simpler than a private equity fund's carried interest. The performance fee is typically paid on both realized and unrealized gains, with no clawback for downturns in aggregate performance over the life of the fund.

Where the fund manager serves as a general partner of a partnership, thereby controlling the actions of the vehicle and subject to unlimited liability, these payments can be structured as an allocation of profits within the partnership, either to the general partner itself or to a special purpose "carried interest partner" acting as a type of limited partner. Structuring as a reallocation, rather than as a fee, can provide far more favorable tax treatment for individual managers. To the extent that the performance component includes unrealized gains, they can be reallocated from the investors to the fund manager without incurring tax until the gain is realized.

Importantly, in the case of private equity funds, these individuals also have access to a particularly beneficial tax treatment – long-term capital gains. The amounts reallocated within a partnership would retain their character as capital gains rather than being converted to ordinary income by payment to the fund manager as a fee. Because of a fundamental distinction made in the tax codes of the United States, the United Kingdom and many other developed countries, between capital gains and ordinary income, recipients of carried interest pay at a lower rate than a professional football player, a Hollywood actress or a Fortune 500 executive.

Pushing aside the increasingly vitriolic rhetoric that built up during the 2012 presidential campaign, the cause of this disparate result is not some obscure loophole buried within the fine print of the tax code. Instead, a fundamental distinction has been made, with broad-based bipartisan support, that different income streams should be taxed differently. For example, the United States has a higher rate applicable to personal income (39.6 percent) and a lower rate of tax for capital gains on investments (15 percent). As a result, just like the entrepreneur who ultimately sells the technology company that he originally started in his garage, the proceeds from the sale of a portfolio company by a private equity fund are investment proceeds. Both are subject to capital gains tax at 15 percent.

It is clear that when Will Smith is being paid for his latest blockbuster picture, or David Beckham for another season of kicking a soccer ball, or the chief executive officer of a large hotel chain or software company for leading his or her business for another year, they are earning an income based on the work they are doing on a day-to-day basis. What is not uniformly clear to all observers is whether that is a fair description for what private equity professionals are doing when they purchase, restructure, recapitalize and ultimately sell a business.

Are private equity and hedge fund managers worth the high fees they earn on the money they manage?

Clearly, a large number of US public pension plans, university endowments and charities, family offices and private banks feel they are. Rightly or wrongly, billions of dollars flow into these funds explicitly accepting that fees being charged are proportionate and fair for the services being provided.

The question of what combination of performance fee and management fees best aligns the interest of fund manager and fund is fundamentally a commercial issue. The two concepts are also linked in the minds of fund managers, who have operation costs to cover and employees to pay. Simply put, any attempt to alter one leg of remuneration will impact the fund manager's position with regard to the other.

In the world of alternative investment funds, the concepts of fees and returns are inextricably linked. Any question raised with regard to one is answered by reference to the other. They are the ying and yang, so to speak, of private equity and hedge funds.

Despite their increasing disagreements over a number of key issues, one point on which both fund managers and investors do agree is their mutual desire to see their funds generate large returns, outperforming by significant margins the returns available in the public markets. This drive for performance immediately distinguishes the sponsor of an alternative investment fund from other traditional asset managers who charge their clients solely on the basis of assets under management. Many mutual funds, for example, must deal with the allegation that they are simply "asset aggregators," seeking out new money from investors, almost indifferent to the actual investment returns.

Asset-based management fees, however, do have an important role to play in alternative investment funds. A fund manager will charge a fixed fee, payable in cash on either a monthly or a quarterly basis and charged as a percentage of the fund's size. The management fee has historically provided the fund manager with a modest revenue stream to cover overhead costs pending the receipt of the first payment of carried interest.

After a number of consecutive years in the late 1990s and early 2000s when allocations to private equity funds by investors (and the size of these funds themselves) grew steadily, the market has now entered a much more difficult fundraising environment. The marketing process for new funds is taking considerably longer. Existing funds are requiring more time to fully invest their committed capital. As a result, there is a large "overhang" in the market limiting the ability of many limited partners to reinvest their returned capital in other funds.

Enter the increasingly savvy investors. These institutions, with their advisers, are now significantly more sophisticated in their understanding of these asset classes, the documentation and the fee structure. Such investors presently have more power in their hands to push for terms (both economic and non-economic) that are more to their liking.

It is useful to remember once again that certain provisions that now warrant the coveted term "market standard" were only adopted in the last few decades. To point out one example in particular, in the case of private equity funds, the not-wholly irrational point that carried interest should be calculated on an aggregated basis (i.e. across all investments made) rather than only with respect to the ones that show a profit comes to mind.

In the sepia-colored early days of private equity as we recognize it today, carry was paid separately on each investor, regardless of how many losers preceded or followed the home-run hit that earned the big money. Eventually, investors were able to move the consensus on this point to have winners and losers netted out against each other.

If returns are meant to justify the fee levels being charged, then it is incumbent on all parties to clearly understand and report these returns accurately.

To measure the performance of a fund, several important pieces of information are required. These include the money provided by investors; when the money was put into the fund (e.g. all at once or in stages) and how the cash was used (e.g. investment or management fees); the distribution of cash and investment held; and the valuation of each unrealized investment currently held. Equally important, this information must be correct, current and complete. In particular, valuation of unrealized, illiquid investments can be the most problematic for both private equity and hedge funds, and leads to potential differences in practice.

Private equity has evolved its own particular means of measuring and comparing performance, which integrates a duration component into the calculation. The key concept in measuring performance in private equity funds is the internal rate of return (IRR). The IRR is the net return earned by investors over a particular period, calculated on the basis of cash flows to and from investors, after the deduction of all fees, including carried interest.

IRR is a time-based concept. As holding periods for investments lengthen, this performance measurement will fall significantly. It is not sufficient to simply know the increase in value of an investment between acquisition and realization (e.g. 2X). One must also know the length of that period (e.g. two years or five years). Simply put, doubling your money in two years is much, much better than doubling your money in five years. This fact goes some way toward explaining certain differences in the investment preferences and behavior of financial buyers, such as private equity funds, and trade buyers.

Recent research has focused on an interesting trait of successful private equity funds. Apparently, the most successful investments of a fund account for a significant amount of its ultimate IRR. As a result, a small number of exceptional realizations can be more important to a fund's success than more consistent performance across the portfolio. This may explain the tendency of many in the private equity industry to focus on big, home-run returns on investments that can do well quickly.

In recent years, IRR numbers for leading private equity firms have become increasingly easy to come by. Notably, a number of US institutional investors (primary public pension plans who are entrusted the savings of teachers, policemen, firemen and other government employees) have begun publishing the performance of their fund participation. A string of legal cases may compel such disclosure where the investors are US public entities subject to state "sunshine" laws. The accumulation of such piecemeal disclosure will have a significant long-term impact on the industry, by driving the overall shift toward increased consistency in reporting performance and, ultimately, benchmarking between funds.

Despite its prevalence, IRR has certain features that are important to fully understand in order to use the data effectively. For example, the ability of private equity funds to distribute shares of portfolio companies to investors in kind can have certain potentially negative impacts on the IRR calculation. Upon an IPO, despite a lock-up period restricting the ability of holders of a security to sell in the market, the value of the security at the time of its distribution is the value used by fund managers in calculating IRR. However, investors may receive significantly less than that amount at the end of the lock-up period when the shares are freely tradable.

Also, the distinction between gross IRR and net IRR is crucial. From gross IRR must be deducted the asset-based management fees, any expenses paid by the fund and, most importantly, the cost of "cash management" relating to the money not yet drawn down by the fund. As the ultimate return to investors will be the net IRR, knowledgeable investors will attempt to focus fund compensation arrangement to the greatest extent possible on net, rather than gross, performance. Effective cash management, which is ultimately in the investors' control, is also crucial to achieving desired rates of return.

Equally important, little insight is typically gained from comparing the funds at different points in their life cycle. As a result, funds are frequently compared against other funds which launched in the same year, giving rise to the concept of "vintage year." Because of the relatively constrained period of time within which a private equity fund must drawdown and invest its capital, the concept of "vintage year" has become a frequent topic of discussion and debate in the industry. Funds with the same vintage year are thought to have experienced similar economic environments, making comparisons amongst them more meaningful.

There is a very important step that must be taken, however, before performance can be calculated – valuation. Without correct values for every security and financial instrument in the fund, any attempt to measure performance will end up a useless nonsense.

Funds must put in place procedures for valuing the investments that they hold. As a result of lack of appropriate knowledge or controls, errors in valuation can arise that materially affect a fund's net asset value. In extreme situations, these inconsistencies can lead to the collapse of a fund. Reliable valuations are, therefore, necessary to maintain investor confidence in the alternative investment funds buying and selling such assets.

While prices for listed securities will be generally accessible, unlisted securities and derivatives can be much more problematic. Where the underlying assets are illiquid (such as interests in unlisted companies) the need for standardized valuation procedures is absolutely crucial. In the absence of an agreed valuation approach, investors in the same asset can receive radically different values for their interests based on the differing methods applied by their fund managers. The increased disclosure from US pension plans mentioned above has further highlighted these disparities.

Valuation guidelines, therefore, are very important. The goals of any valuation guidelines are quite straightforward: transparency, comparability, and consistency. However, the role of the fund manager's judgment will always play a key role in the valuation process. This is unavoidable, given their extensive prior history with the investment. As a result, specially constituted valuation committees, staffed by select fund investors, are increasingly being established to adopt and monitor the valuation policy to be followed by the fund manager.

Unlike private equity funds, hedge funds typically hold highly liquid, readily valued investments. However, at times they may instead hold thinly traded illiquid investments. In such instances, these investments may be held in separate accounts known as "side pockets," which can impact the timing and amount of redemption proceeds returned to investors over the course of their investment. Without side pockets separating the illiquid investments from the liquid portions of the portfolio, it would be very difficult for these hedge funds to continue honoring the redemptions they received, without potentially harming the interest of the non-redeeming investors.

For any fund holding assets that are not freely transferable, whether that is illiquid, thinly traded securities held by a hedge fund or investments by private equity funds in companies that have not yet been exited, this "unrealized portion" of the fund's portfolio is a crucial factor in ultimately determining both the past and the future performance of the fund.

Valuation of the unlisted portfolio companies that are at the heart of most private equity funds can be a surprisingly subjective business. As Julie Creswell of *The New York Times* aptly pointed out in January 2011 in connection with the private equity acquisition of Freescale Semiconductors, "The owners – the Blackstone Group, the Carlyle Group, Permira Advisers and TPG Capital – disagree on its value. What they do agree on is that the deal, one of the biggest buyouts of all time, has been a troubled investment. Blackstone calculates that each dollar of its initial stake in Freescale is now worth 45 cents, Carlyle and Permira value their positions at 35 cents on the dollar, and TPG at 25 cents, according to investors in the buyout funds."

Determining what a private company is actually worth is actually quite tricky. For a public company listed on a stock exchange, there may be hundreds or thousands of purchases and sales each day upon which to base a price. Unfortunately, unlisted companies are more like real estate, in that the true prices can only be determined when they are ultimately sold. Until then, estimates can be made based on comparable houses that have sold, even if they are substantially different.

According to Steve Judge, head of the US trade association for private equity firms, "Private equity firms work hard, with auditors and company managements, to provide accurate valuations of their largely illiquid holdings to their investors." Fund managers often use complicated formulas in the valuation of their investments. These formulas can include a number of subjective factors. As a result, the values established by these procedures are not beyond question. Two private equity firms investing in the same company could, and often do, value that company quite differently.

What harm, though, do interim estimated values actually cause in a private equity fund, since the fund manager's carried interest depends on the amount finally realized when the company is actually sold?

As Creswell went on to explain, "Most big institutions that invest in private equity do so for the long haul. They rarely worry about how an investment performs over one quarter or even one year. What matters is the final payoff – the return when a private equity firm exits an investment, either by taking the company public or selling outright to another buyer. But interim performance figures – akin to the score in the fifth inning of a baseball game – do sway decisions. They influence how pension funds and others allocate their money."

Valuation, therefore, is a very important issue that must be understood by fund investors, or else the mistakes that they make when evaluating a fund manager's progress can seriously compromise their investment goals. Since most investments made by a private equity fund are highly illiquid, the process of establishing what they are worth before they are finally sold is, therefore, very convoluted and subjective. If the values of these unrealized investments are inflated, then investors may be misled to invest in subsequent funds launched by the same firm because they will overestimate the interim performance of the existing fund.

Talking about performance abstractly is not particularly rewarding. What investors and managers want to do is make comparisons of one set of performance numbers with others. As a result, benchmarking can be useful to investors, both as a means of understanding what is happening to an asset class over time and as a tool to assist in the decision-making process regarding whether to invest in a particular fund.

The phrase "top quartile" is used frequently in the world of private equity and hedge funds. Some might contend that it is over-used. Regardless, it resonates with wavering investors and appears repeatedly in marketing materials. Due to the nature of both alternative investment funds and the underlying investments themselves, there can be a great opacity and arbitrariness with regard to performance measurements. The question of whether a fund's performance is "top quartile" is always based on a comparison of the particular fund to a wider universe of other similar funds. Defining that universe correctly is very important. Inappropriate comparisons are of little use to prospective investors. A hedge fund investing in Japanese equities on a long-short basis can be compared to other Japanese funds or other equity long-short funds. A private equity fund launched in 2012 to invest in companies operating in the health care industry in North America can be compared to other 2012 vintage funds or other health care funds generally.

As a result of this deep-seated need to make comparisons, the track records of funds can actually develop real economic value and immense strategic importance. The issue of past performance is a particular concern where a group of investment professionals are starting up a new firm. As hard as it is to believe, at some dim date in the not-so-recent past, firms such as the United State's Tiger Global Management and Providence Investment Management and Coatue Management, and the United Kingdom's Brevan Howard Asset Management, BlueCrest Capital Management and Capula Investment Management did not yet exist. Their initial founders still had to make the leap from their current places of employment to their new platforms. The ability of these men and women to point to their past track records can be a key factor in their ultimate success.

Where the individuals have worked together before at a prior firm, it is not uncommon to use the track record of their prior work together in marketing and promotional materials on a selective basis. Investors may express concern, however, where the individuals previously worked for different firms, rather than as a team in their own right, but still want to present some carefully constructed numbers as their own. This would be done by way of building up a hypothetical composite of their prior performances for the purpose of providing a "historical" view of the current team.

Legitimate questions can be raised about how useful or appropriate such numbers are to a prospective investor.

Similarly, where a new fund is to be established that differs significantly in its investment strategy from earlier funds, a fund manager may wish to present the prior performance of only those transactions that fall within the new strategy. This is also subject to great risks. The concern is "cherry picking," where only the better performing deals and transactions are selected. As a result, very clear disclosure should be provided to would-be investors indicating precisely how particular selections were made. Otherwise, the fund manager and its principals will leave the door open to potential litigation later on, when disgruntled investors come across the cherry picking.

Without a doubt, money is the primary driving factor in private equity and hedge funds. Lucrative fees are paid to talented fund managers by investors eager to earn high returns on their investments. As a result, the economics of alternative investment funds are a worthwhile topic for detailed study.

As discussed earlier, management fees calculated in reference to the entire sum of money in, or committed to, a fund are typically paid on a monthly or quarterly basis. Traditionally designed to permit the struggling manager to "keep the lights on" until the performance fees are paid, a 2 percent fee has been the *de facto* standard for private equity and hedge funds for many years. However, with the rise of "mega funds" and the continued presence of significantly smaller start-up managers entering the market to focus on niche opportunities, 2 percent is often too small for small funds and too large for large funds.

The math is straightforward and compelling. For a $1 billion fund, a 2 percent management fee would see the fund manager earn $20 million every year, regardless of how the investment strategy actually performs.

Different types of fund approach the mechanics of calculating and paying these fees in slightly different ways. In a hedge fund, mechanisms are put in place to take account of subscriptions and redemptions within the quarter, in order to ensure that fees are only paid on money actually at work in the fund during the period in question. For private equity funds, with drawdown and harvest of potential investments within a particular investment period, it is common to see the management fee being charged, after the investment period has passed, only on actually invested capital. As a result, the total amount payable would decrease as underlying investments are harvested. In addition, the rate of management fees might also decline upon the launch by the fund manager of a follow-on fund. This is due to the additional revenue stream coming in from the new commitments obtained, often by many of the same investors who have "re-uped" into the new fund.

Given the significant sums of money that can be paid over by investors as the years go by, limits and carve-outs on management fees have evolved to protect investors. For example, management fees are frequently offset by other revenue received by the fund manager in connection with the operation of the fund. In the rapidly evolving world of modern finance, there are a surprising number of ways Wall Street investment bankers have devised to get paid along the way while a deal is getting done. Many of these payment streams have migrated into private equity deal-making, including transaction fees, monitoring fees, investment banking fees, director's fees and break-up fees. The receipt of these additional revenue streams will need to be disclosed to the fund and its investors in the offering memorandum, because of the potential for conflicts of interest to arise. The amount of offset has ranged from 50 percent to 100 percent and is often a point of negotiation at the fund's launch.

In addition, certain large investors will often be able to negotiate sufficient management fee offsets and rebates across their portfolio of fund investments to materially lower their overall costs of investment in alternative investment funds. Bulk buying can have the same economic benefits in money management as in most other industries. As a result, the investors in the same fund can have materially different returns based on discounts obtained against fees.

The amount of money a fund manager will earn in management fees from a particular fund is determined by simply multiplying the management fee rate by the size of the fund. As a result, fund size has become a more frequent topic of negotiation over the past few years, particularly in the private equity and venture capital area. Unlike hedge funds, which earn their performance compensation on an annual basis, these funds typically receive carried interest only on the realization of the underlying investment. For many of these funds, management fees have become an important source of profit, independent of the success of the fund manager in delivering the promised outsized returns.

Assets under management (AUM) is the principal meter stick against which many money managers, whether traditional or alternative, are measured. AUM increases either when the assets overseen by the manager increase in value, or when subscription money from existing or new investors pouring into the fund is more than the redemption money being pulled out of the fund. On the other hand, AUM will decrease either when the assets decrease in value or redemption requests outnumber new subscriptions. Where a manager only charges a management fee on the assets it invests for clients, AUM is the sole determinant of its revenue. Where a performance fee is charged, higher AUM can in fact be a burden by acting as a drag if there are insufficient high-yielding investment opportunities at any one time.

Can a fund be too big?

Given the 2 percent management fees that many managers earn off their assets, the initial answer might be "no!" However, on closer reflection, most managers and investors often agree that being too big creates more problems than it solves. The reason is relatively straightforward – every new dollar in a fund must be put to work in such a way as to earn a return at least as high as was being earned on the earlier dollars. Otherwise, the overall performance of the fund will quickly be dragged down.

For example, if a fund is earning a 14 percent return on its investments and new money coming in must sit in a bank account or in Treasury Bills, earning only 2 percent, until new investment opportunities are identified, then the fund's overall performance may drop, for argument's sake, to 13 percent. This will impact the calculation of the performance fee and may actually result in less money being paid to the manager than on the earlier (lower) amount.

Many investors prefer managers who "stick to what they know," so to speak, rather than being forced to make investments in different sectors or styles just to keep the money in motion. Investors will generally have their money with several different managers at any one time, and rather than see a portfolio manager focused on equities begin dabbling in mortgage bonds in search of returns, they will typically prefer that the manager does less, but does it very, very well.

A fund manager with too much money, therefore, can be in a position where the best thing for it to do is to simply give some money back to investors. In September 2011, Brevan Howard, the leading UK hedge fund firm, agreed to return $2 billion to investors in its fund, in order to keep assets at a maximum of $25 billion. The fund had been in positive territory each year of the financial crisis, distinguishing it immediately from many other funds.

Another approach is simply to shut the door on any further subscriptions and allow the fund to continue investing only the money it already has. For example, in order to avoid a slide in performance during the years immediately following the financial crisis, a number of other managers also closed their funds to new investors, including CQS and SAC Capital.

In addition, a particularly dangerous side effect of growing too fast is that new money in a hedge fund, which has not in the past benefitted significantly from the manager's skill, may bolt immediately should the fund suffer a significant loss. Sudden large redemptions can be devastating to a fund in the best of times.

The "winter of discontent" of 2008–09 demonstrated the fatal damage that a flood of redemption requests could inflict on otherwise healthy hedge funds. As a result, fund managers often deliberate long and hard about the best size for each of their funds, as well as the most appropriate investor demographics, in order to ensure that they are optimal.

An important distinction can be made between hedge funds and private equity funds when it comes to fund size. Due to the drawdown structure, uninvested money does not serve the same role as a drag on performance calculation in private equity funds as excess capital does in hedge funds. As discussed earlier, IRR only calculates the investment returns once a new portfolio company has been identified. Over the past decade, many private equity funds have chosen to raise larger and larger funds, on which lucrative management fees will be earned with reference to all of the undrawn committed capital. As buyout funds now routinely raise funds measured in billions of US dollars, the fee revenue stream to the fund manager can be substantial.

However, prospective investors in private equity funds are increasingly voicing concern over the prospect of ever-larger funds. Of particular concern are situations where management fee revenue levels exceed the fund manager's carried interest payments. The fear is that the guaranteed income stream provides too many mediocre managers with too great a reward for simply doing nothing.

In light of these concerns, and the difficult fundraising environment since the global financial crisis first arrived in 2008, some funds have shown a willingness to reconsider the size of their funds and the impact on management fees. This can be accomplished either through the lowering of undrawn capital commitments for each investor or by negotiating down fee levels.

Despite concerns over fees and the potential for misaligned incentives, investors continue to demonstrate a fundamental belief in private equity and hedge funds. These intrepid investors are willing to make the sizeable commitments and pay the significant fees required to have access to fund managers in the proverbial "top quartile." As many investors show a marked preference to brand name fund managers, this process of increased fund sizes is further reinforced as new money follows old money disproportionately into the funds of established firms.

A similar problem relating to the relative incentives provided by management fees and carried interest arises in circumstances that are not related to fund size. Where a private equity fund is in a position where carried interest is no longer a viable possibility, their dependency on management fees may become overwhelming. The concern here is that reasonable offers from prospective buyers of their underperforming investments may be waived off by the fund manager in order to preserve the management fee revenue stream. Rather than risk the loss of fee revenue when the proceeds of such a realization are then distributed out to investors, fund managers may prefer to wait for the life of the fund to wind down.

Increasingly, investors are applying the painful lessons they learned during the early years of the global financial crisis to their investments in new funds today. They are requesting more detailed information about the fund managers' operating expenses and overheads as a way of tying the management fee calculations to something more tangible. They are asking better questions of their fund managers about their cash flow needs and budgeted expenses, in order to make certain the fee mechanisms are appropriate and not excessive. For example, where investors in a private equity fund are pressing for a step-down in the rate of management fees once all the committed capital is invested, more thought is now being given to the potentially perverse incentive that this creates to draw all but the final amount of capital.

Determining when, precisely, a fund has delivered a true profit, rather than simply benefiting from a rising market, is an important issue that warrants further exploration. When is an increase in the assets of a fund actually a profit worthy of granting the fund manager payment of incentive compensation? To answer this question, two different mechanisms have evolved in private equity funds and hedge funds to address these concerns – preferred returns and high water marks.

Because a hedge fund is open-ended, and operates based upon regularly occurring dealing days which permit new and existing investors to subscribe and redeem from the fund, the cash flows for these funds are relatively straightforward. Private equity funds, due to their closed-end, fixed-life structure, pose unique problems which must be addressed in their structure and operation. The partnership agreement will provide in detail for the manner in which distributions will be made to investors. These provisions are often referred to as the "waterfall." Money received from realized investments flows down the list of recipients who participate in different ratios at different levels.

Typically, the timing of any distribution to private equity fund investors will be at the sole discretion of the fund manager. However, following the realization of an investment, a specified time limit is usually imposed which mandates when those particular cash proceeds will need to be distributed. Amounts can be retained in certain limited circumstances, such as to cover expenses of the fund and the fund manager, if explicitly provided for in the partnership agreement. Distributions are generally made in cash, although a provision may be included for distribution of certain assets "in specie." For example, in the context of venture capital funds, shares of a technology company recently listed on a stock exchange may be distributed to investors rather than the cash proceeds obtained on their sale.

The function of the waterfall is to establish how profits from investments will be divided between the investors and the fund manager once an investment is realized. It is by way of the waterfall that the fund manager and its individual principals receive their carried interest. The first step will be a repayment to the investors of the capital that they have provided to the fund. A preferred return (e.g. 8 percent) may be required to be paid to investors as well, before any performance-based compensation is paid to the fund manager.

The preferred return has an important role to play in the timing of distributions to investors. Preferred returns reward fund managers for attaining higher returns and forego compensation for returns at or below the threshold. The amount of the preferred return can vary from fund to fund and asset class to asset class. Higher preferred returns can be viewed by potential investors as the *quid pro quo* cost to a fund manager for higher performance-based remuneration.

It is very important, though, to clearly distinguish between preferred returns and hurdles. Preferred returns are a common feature of carried interest calculations in private equity funds. In practice, however, a hurdle can be implemented in widely divergent ways. At the two extremes, the preferred return can either be a permanent feature with only profits in excess of the preferred rate being subject to an 80/20 split to the fund manager, or simply a trigger mechanism that must initially be hit to allow the 80/20 split to commence. In the case of the former, a fund manager's carried interests will approach, but never actually reach, 20 percent of the profits of the fund, since the profits earned below the preferred return are not shared by the investors. In the latter, after a "catch-up period" upon the preferred return being hit, where the fund manager receives all net profits to attain parity, the fund manager will be provided his full 20 percent carried interest in net profits.

An awkward question arises, then, with regard to the preferred return. Should a fund manager earn a carry on this initial level of performance covered by the preferred return? Where the answer is "yes," a catch-up provision is included whereby the fund manager will receive an extra portion of the profits thereafter until the amount equal to a carry on the preferred return has been distributed. Thereafter, all profits will be divided between the investors and the fund manager in line with the carried interest (e.g. 80/20). Where the answer is "no," the ability of a fund manager to receive any earned interest is explicitly predicated on outperforming the preferred return.

As discussed above, a potential side-effect of the preferred return (which is shared with the high water market discussed below) is that when the value of a fund declines to such a point that it is unlikely to generate a return in excess of the preferred return, the fund manager may lack incentive to continue managing the fund for the remainder of its term. Unfortunately, unmotivated investment personnel generally provide mediocre services to their clients.

Preferred returns ensure that a fund manager only receives performance-based remuneration when the value of the fund exceeds the pre-agreed threshold (e.g. 8 percent). However, this threshold will increase with time, where the preferred return is measured over the life of the fund (as is the case with private equity funds). More delays in realizing a particular investment and returning capital plus profit to investors will mean a higher threshold to overcome before performance-based remuneration is paid. The effect of a preferred return, therefore, is either to reduce materially the carried interest received by the fund manager or to alter significantly the timing of such distributions during the life of the fund.

Hurdles, on the other hand, can be seen across a wide range of fund structures and styles, and function significantly differently. Investors often place money with funds on the premise that the strategies to be followed should outperform investments in other assets or strategies. Like so many other features of hedge funds, the principal limitations on hurdle rate mechanics are the negotiating position of the investors and the imagination of the draftsman.

A hurdle rate could be fixed or based on an index. A potential anomaly resulting from the latter is that where an index has declined and the fund has declined by less, the fund manager may be entitled to a performance incentive where the investors have lost money for the period. Another variant is the distinction between whether the performance allocation is made on the entire profits of the fund upon the fund passing the hurdle rate or only on the performance in excess of the hurdle rate.

High water marks operate differently from preferred returns, but are based on similar investor concerns. They protect investors from having to pay performance fees twice where there has been a decline in the value of a hedge fund, followed by a further rise. This will be an issue in hedge funds because performance fees are typically paid on both realized and unrealized gains.

The principle underpinning the high water mark is very simple. A fund manager should not be paid twice for the "same" performance. Where losses have followed a period of gains in which a performance incentive has been paid, a further payment would not be made by the fund simply for returns that place the fund back where it was. Such a payment seems intuitively unfair. At launch, the high water mark is set at the initial net asset value and is subsequently increased at each performance period end when an incentive payment is made.

A side effect of high water marks is that after a significant decline in net asset value, due to market corrections or other factors, the fund manager (and the senior investment professionals who show up to work every day) may no longer feel that it is in its interest to continue to manage the fund. The period necessary to "earn out" the loss and get back up over the high water mark could simply appear too long. This is especially problematic for fund managers with large staffs who depend on the performance fee to motivate their teams.

Press reports in November 2011 recounted how profits at Fortress International Group significantly declined in the third quarter. Declines in certain of its hedge funds meant that they were below their high water marks and as a result Fortress would not be entitled to earn performance fees until those losses were made good. Man Group in London also posted a significant drop in profits at this time. As a publically listed company, the market quickly became very interested in how this would impact future revenue streams.

A cartoon that circulated several years ago encapsulates the powerful protection that high water marks provide investors. A man is dressed in academic regalia and is speaking to a large group of university students on their graduation day. Surveying the crowd, he says sagely, "The most important thing I have learned so far in life is that if you are 70 percent down, and then 70 percent up, you have *not* broken even." Losing money is particularly damaging precisely because to earn a desired return on the original amount, you need to produce a significantly higher return on the reduced amount.

In the past, it has not been uncommon for some fund managers to wind down the "underwater" fund and relaunch a new fund, granting existing investors the opportunity to invest in the new vehicle. The practical effect of this elaborate exercise is to reset the high water market in reference to current market conditions. Recently, some fund managers have begun to include explicit reset mechanisms in their new funds as a way to deal with this commercial point in a less costly and time-consuming manner. In these circumstances, a limited loss carry forward is adopted to reset the high water mark in certain circumstances. After a certain period has passed following large losses, the new water mark will be reset and a performance fee will be earned from any growth in NAV that follows.

The time value of money is central to all investing, but has a particular importance in the area of private equity. Interestingly, the practice in the United Kingdom and Europe with regard to the payment of carried interest in private equity funds has differed historically from the practice in the United States. In the case of the former, a "fund-as-a-whole" approach was followed, whereby all of the capital contributions of investors are returned before the fund manager begins to participate in any of the carried interest. In the latter case, a "deal-by-deal" approach has been standard for some time, under which a fund manager participates in the carried interest upon each realized investment to the extent that capital is returned in excess of the capital originally drawn down from investors to acquire the investment, thereby accelerating the receipt of carried interest by individual participants. As a result, the approach in the United States is much more "pro-GP," while the approach taken on the other side of the Atlantic and elsewhere is considerably more "pro-LP."

To remedy potential unfairness in the operation of the deal-by-deal approach in practice, each subsequent realizations of a portfolio company will be aggregated with earlier realizations. Simply put, carry is recalculated and paid on all deals that have realized to date. This enables a significant loss to be set off against either previous or successive gains.

As a result of these recalculations, a fund manager who earned and received carry payments in regard to investments 1 and 2 may find that the loss suffered when selling investment 3 is so large that when carry is recalculated across all three, it turns out that *none* is due and payable. So what happens to the money already paid out to the fund manager?

Where earlier carried interest payments to the fund manager in hindsight appear to be overpayments, a "clawback" obligation is imposed on the fund manager. This clawback requires the repayment of any excess carried interest payout from the fund. Often, investors want to rely more on just the creditworthiness of the individual principals at the fund manager. As a result, the clawback may be supported by either an escrow of some amount of the carried interest with a third party bank, which will not be released to principals of the fund manager; guarantees from the individual principals to repay any amounts of carried interest distributed to them; or a holdback within the fund's bank account.

However, very soon after carry payments are received by the individual principals, they each (on the advice of their accountants) will promptly pay a significant part of the money into the government as taxes. To do otherwise would run the risk of invoking the rage of the IRS or HMRC!

The receipt of carried interest by the fund manager and its individual principals will often be a taxable event for them. Therefore, the possibility exists that clawback obligations may imply an obligation to repay gross amounts of money upon which tax has been paid. However, it is customary to make clear that only after-tax amounts received by the fund manager and the individual principals must be repaid.

A widely observed trend in recent years has been to focus more and more time and attention on the practical mechanics of clawback provisions, specifically the inclusion of annual "true-ups" and more escrows. Prior to 2008, these provisions were frequently included simply as a formality, with little anticipation that they would ever need to be invoked.

With more volatile markets since the start of the global financial crisis, clawback enforcement has now become an unfortunate feature of many funds' lifecycle. The reason is quite simple. Often, it is the most successful companies that are exited earliest and with the highest multiples. The portfolio companies left to the final years of a fund's life may significantly drag down overall performance, should they be written off or exited at a fraction of their acquisition costs.

For example, in 2010, Blackstone was required to refund approximately $3 million of its carried interest, received from the Blackrock Real Estate Partners International LP. Initial deals had done well, but the remaining deals in the fund performed less well, taking the overall fund performance down below the level at which carry was payable.

Where invoking a clawback obligation begins to appear likely, a fund manager may consider waiving some portion of future management fees as a means to lower the amounts of clawback. Separate steps may also be taken by the fund manager in connection with distributed carry to individual principals, by inserting provisions in their documentation to require a "true-up" in anticipation of the clawback being invoked.

In the late 1990s, certain UK and European private equity houses began to launch funds following the "deal-by-deal" method, despite some vocal complaints by annoyed prospective investors used to the "fund-as-a-whole" approach. The impact, however, on market terms was limited. More importantly, when the market began moving against fund managers after the start of the global financial crisis in 2008, a number of recent funds have been raised in the United States under the "fund-as-a-whole" approach. This has been driven by the prolonged and mounting insistence of reluctant investors who had bad experiences with clawbacks in practice.

Investors successfully pushing for the "fund-as-a-whole" approach argue that it incentivizes fund managers to be focused on the performance of the entire fund, as well as accommodating a desire among individual principals to avoid the painful exercise of clawback rights against them, as has occurred frequently in recent years. However, postponing the timing of carried interest payments toward a fund-as-a-whole model has made many fund managers less likely to agree to parallel cuts in the annual management fee. This income in a fund's early years becomes the only source of employee and principal compensation, which has traditionally been one of private equity's strongest recruiting tools to acquire new talent.

The flipside of the fund manager's obligation to return money to the fund when carried interest payments are recalculated is an obligation on the part of the fund investors to return money to the fund if there are subsequently incurred costs or liabilities at the fund level which are the obligation of the investors to pay. The obligation of investors to return distributed money back to the fund has become increasingly accepted in the United States, although practice is more diverse in the United Kingdom and Europe. The basis for this obligation is that the possibility exists for liabilities to arise (such as, for example, indemnities) to the fund which, in the absence of sufficient assets, could fall to the general partner, who is subject to unlimited liability for the debts of the partnership, where the fund is structured as a partnership. Many general partners view the investor giveback obligations as the necessary *quid pro quo* for their own obligations under the clawback provisions. The focus of negotiations frequently centers upon time limits and caps on the amount to be returned.

The investor giveback effectively protects the carried interest entitlement of the fund manager from loss incurred by the private equity fund, after significant distributions had been made out of the fund to the investors. Without such mechanisms, the fund manager, as general partner of a partnership, would be wholly liable for such losses, with the investors enjoying limited recourse because of their position as limited partners. Such losses could arise in a number of circumstances, including breach of warranty by the fund in the sale of an investment, or an environmental liability stemming from an investment, and could otherwise have a highly punitive effect on the fund manager.

No matter how well crafted a set of waterfall provisions in a private equity limited partnership agreement is, there is always the possibility that too much money may be released to some of the partners too early. As a result, the basic economic agreement between the general partners and the limited partners will be undermined. Each of the clawback and the giveback provisions attempt to put the fund manager and the investors back in the same position as if the amount of the losses had never been distributed. The investor giveback provisions remain highly contested and resisted by certain limited partners, often only being agreed subject to predetermined percentage and "sunset" limitations.

Hand in hand with the question of how much a private equity or hedge fund manager should earn is how much tax they should pay on those earnings. This debate has increased significantly in recent years, as the high paychecks of more and more alternative fund managers have been reported in the mainstream press. With Mitt Romney's run for the White House in 2012, the attacks became more focused and highly personalized.

The debate over carried interest taxation reopened again in the summer of 2011, putting two of the biggest names in investing into opposing corners – Warren Buffett of Berkshire Hathaway and Stephen Schwartzman of Blackstone. Warren Buffett's op-ed piece in *The New York Times* in the summer of 2011, entitled "Stop Coddling the Super Rich," re-ignited the debate over the proper categorization and treatment of carried interest. The billionaire Buffett revealed that he paid tax at a rate of 17.4 percent, which was the lowest of anyone in his company. Schwarzman quickly countered Buffett's claim by disclosing that he was currently paying tax at a combined federal and state rate of 53 percent. According to Schwarzman, "I'm not feeling undertaxed."

Earlier that summer, President Obama made clear to Americans that carried interest was in his sights. "How can we ask a student to pay more for college before we ask hedge fund managers to stop paying taxes at a lower rate than their secretaries. It's not fair. It's not right." Buffett's op-ed played squarely into Obama's attacks on carried interest, although it is interesting that he chose to incorrectly reference "hedge fund managers" as his attack target. In fact, hedge funds rarely earn revenue that would qualify for capital gains treatment. Perhaps his speechwriters believed that sound bite would resonate better than a more correct reference to "private equity managers."

In September 2011, the Obama White House took advantage of the publicity being generated around the Buffett/Schwarzman kerfuffle and announced, as part of a tax package that was an attempt to pay for a new stimulus package, a proposal to raise the tax rate applied to carried interest payments. In addition to hedge funds and private equity funds, venture capital funds and real estate funds would also be covered.

Of course, rumors of carried interest's imminent demise have been circulating for several years. Opponents of private equity estimate that over $20 billion could be raised in taxes over the next decade if this so-called "loophole" was closed. Since 2007, the tax treatment of carried interest has been repeatedly in the cross-hairs of Washington politicians looking for new ways to balance the nation's worsening budget deficit.

As Steve Judge, head of the Private Equity Growth Capital Council, remarked in the autumn of 2011, "Proposals to raise taxes on carried interest have consistently been rejected over four years because raising taxes on investments would only sideline employees and investors and create further uncertainty in an already struggling economy."

The underlying issue here is surprisingly simple and straightforward – the difference between the capital gains rate and the ordinary income rate, and why that difference is maintained. Currently carried interest is taxed in the United States at the capital gains rate of 15 percent, rather than the ordinary income rate of 39.6 percent. Despite this simplicity, the debate over raising taxes on carried interest remains highly emotional.

Defenders of the status quo warn that such changes could have a chilling effect on economic recovery, significantly slowing the flow of capital into companies that would ultimately fail without such support, eliminating much needed jobs. Controversially, Stephen Schwarzman of Blackstone went so far as to compare Obama's proposal to increase taxes on carried interest to Hitler's 1939 invasion of Poland.

Despite the heated rhetoric on each side, a simple fact of legislative life remains inviolate – changing the tax code is always difficult. There is tremendous legislative inertia when it comes to making changes to a law as significant, and with as many highly entrenched constituencies, as the tax code. The US provisions governing partnership tax on which the carried interest tax treatment is based pre-date the rise of private equity funds in the 1970s, and these funds and their general partners are reluctant to see any changes. UK tax rules addressing private equity funds were adopted in the late 1980s to provide a tax treatment that made sense in the pre-existing British fiscal regime.

At its heart, the debate over carried interest taxation is more a problem of public relations than of fiscal policy. This became even more evident as the race for the White House picked up steam in early 2012.

Clearly, if private equity firms want to retain these benefits, they need to make the case to each taxpayer, clearly and effectively, that the benefits they bring to the economy outweigh the billions in tax revenue that is not collected from them. Not a simple task, but a fight worth fighting for those who believe that there is real value in the corporate rescues that private equity firms conduct.

Fund investors will be vital in this debate and will also have a case of their own to make to tax authorities. Fortunately, none of the proposals for taxing carried interest as ordinary income made so far would deny investors in these funds of capital gains treatment for their investments. However, as US public pension plans, university endowments and charities and other institutional investors become more dependent on the promise of high returns that are offered by private equity firms, it seems unlikely that these investors will stand idly by as money is taken out of fund managers' pockets. Especially since the most likely place for these fund managers to replenish that money is to look very closely at the money remaining in these investors' own pockets.

It is perhaps worthwhile to take some time to actually walk through the relevant tax provisions to get a better feel for what their intentions really are. If the tax codes are appropriately categorizing the money earned by private equity and hedge fund managers, then the allegations lobbed at them are unfounded. If these categorizations are incorrect, then there are concrete steps that can be taken to change the tax codes and adapt them to the reality on the ground.

Under general US tax rules governing partnerships, which apply with equal force to all private equity and hedge funds set up as partnerships, income or gain is allocated directly to each partner, including holders of a carried interest. The vehicle itself is ignored. Therefore, the character of such income or gain passes through to the partners. As mentioned above, where this income is derived from long-term capital gains, an individual receiving carried interest pays tax on this income at a 15 percent rate, rather than the higher 39.6 percent rate applicable to compensation income.

In addition, the fund manager entities often elect partnership classification for tax purposes as well. This is done in order to permit principals who own an interest in that entity to benefit from this tax treatment for any carried interest held by the fund manager. If the fund manager were itself not a partnership for tax purposes, then the character (capital gains) of the carried interest would not "pass through" to the individual principals. They would have to take those cash flows as ordinary income through the payment of performance fees, like a hedge fund manager would. There are other benefits as well. Where capital gain income is not treated as compensation, it has the additional benefit of not being subject to "self-employment taxes," such as the 2.9 percent Medicare tax generally payable on all compensation income in the United States, or National Insurance contributions in the United Kingdom.

Clearly, the distinction between capital gains and ordinary income adds significant complexities to the tax codes, and as a result opens up the potential for abuse. However, the foundation of this distinction is recognition that the potential for double taxation can dissuade people from investing their money, rather than simply spending it now.

This can best be seen in a simple example. Imagine that you earn $10,000 for work that you have done assisting a small chain of wine shops update their computer systems. You pay tax of $3,500 on that money (at the rate of 35 percent, for simplicity's sake) and so you will have $6,500 remaining. You could choose to spend that on a new home entertainment system, including a large flat screen television, or you could instead decide that rather than "consume" now, you will put that to work by buying the shares of the company that makes the flat screen television that you considered buying. In a year the company's share price doubles, and that $6,500 is now $13,000.

You already paid full tax on the first $6,500, so how much should you pay on the second $6,500?

The lower capital gains rate recognizes that by investing, you decided to forgo an immediate benefit for the possibility of a larger benefit in the future. The lower rate rewards this decision and incentivizes you to do it again in the future.

Of course, the above example is necessarily a simplification of dozens of factors at work in these decision-making processes, but incentivizing investment over immediate consumption is at the heart of the justification for the lower capital gains rate. Some commentators, however, have made clear their views that the lower capital gains rate is a mistake. According to Paul Krugman, *New York Times* columnist, "In short, the low tax rate on capital gains is bad economics, even ignoring who it benefits."

Meanwhile, the distinction between income and capital treatment is important in the United Kingdom, just as it is in the United States. The introduction of a flat 18 percent capital gains tax rate for individuals in April 2008, increased in 2010 to 28 percent for higher rate taxpayers, created a significant difference between the taxation of income and capital gains. Immediately after the outbreak of the global financial crisis, the top UK tax rate was raised to 50 percent. As in the United States, when not treated as employment income, carried interest also enjoys the additional benefit of not being subject to UK National Insurance contributions. By contrast, hedge fund performance fees attract National Insurance contributions when paid to managers, since it is categorized as ordinary income.

The UK tax treatment of performance fees or carried interest also depends on the structure of the fund, the nature of the fund investments and the fund's investment strategy. Together, these factors determine whether the performance fees or carried interest received by the manager will be treated as income for UK tax purposes, as in the case of most hedge fund performance fees, or as a capital gain, as has been the case with private equity funds since 1987. This was the year in which a Memorandum of Understanding was agreed between the Inland Revenue (the predecessor of today's HMRC), the British Venture Capital Association (BVCA) and the Department of Trade and Industry (the 1987 MOU). Importantly, the capital gains tax treatment for carried interest was reaffirmed in 2003 in a further memorandum between HMRC and the BVCA on the occasion of the introduction of the employment-related securities regime in the Finance Act 2003 (the 2003 MOU).

This significant difference in tax treatment follows from the different structural set-up of hedge fund and private equity fund management entities. Performance fees paid, for example, by offshore hedge funds to UK investment managers are contractually structured as fees for services provided, and as such are classified as ordinary trading income for UK taxation purposes. Carried interest awards of private equity funds making long-term investments, on the other hand, are typically structured as limited partnership interests in the investment fund itself.

Where the private equity fund is structured in accordance with the 1987 and 2003 MOUs, gains allocated to individual UK managers via their partnership holdings when fund investments are sold will be treated as arising to the managers directly, and are normally treated as capital gains.

Importantly, the 1987 and 2003 MOUs only apply on their face to fund arrangements that are structured in line with the fund model described in detail in the memoranda. Material deviations in structuring might not benefit from MOU protection. While HMRC have not to date required strict compliance with the MOU structure, as the market has evolved in recent years, care is always to be taken to ensure that the carried interest when paid out would, in practice, also be taxed as a capital gain and not as income.

Negotiating a path between tax categorizations and jurisdictional reach is always a challenge for private equity and hedge funds, especially in a rapidly changing world with overlapping rules and regulations. Recently in the United States, there has even been tax competition on the state level.

As state tax revenues continue to fall as a result of the destruction of asset value that has followed the onset of the global financial crisis, state legislators have begun looking around for potential new taxpayers and employers to lure into their states. Unsurprisingly, their eyes soon fell upon hedge fund managers and private equity funds.

In July 2010, Connecticut sought to gain the upper hand on New York in a battle for the hearts and minds of hedge fund managers and private equity professionals. And their wallets. New York, facing a budget shortfall, was looking for extra tax receipts. One idea that eventually surfaced was to try to collect an extra $50 million in income taxes from so-called "alternative" fund managers who work in New York but live elsewhere. They soon focused like a laser beam on the holy grail of compensation – carried interest.

New York's controversial proposal required that out-of-state commuters be taxed on these profits instead at the higher ordinary income tax rates, in line with New York residents. New York already levies a higher top income tax rate (nearly 9 percent) than Connecticut (6.5 percent). Connecticut, unsurprisingly, realized the competitive advantage that such a fiscal misstep potentially provides them. "Connecticut welcomes you!" as their governor quickly made clear to wavering managers.

New York City Mayor Michael Bloomberg also expressed his concern, querying why any manager would continue to commute into the state if it would mean a higher tax rate. Talented high-earning individuals provide a clear boost to the economy of the place where they live. Whether they are NBA basketball players, movie stars or hedge fund managers, the local shops, restaurants and countless others benefit from their presence. And New York City is particularly dependent on these elite taxpayers.

Despite the lingering effects of the global financial crisis, with its jobless recovery and lingering fear of an impending double dip, astute fund managers have been profiting from the fear and inertia of others. These men and women have choices as to where they live, and where they pay taxes.

Tax authorities around the world – whether they are large or small, onshore or offshore – that think they can fill their emptying coffers by taxing these highly mobile individuals may find that their search for taxes will do more harm than good. However, this is not to say that there are not instances where tax laws are being violated and steps must be taken to protect the integrity of national finances. Where illegal tax avoidance occurs, it must be punished. Sometimes, even the best tax planning gets called into question by a prosecutor, if not by the IRS itself.

As many private equity professionals were finalizing their plans for enjoying the upcoming Labor Day holiday weekend, the New York Attorney General's office was busy issuing subpoenas in late August 2012 for many of the largest and most well-known private equity firms. Attorney General Eric Schneiderman was looking for documents that would reveal the inner working of a tax strategy that allowed them to convert management fees, normally taxed as ordinary income, into direct investments in their fund. The result was that this money would be taxed at the lower capital gains rate. Schneiderman has made tax evasion a top priority for his office.

Under a process known as "management fee waiver", a portion of the regular payments made by investors to fund managers of their funds are reallocated to investments in portfolio companies within the fund. As a result, these individuals received direct interests in those companies, rather than cash. Since these private equity professionals do not receive those fees before their conversion, they are not taxed on them at that time. Instead, they will be taxed on the capital gains derived from those investments at some point in the future when those companies are eventually sold.

As discussed above, the argument in favor of capital gains treatment is that the money in these portfolio companies is at risk of loss and, accordingly, deserve the incentives embedded in the lower tax rate to encourage them to put money at risk, rather than simply spending or saving it. The conversion practice has been well known within the industry, and by the IRS, for many years. Critics allege that there is little actual risk for private equity firms since the conversion is often optional, and therefore would only take place if the fund is clearly "in the money." Until Schneiderman decided to send out his subpoenas, however, little official attention had been focused on these arrangements.

Importantly, though, there is a more simple commercial argument that can be made by fund investors against the conversion process, particularly in the case of newer or smaller funds. By requesting that some portion of management fees are converted into fund investments, the fund manager is explicitly acknowledging that this amount of money is not necessary for the day-to-day management of the fund. Aggressive investors can push back against this approach by claiming that, in effect, they are subsidizing the fund managers' "skin in the game" and therefore denying themselves the alignment of interest that these co-investments are supposed to provide. It will be left to the fund managers to defend the economic advantages that this arrangement gives them.

In light of the growing concerns that investors are having about excessive management fee revenue streams resulting in misaligned incentives for fund managers, it is likely that the fee levels necessary to support the practice of fee waivers will continue to come under scrutiny from investors, regardless of the ultimate success of Schneiderman's subpoenas.

What would actually happen, though, if Congress raised taxes on private equity? Would it be the end of life as we know it? Would financial activity on the planet violently seize up and stop?

David Rubenstein of Carlyle doesn't think it would be very complicated. In January 2012, he remarked during the gathering in Davos of the world's leading business people and politicians, "If you change the law, we'll pay the taxes." This position has the immediate and tangible benefit of avoiding what is known in some circles as the "Wesley Snipes outcome."

The sums involved are, of course, substantial. A study conducted by the London School of Business concluded that US private equity professionals earned almost $140 billion in the fifteen years leading up to 2004. Other countries with thriving private equity industries charge higher rates of tax on carried interest. The United Kingdom and Sweden charge 28 percent and 30 percent respectively. In 2010, the rate in the United Kingdom was only 18 percent, but political pressure saw it rise for the highest earners. Even China has a 20 percent rate for carried interest. But other countries do have lower rates, with both Switzerland and Hong Kong having 0 percent rates on their books.

According to Mario Giannini, head of Hamilton Lane, "I have yet to see the prospect of higher taxes reduce incentives for those running private equity firms." Even Mitt Romney's campaign adviser, N. Gregory Mankiw of Harvard University, admitted that "[n]ot all problems have easy answers," and "some reform may well be appropriate" for tax rules governing carried interest.

It may be in the best interest of private equity firms to ultimately accept that something needs to be done on the tax issue. The public relation benefits could be substantial. Ignoring negative sentiment opens the industry up to larger risks. According to Joe Dear, CalPERS' investment chief, "They risk becoming the robber barons of the twenty-first century if they are not careful."

Given the increasingly politicized tone of the debate surrounding Wall Street and the City of London since the onset of the global financial crisis, all private equity and hedge fund managers must bear in mind the perception of their industries by a wider group of concerned individuals. The most important asset they have in winning the hearts and minds of their critics is the testimony, and ongoing support, of their satisfied customers – namely, the institutional investors who regularly entrust them with their money.

Accordingly, our attention now turns to the variety of different public pension plans, university endowments and charities, family offices and other investors who pay the managers so generously for the opportunity to invest in their private equity and hedge funds.

5: I GET BY WITH A LITTLE HELP FROM MY FRIENDS

Investors in Funds, Who They are and What They Expect

Pension managers – especially at public pensions – lack the resources, expertise and time to keep a close eye on the people managing their money.
Henry Sender, *Wall Street Journal*, September 2006

I worry that institutions are betting on an asset class that is not well understood. We know that the real long-term source of performance is not picking someone good at beating the market, it's taking risks on meat and potato assets like stocks and bonds.
William Goetzmann of the Yale School of Management

A yellow Lamborghini is an impressive sight to behold on any road. In the small southern city of Columbia, capital of South Carolina, such an exotic sports car makes a clear and unequivocal statement.

Robert Borden, who spent several years as the investment chief of the South Carolina Retirement Systems and oversaw the pension money for over 500,000 state employees, wasn't afraid to make such a statement. In 2009, the South Carolina pension plan was named "Large Pension Plan of the Year" and Borden accepted the trophy at an awards ceremony in California. His $500,000 a year salary made him one of the highest paid public officials in the state.

Eventually, concerns were raised over the high fees the state was paying for what appeared to be unexceptional returns. Borden soon fell out with various politicians and watchdogs and resigned as a civil servant in December 2011, to take a job in the private sector.

Since a significant amount of the money invested in private equity and hedge funds originates from public pension funds, which hold the retirement savings for government employees, it was probably inevitable that one day scandals would eventually emerge involving wayward public officials and shadowy middlemen. In the years since the start of the global financial crisis in 2008, more troubling stories relating, directly or indirectly, to US public pension plans investing in private equity and hedge funds began to enter the mainstream press.

Many laypersons inexperienced with alternative funds are often quite surprised when they first learn that the retirement plans of teachers, police officers and sanitation workers serve as the foundation for these financial high fliers. The difference in remuneration is only one of the many, many ways the world of government differs from the world of alternative investment funds. What brings these two very different worlds together is central to understanding the key dynamics in the industry and the growth of these funds in recent years.

Simply put, US public pension plans are in a race against time. An estimated $1 trillion short of the money they need to cover pension entitlements for a growing number of government employees, these plans are turning to private equity and hedge funds for the large returns they need in order to close the funding gap. As a result, hedge funds have come in from the shadowy fringes and joined private equity funds at center-stage with institutional investment portfolios. 2011 saw Illinois, New Jersey and Texas increase their pension plan exposure to hedge funds. New York City's pension plan also announced that it was contemplating a ten-fold increase in its hedge fund allocations.

As public pension funds are increasingly being asked to achieve higher and higher investment returns in order to deliver retirement benefits to their beneficiaries, these retirement plans are being forced to allocate more of their money to riskier and riskier funds. Unfortunately, the results are not as clear-cut as many would like.

One phenomenon that became increasingly common in 2012 was the awkward case of pension funds focused on traditional investments having a better return than those pension funds paying higher fees to participate in private equity and hedge funds. The Pennsylvania State Employees' Retirement System, for example, posted an average return of 3.6 percent over the past five years, well below the 5 percent average of all public pension funds, despite almost half of its assets in alternative investments. However, the $26 billion fund still had to pay over $1 billion in management fees during this period. Research suggests that pension plans with significant participation in alternative funds may pay as much as four times in fees than more conservative funds.

Some critics have raised concerns over these developments. According to William Goetzmann of the Yale School of Management, "I worry that institutions are betting on an asset class that is not well understood. We know that the real long-term source of performance is not picking someone good at beating the market, it's taking risks on meat and potato assets like stocks and bonds."

With interest rates at record lows and pension costs rising, public pension funds continue to struggle with their investment returns. The California Public Employees Retirement System (CalPERS) increased its exposure to alternative funds from 16 percent in 2006 to 26 percent in 2010, but at the same time saw the fees it paid double. Joseph Dear, chief investment officer of CalPERS, has an eye on costs, though. "I think it's part of our job for public fund managers to do our best to drive a better bargain."

Institutional investors across the United Kingdom, Europe and other leading industrialized countries are also facing similar short-falls and similar drives for higher and higher returns. Although US public pension plans have always been at the forefront of investing in private equity and hedge funds, many of the challenges they are facing in this area apply equally to institutional investors around the world.

Alternative investment funds have historically been the domain of either high net worth individuals, predominantly in hedge funds, and institutional investors, primarily in private equity and real estate funds. Institutional investors include public and private pension funds, endowments and foundations, insurance companies, banks and financial institutions, and corporations. High net worth individuals have either invested in hedge funds directly or indirectly, through family offices located in Philadelphia or Boston, Mayfair or Monaco, or through Swiss private banks.

Recently, institutional allocations to hedge funds have accelerated rapidly and are now recognized by the industry and its regulators as a principal driver for future growth. In the last decade, hedge funds have quadrupled, driven primarily by large institutional investors who now provide over half of the money sitting in hedge funds.

Between 2006 and 2011, it has been estimated that public pension plans increased their allocations to hedge funds from $28 billion to $63 billion. This is a marked change from the early days of hedge funds, when almost all of the money came from high net worth individuals. Institutionalization of the investor base for hedge funds has contributed to more sophisticated business practices, increased transparency and overall professionalization. Attracting institutional investors requires significant investment in business processes, together with increased legal and compliance costs.

As a result of these important trends, it is very important to take a long and comprehensive look at who is actually writing checks to the private equity and hedge funds, in order to form a complete and accurate judgment on the role these funds actually play in the broader society. Since the United States remains the primary market for alternative fund investors, it makes sense to begin the analysis there, before expanding out around the globe.

A wide variety of corporate pension plans invest in private equity and hedge funds. Industrial giants include Mercedes-Benz USA, Boeing, 3M, General Electric (GE), Citigroup, Northrop Grumman, Verizon Wireless, Lockheed Martin, Eli Lilly & Co., Honeywell, Bristol-Myers Squibb, Dow Chemical Company, Raytheon, Weyerhaeuser and International Paper Company. Technology companies such as Hewlett Packard (HP), International Business Machines (IBM) and Navistar also invest frequently. Well-known brand names such as Tyson Foods, Wells Fargo, Coca-Cola, UPS, PepsiCo, General Motors, Ford Motor Company, Campbell's Soup Company, MetLife and Allstate are also entrusting significant sums to private equity and hedge funds.

University and college endowments of all sizes also entrust significant portions of their investment portfolios to private equity and hedge funds. Ivy League colleges such as Princeton, Columbia, University of Pennsylvania, Harvard and Yale are all frequent investors, as are a number of other leading universities, such as Stanford, New York University, Georgia Institute of Technology, Emory University, Boston College, Massachusetts Institute of Technology (MIT), Tufts University, Wellesley College and Brandeis University. It would be a mistake, however, to see investment in these funds as the exclusive domain of expensive private schools. Many of the largest public universities in the United States, such as University of Michigan, Michigan State University, University of Minnesota, University of Virginia, University of Florida, University of Alabama, Auburn University, UCLA, Pennsylvania State University, University of Texas, Ohio State University, Washington State University and University of Washington, also allocate significant sums to private equity and hedge funds.

However, the most significant group of investors in these funds remain the large US public pension plans, whether on the west coast (CalPERS, California State Teachers Retirement System (CalSTRS), Los Angeles County Employees Retirement Association (LACERA), Los Angeles Fire and Police Pensions (LAFPP), San Diego County Employees Retirement Association (SDCERA),

Sacramento County Employees Retirement System (SCERS)), the east coast (Massachusetts Public Employees, New Jersey Division of Pension and Benefits, New York State and Local Retirement System (Common Fund), New York City Retirement Systems (NYCRS), Virginia Retirement System (VRS), Florida Retirement System) or from points in between (Michigan State Office of Retirement Services (ORS), Missouri Public School and Education Employee Retirement System (PSRS/PEERS), Missouri State Retirement Systems (MOSERS), Ohio School Employees Retirement System (SERS), State Teachers' Retirement System of Ohio (STRS), Texas Teacher Retirement System, Texas County & District Retirement Systems (TCDRS), Employees Retirement System of Texas (ERS), Illinois Teachers' Retirement System, State Retirement System of Illinois, Illinois Municipal Retirement Fund).

Many of these public pension plans are seeking to provide retirement benefits to enormous groups of beneficiaries. As a result, they are often quite large. CalPERS, for example, has over $200 billion to invest and manages retirement benefits for 1.6 million Californians. The City of New York has five separate pension funds for over 500,000 beneficiaries, with assets of approximately $120 billion. The plans are estimated to pay $400 million each year to various investment advisers. In 2011, Mayor Michael Bloomberg stated his desire to improve performance of the city's pension plans, which had been mediocre at less than 3 percent per year over the past ten years, by streamlining and de-politicizing the plans and their selection of fund managers.

Importantly, a growing segment of private equity and hedge fund investors is comprised of sovereign wealth funds. These entities manage the great pools of wealth that can be accumulated by states that are monetizing their natural resources. For example, the Abu Dhabi Investment Authority (ADIA), which is wholly owned by the Abu Dhabi government, invests in substantial assets across a number of asset classes, including private equity and hedge funds, as well as listed equities, fixed income and real estate. Kuwait Investment Authority, the Government of Singapore

Investment Corporation and the China Investment Corporation are also active investors.

Why invest in alternative investment funds at all? Perhaps by better understanding what these investors believe they will gain from entrusting their money with these entrepreneurial firms, it will shed light on the underlying drivers that have led to the relentless growth of private equity and hedge funds during our lifetimes.

The simplest answer would, of course, be high investment returns. Dressing this obvious conclusion up a little bit more, the benefits of private equity and hedge funds to investors purportedly include attractive risk-adjusted returns, downside protection, low correlation to other asset classes, diversification and access to exceptional investment talent.

As participation in alternative investment funds has increased over recent years, investors have gained invaluable experience and knowledge about how these funds operate. Although one by-product of this development could have been a rapid evolution in the structure of these vehicles, this has not occurred. The fundamental structure of private equity and hedge funds remains largely unchanged, with the principal economic motivation of fund managers continuing to be the opportunity to receive substantial performance-based compensation.

So how does an institutional investor enamored by alternative investment funds start the process of successfully building a portfolio of private equity and hedge funds producing eye-wateringly high investment returns?

Many US university endowments, as well as other large institutional investors around the world seeking higher returns for their nest eggs, have looked to Yale University, and in particular its chief investment officer David Swenson, as a source of inspiration. Over the two decades from 1985 to June 2008, Yale's endowment multiplied twenty-fold as Swenson pushed it toward private equity and hedge funds. Unfortunately, the market collapse that initiated the global financial crisis didn't leave Yale unscathed. Swenson estimated in 2009 that the endowment was down 25 percent.

After years of other universities debating whether or not to be more like Yale, many are now instead questioning whether alternative investment funds actually deliver enough return to account for the potential risks. The most difficult question presented by the global financial crisis to institutional investors is, simply put, "Can you live with the new realities of growth?" For those brave investors who want higher returns, the next question is, "Which private equity or hedge fund should you actually pick in order to achieve those higher returns?"

The decision to invest in alternatives is only the first of a long series of questions that necessarily follow. There are literally thousands to choose from (with new funds being launched each and every month), so it is not a simple process. Several factors drive a prospective investor's decision to allocate money to a particular private equity or hedge fund manager. These include their assessment of the manager's track record and prior experience, the particular investment strategy the manager proposes to follow, and the organizational infrastructure supporting the manager's business.

Importantly, since the beginning of the global financial crisis, more and more attention has been spent by investors on understanding how the funds operate and locating areas of particular risk. For many, the fallout from the crisis has provided them with a very, very expensive education! Investors contemplating allocations to these asset classes today are increasingly allocating more and more time to understanding the risks each fund poses.

According to Swenson, "The investment management world is a strange place in that the right solution is not in the middle. The right solution is at one extreme or the other. One end of the spectrum is being intensely active. The other is being completely passive. If you end up in the middle, which is where almost everybody is, you pay way too much in fees and end up getting sub-par returns." How different investors follow this advice when structuring and negotiating their participations in private equity

135

and hedge funds will be a recurring theme of this chapter, as well as the chapters to follow.

As discussed above, much of private equity's money, and a significant portion of hedge fund's money, comes from US public pension funds. Typically, pension plans that invest in alternative investment funds are defined benefit plans, rather than defined contribution plans. The distinction between these two plans is very important. Defined benefit plans, which provide set payments to recipients at the end of their working life, are better suited to the liquidity demands of these funds. As pension assets continue to shift from defined benefit to defined contribution in the United States, fund managers are hoping that pension plans in other markets, such as the United Kingdom and Europe, will allocate to alternative investment funds to make up for the loss of assets.

It is important to recognize one of the most important drivers to the private equity and hedge fund industries that is overlooked again and again by observers, commentators, legislators and academics attempting to evaluate these funds – namely, that much of the profits earned from a successful "buy-strip-flip" of a hundred-year-old business in a contracting industry that has fallen on bad times, or the relentless short-selling strategy that forces the collapse in the share price of a previously favored technology company, go overwhelmingly to New York teachers, Colorado firefighters and Californian civil servants. These are the constituencies who most directly benefit from the outsized returns and it is surprising how rare it is for both groups on either side of the money equation to be mentioned in the same breath.

It is, therefore, worth stressing again this fundamental linkage between highly remunerated financial professionals and large numbers of public employees with generous retirement benefits that must eventually be paid out. If the hedge fund managers and private equity professionals are not able to make up the difference between what is in these pension pots today and the contractually mandated retirement benefits, then all taxpayers, regardless of their own personal pension entitlements, will be expected to make up the difference.

This symbolic relationship between private equity and hedge funds on the one hand, and public pension funds on the other-hand, leads to a number of other awkward conclusions. First, as Henry Sender notably reported in *The Wall Street Journal* in October 2006, "Pension managers – especially at public pensions – lack the resources, expertise and time to keep a close eye on the people managing their money." In other words, although legally entitled to be categorized as sophisticated investors, these pension fund trustees may not have the actual ability to adequately oversee and monitor the firms with which they entrust their money. Of course, what they don't lack is the money to hire such expertise in order to protect themselves. Second, the public policy choice to rely on these managers to provide the high returns in order to fulfill the obligations that these governments have to their former employees means that these funds are directly influencing, and are influenced by, the decisions of political officeholders. The scale of this influence should not be underestimated.

Conventional wisdom holds that in the United States approximately two-thirds of the money in private equity and venture capital funds comes from tax-exempt investors such as pension funds and university endowments. A curious feature of these institutional investors is that, unlike the fund manager who ultimately manages the money, it remains relatively uncommon for the investment professional within these pensions and endowment funds to receive bonuses linked to performance. This lack of performance-based remuneration can place these institutions in an unfavorable comparison to funds of funds and other firms willing to provide fuller compensation to these individuals. The war for talent that is often discussed in connection with private equity and hedge funds often includes accomplished individuals on the investor side.

Interestingly, despite the prevalence of college students among the Occupy protesters, and growing opposition to Wall Street firms recruiting on college campuses, US universities, such as Harvard, Yale, Dartmouth, Indiana, Illinois and Texas, are very active investors in private equity funds. Their endowments have often significantly outperformed public pension funds, the other most frequent participants in private equity and hedge funds. Yale earned over 10 percent on its endowment over the past decade. Harvard's endowment earned approximately 9.4 percent on average over that period.

The underlying dynamic between fund managers and fund investors is absolutely crucial to any attempt to understand how private equity and hedge funds operate in the world and what drives decision-making at either end. Far too often, however, the role of investors in these structures is ignored or minimized. Perhaps this omission stems from simple ignorance, but there is a risk that these omissions are made purposefully as a way of providing a narrative about the nature of private equity and hedge funds that lends itself more readily to certain partisan political viewpoints.

Over thirty years ago, the relationship between US public pension money and private equity investment acumen began. In 1981, KKR used money provided by the Oregon Investment Council to acquire the retailer Fred Meyer. Since then, the relationship has deepened and broadened considerably, driving the alternatives industry forward.

When a public pension plan invests in a private equity fund or a hedge fund, the retirement savings of millions of government employees are often handed over to a small handful of millionaire (or billionaire) investment professionals who stand to earn staggering sums of money if they manage to generate significant returns for these working-class beneficiaries. Pension funds are in desperate need of high yields on their investment portfolios, and they are willing to pay handsomely to get it.

How much money is being paid? A 2010 *New York Times* study found that for the ten years between 2000 and 2010, the ten largest public pension funds paid approximately $17 billion to private equity firms in connection with their investments. However, it is important to keep in mind that these pension plans hold vast portfolios of investments. For example, the Teachers Retirement System of Texas manages over $100 billion in assets, while the New Jersey Division of Investment has approximately $66 billion in assets. It is also important to remember that for every dollar of profit generated from a leveraged buyout, 80 cents goes to investors, such as public pension plans. In January 2011, CalPERS announced an annual return of over 12 percent on its investments, even in the face of punishing losses in real estate and having lost a quarter of its money in the early years of the financial crisis.

Increasingly, public pension plans are expanding their relationships with the top tier of private equity firms to include a broader range of investment objectives and potentially lower fees. In December 2011, the New Jersey Division of Investment gave Blackstone an approximately $1.5 billion mandate to invest across a number of strategies, including private equity. Notably, the pension plan is run by a former Carlyle partner, Robert Grady. The previous month, the Teachers Retirement System of Texas (TRS) gave a similar $6 billion mandate to KKR and Apollo. TRS referred to these two private equity titans as "among the most reputable and successful private management firms in the world."

Underfunded, but still in pursuit of returns of 8 percent or more, public pension plans have put their money to work in private equity funds and increasingly hedge funds in a desperate effort to close this gap. How successful have the pension plans been in achieving these goals? Industry researcher Preqin reports average pension plan returns on private equity, but some plans have significantly outperformed the benchmarks. The Texas Retirement Fund claims a 13 percent per annum return, while CalPERS boasts an 11 percent average return since it first began investing in "alternative" investments in 1990.

As noted earlier, US public pension plans remain the largest investors in private equity funds, although the relationship between client and money manager has diversified as private equity firms have expanded their offering from traditional leveraged buyouts to include real estate, hedge funds and customary money management. Given this significant flow of funds, a legitimate question would be how much influence do the public pension plans have on fund managers and their decision-making? This question goes to the heart of the structures used for these funds, as well as opening up several important follow-on questions.

For example, what recourse does a public pension fund, or any investor in a private equity fund or a hedge fund, have if the fund loses money? In practice, only limited remedies will usually be available to a fund investor looking at large losses. In 2004, for example, the State of Connecticut went so far as to actually sue the private equity firm Forstmann Little for making investments that were significantly riskier than what had been promised to investors. In an ambiguous result, the court found in favor of Connecticut, but no damages were awarded. Forstmann Little founder Theodore Forstmann announced soon thereafter that he would not be raising a follow-on fund.

The money flows both ways in private equity and hedge funds. This two-way flow invariably raises concerns over conflicts of interest. Mixing low paid government employees with highly paid Wall Street types seems a sure-fire recipe for scandal. Unsurprisingly, in the early years of the global financial crisis, the attention of law enforcement officers and public sector watchdogs turned toward public pension funds and the alternative investment equity funds with which they entrust their beneficiaries' money.

In 2009, scandals involving large public pension plans erupted in both New York and California, revealing the significant risks present when large sums of money are being allocated by government employees to alternative investment funds in pursuit of stellar returns. In each case, middlemen profited by delivering large investments from these pension plans to particular fund managers, who subsequently earned large fees for managing this money. Allegations made against politically connected intermediaries included bribery, securities fraud and even money laundering. As an indication of the political reach of these accusations, the private equity firm Quadrangle Group, co-founded by Obama's auto-czar Steven Rattner, was also swept up in the investigations. Eventually, if perhaps belatedly, even the SEC became involved in these investigations.

For many years, placement agents earned lucrative fees by helping managers find new investors for their funds. Like those who perform a similar role in connection with equity and bond underwriting, fund placement agents typically earn a small commission (often 1 to 2 percent) off each dollar that is put in the fund. The industry had accepted these practices as legitimate and necessary for many years. However, at times, such arrangements can cross the line into allegations of kickbacks and pay-to-play. In addition, since many elected state officials can potentially influence, however remotely, the investment decisions of a pension fund, questions can also be asked about the influence of campaign contributions on the allocation process.

Crime blotter-style stories eventually began running in leading newspapers week-in and week-out, focusing on a potentially corrupt web of relationships between a cabal of individuals who wear multiple hats in political fundraising circles, powerful unions, the public sector and private industry. These reports did little to reinforce and bolster the credibility and luster of the large pension plans involved. Public confidence in the security of pension plans can arguably be harmed even by the mere appearance of cronyism and bias.

Subsequent to the 2009 scandals, many US public pension plans now ban any manager with whom they invest from using placement agents. Even where existing laws are not directly broken by these activities, advocates of transparency and accountability stress that even the appearance of impropriety undermines the good functioning of government.

Unfortunately, issues involving illegalities concerning pension funds continued as the financial crisis wore on. In January 2011, it was reported that the SEC was investigating whether the State of California violated federal securities laws when it failed to provide full and complete information about CalPERS. California is ultimately responsible for ensuring that retirement payments are eventually paid to entitled beneficiaries, and if there is a shortfall, California taxpayers will have to make up the difference. At the same time, the California Attorney General was conducting his own investigations on conflicts of interests between CalPERS and its service providers.

In April 2012, the SEC charged Federico Buenrostro, former chief executive of CalPERS, with defrauding private equity giant, Apollo. Buenrostro and his friend Alfred Villalobos allegedly fabricated certain documents in order to induce Apollo to make payments to Villalobos, a former CalPERS board member. It was believed that Apollo paid Villalobos almost $50 million in connection with various CalPERS investments. Notably, CalPERS is also a direct shareholder in Apollo, in addition to being a frequent investor in its funds. In 2007, CalPERS bought 9 percent of Apollo for an estimated $600 million.

The Buenrostro/Villalobos prosecution was part of a nationwide trend by regulators and law enforcement to more closely police the placement agents, finders and gatekeepers who profit by directing public pension money to private equity and hedge fund firms. Critics call such activities "influence peddling", which violate laws against corruption in government. These prolonged scandals in California and elsewhere, involving allegations of conflicts of interest regarding the selection of fund managers, led to the eventual adoption of new requirements that placement agents who get paid to find public pension plans to invest in funds will need to get officially registered as lobbyists.

Even where there is no fraud or malfeasance, public pension funds and other institutional investors must balance themselves on a tightrope in order to ensure that these investments deliver what they have promised. For example, a feature of recent years has been the phenomenon of "denominator destruction," whereby due to a decrease in the value of one class of investments held by a particular investor (e.g. public equity), such investor becomes "over-allocated" in other asset classes (e.g. private equity or real estate). As a result, pension fund trustees must keep a close watch on their portfolios to ensure that they are not inadvertently "doubling down" on one asset class because of the collapse of other asset classes.

Being a pension fund trustee who invests in private equity and hedge funds is not a job for the faint-hearted. By their very nature, investments in alternative investment funds may demand a disproportionate amount of time and resources of an investor, both in making an initial allocation and in monitoring the allocations going forward. The answer to this demand can be either an increase in personnel and capabilities internally or investing by way of fund of funds or other multi-strategy products. Neither approach, however, is without cost.

Funds of funds, for example, can play a crucial role in providing full-time oversight of an allocation to alternative investment funds. They offer investors a variety of services including sourcing funds with available capacity, monitoring their performance over time and, when appropriate, realizing the profits from the fund and reallocating. Unfortunately, as the dire fate of several fund of funds involved in the Bernard Madoff debacle clearly demonstrates (and which will be discussed in subsequent chapters), they are not always a foolproof solution that can guarantee the desired results.

Nowhere are the principles of supply and demand more evidently in operation than in the process of securing a prospective investor's participation in a new private equity or hedge fund. During a particular fundraising cycle, it is not uncommon to see a very small number of elite fund managers facing massive over-subscription, while a significant number of others have difficulties obtaining money sufficient to even launch their funds. The practical implications of this tendency for investors to adopt a "herd mentality" around established brand names, influenced, in part. by subjective factors such as perceived exclusivity, arguably grants too many fund managers the higher ground when it comes to negotiating the commercial and legal details surrounding the actual investment in the fund.

Even at the best of times, the process of investing in a fund can be a time-consuming ordeal for all parties involved. Due diligence demands have been steadily rising since 2008 as institutional investors become better educated about what separates successful funds from unsuccessful funds. Investors are asking more and more sophisticated questions about how fund managers create value for their funds. Investors want to understand whether past performance was driven principally by benefiting from a "rising tide" or whether it is reproducible in years to come.

An ongoing debate centers on the relative balance of power between investors and fund managers at any given time. Principally, the focus has been on objective, economic factors, such as the ability of investors to demand lower fees. However, issues of fund governance and ongoing oversight of the fund managers increasingly arise when discussing relative negotiating leverage today.

As discussed earlier, because of the difficulty that certain new fund managers face in raising their first fund, it is not uncommon to reward a cornerstone investor, who provides the fund with "proof of concept," with something to compensate for the value they create by way of their participation. This could include a discount on the management fee, a participation in the performance remuneration or an equity stake in the fund manager itself. However, preferential terms may create a subtle, but real, impediment to other investors' participation in the fund. This is based, in part, on the recognition that because of these terms, the interests of the cornerstone investor and the remaining investors are no longer fully in-line.

Of course, any new fund managers will need to consider the relative costs and benefits of providing fee discounts or ongoing capacity guarantees to early investors in exchange for receiving the assets necessary to launch their initial fund. Any arrangement with regard to fee discounts will need to be examined in light of the fund's overall capacity constraint. Allowing too much of a strategy's ultimate capacity to be taken up by investors paying sub-optimal fees can have long-term implications on a fund manager's profit and, in extreme cases, viability.

For example, after years of investing in various private equity funds, two of the world's largest sovereign wealth funds took the next logical step and purchased a 5 percent stake in private equity giant TPG. Kuwait Investment Authority and the Government of Singapore Investment Corporation paid $500 million for their stake in the firm, valuing TPG at $10 billion. China Investment Corporation has also taken a stake in Blackstone, and the Abu Dhabi Investment Authority invested directly in Apollo as well. Public pension plans had previously taken this step before the global financial crisis set in, with CalPERS purchasing small stakes in Carlyle and Apollo.

In February 2012, TRS made news that it was taking a stake worth $250 million in Bridgewater Associates. As a result, TRS (and the Texas teachers whose retirement benefits it provides) now can share in the profits associated with Bridgewater's future success. As discussed earlier, in return for giving up equity, a fund manager can use outside investment to monetize one or more founders, as well as ensuring an adequate pool of long-term capital.

However, buying into a hedge fund manager or a private equity firm can be a very tricky business. No less an intellectual powerhouse than Goldman Sachs invests directly into fund managers, and although some have been good performers, others – such as Shumway Capital and Level Global – were disappointments. Morgan Stanley also had a troubled history when it bought FrontPoint Partners in 2006, only to exit after taking a significant loss on its investment.

Are private equity and hedge funds ultimately "bought" or "sold"? This surprisingly tricky question sits at the heart of many difficult issues that arise in and around both the fundraising process and the correct expectations to place on institutional investors who are entrusting their beneficiaries' money to alternative investment funds.

With insufficient planning and forethought, the distribution of a new fund can become a time-consuming and expensive ordeal for the fund manager. Realistic decisions will need to be made about the demographics of the prospective investors. The fund will need to be structured to comply with their tax and regulatory requirements. Investors will need to be courted over long periods of time to convince them of the appropriateness of this particular fund in their vast portfolios.

Based on the fund manager's particular needs, third party distributors may need to be hired to add credibility and recognition to the launch, as well as accelerating the fundraising process. Especially where investors are being sought on a global basis, numerous practical difficulties (such as competing demands on their time) must be overcome by the individual principals seeking to raise funds on their own. Simply put, the function of the placement agent is to provide the fund manager with access to investors and their money.

Placement agents provide a number of interrelated services to funds and fund managers they assist, including identifying and pre-qualifying investors, preparing marketing materials, assisting fund managers with preparations for the investor presentations and managing the subscription process during the initial launch period. Placement agents may be either small and highly focused boutiques or global teams within large investment banks. They will have different strengths among the various categories of prospective investors, such as private banks, family offices, independent financial advisers, pension trustees and insurance companies. Certain placement agents may provide other valuable services to new managers, including infrastructure, risk management and compliance oversight.

Leading fund placement agents include Triago in Europe, Hyde Park and Aravis Partners in the United Kingdom, and global players such as the dedicated teams at UBS, Credit Suisse and Lazards. With institutional investors more hesitant to commit their money to funds since the commencement of the global financial crisis, the importance of a placement agent increases as the fund-raising period lengthens.

The economics of placement agent remuneration are varied, and can include either one-off commissions, revenue co-participation or equity stakes in the fund manager, based on the nature of the distribution platform. For hedge funds, it is common to see distributors request 20 percent of the remuneration received from investors who they introduce. In private equity funds, a fee of 2 percent of capital is common, to be paid either in full at launch or in instalments over two to three years.

As discussed earlier, the distribution of alternative investment funds is principally conducted by way of private placements to non-retail investors. With limited exceptions, this is driven by detailed restrictions on public marketing efforts imposed by financial regulators. Regulators generally limit access to these funds by either establishing high minimum subscription levels or setting qualification standards for each investor which must be met before he or she can invest.

Often, when an established fund manager is launching a new fund, the logical place to look for investors is to approach current investors in the manager's existing funds. One measure of success of a private equity fund, for example, is what proportion of existing fund investors invest in the fund manager's subsequent fund (known as "re-ups"). Questions may be raised in circumstances where a significant number of existing investors do not re-up. The view of an increasing number of investors, however, is that re-ups must be earned and not simply presumed to be the default.

As a result, a fund manager may find that if it is seeking a broader, global investor base or still lacks the reputation in the market to raise money solely on its personal track record, the service of a placement agent will be invaluable. The role of the placement agent is to bridge the gap between fund manager and potential investors. The fundraising process is merely one aspect of the fund manager's overall role.

Placement agents can also serve as a means for information to be exchanged more efficiently between fund managers and investors, especially with regard to changes in market practice. With demands by experienced institutional investors for both qualitative and quantitative due diligence increasing, placement agents can serve a valuable role in addressing queries.

Placement agents can expedite the due diligence process by preparing the fund manager in advance for the level of disclosure that will be required by prospective investors. As investors become more familiar with the alternative asset classes, through their knowledge of past pitfalls and shortcomings, their questions for fund managers are becoming more precise and more detailed. Placement agents can also assist fund managers by advising a variety of fund structuring issues of particular concern to investors in recent years, particularly issues that emerged as a result of the global financial crisis, such as investment committee composition and innovative remuneration structures that may appeal to otherwise reluctant investors.

From the investor's standpoint, the fundraising process is also a lengthy and demanding process. Before any decision can be made by any pension fund, university endowment or other charity about whether to invest in a particular fund, it must be determined whether the trustees will need to be educated generally regarding alternative investment funds. As discussed earlier, to the extent that trustees are elected or appointed by way of a public process, the current political climate in the relevant state capitals may be relevant to their actions. In addition, public pension funds may be subject to "sunshine" laws requiring that their deliberations and decisions be open to the public.

The steps necessary for approving an investment in a new private equity or hedge fund can be complicated and lengthy. A combination of external consultants and internal staff may be used to compile a "request for proposals," which can then be sent to potential managers for completion. Certain fund managers may decide that such demands make public pension funds unsuitable investors for them. The rise of questionnaires, either from investors themselves or their consultants, have led some critics to accuse fund investors of falling into a "check-the-box" mentality, when a more robust and wide-ranging analysis is necessary. The focus of these questionnaires includes useful information such as historic track records, propensity for style drift, and composition, experience and remuneration of the fund manager's team. The more important question, though, is how this data is ultimately used by the investor prior to signing the subscription documents and sending in the check.

As investors come to the table today with increasing demands for information and accommodation, they are also recognizing that the very successful managers will be less in need of any particular investor's participation. As a result, investors will need to prepare themselves for the curious circumstance whereby the fund managers most willing to meet the present demands could be managers well outside the top tier. This can add an important further dynamic to these negotiations.

Regardless of the asset class or type of fund, due diligence has become a more common activity of investors since 2008. Due diligence consists of the commercial and legal review of a prospective alternative investment fund and its managers prior to investment. In part, this exercise is driven by an increase in knowledge concerning the alternative asset classes amongst investors, and in part this is a result of an increase in funds (and managers) competing against one another for investor allocations.

Information is now more readily available to investors today than in the past. In addition to quantitative analysis of past performance, due diligence can involve an examination of numerous qualitative factors, including the manager's background, the investment strategy of the fund, the legal documentation related to the fund and the structure of the fund that has been selected.

Although due diligence efforts can successfully uncover material issues with a proposed fund investment, there are necessary costs involved, either in internal time and resources dedicated, or external advisers retained. The costs can be viewed as a necessary feature of forgoing the initial and ongoing review and oversight provided to regulated funds approved by the government for sale to retail investors, such as Uncle Edgar and Aunt Edna. For example, certain investors may require the fund's lawyers to prepare a legal opinion regarding the formation of the entity being used as the fund vehicle, compliance with applicable laws, the limited liability of the investors in the fund and the tax status of the fund vehicle. The use of offshore or cross-border structures can increase the number of lawyers and legal systems involved, as well as the time and cost requirements associated with the provision of such opinions.

The practice of due diligence will vary greatly in scope and depth from one investor to another, based on its experience, risk tolerance and recent history during the global financial crisis. Efforts have been made over the years to standardize the approaches among investors and across asset classes. Recent events, such as the Bernard Madoff debacle, as well as the earlier meltdowns of Amaranth Advisors (2006) and Long Term Capital Management (1998), have highlighted the shortcomings of a limited due diligence based on untested presumptions and excessive confidence in the earlier efforts of other investors.

Importantly, the limitations discussed earlier on the type and number of prospective investors who may participate in private equity and hedge funds is based, in part, on the belief by regulators in the United States, the United Kingdom and elsewhere that such persons can and will ask for and review relevant information about a fund's track record, compliance, controls and risk assessments. Failure by a prospective investor to conduct such a review undermines the very basis upon which such exemptions were originally conceived.

Of course, due diligence cannot be guaranteed in all circumstances to reveal all flaws or shortcomings in a prospective fund or its manager. Although it must be acknowledged that anticipated fund performance will always be the primary factor in selecting a private fund for investment, the due diligence function can and should be expanded by motivated investors to analyze and address fund governance concerns as well. A well-governed fund with poor performance will appeal to few discerning investors, but the risks to retaining a high return after a significant governance failure are substantial enough to warrant a reasonable allocation of time and attention to ensure the appropriate oversight mechanisms are in place.

For example, one potentially thorny question that institutional investors need to address alongside their increased allocation to private equity and hedge funds is their own internal staffing levels. Underlying significant numbers of frauds, malfeasances and failures in recent years is the lack of appropriate individuals at the investors with the required skills and supervision to do their jobs.

As David Swenson, CIO of Yale University, observed about university endowments in a February 2009 interview with ProPublica.org, "If I had to generalize, I would say institutions have been slow to commit the resources to hire dedicated investment staff. I think that once you get to the $500 million to $1 billion range, you should be moving in that direction. A consultant probably seems like an easier, cheaper alternative, but I think you realize enormous benefits from having dedicated investment staff if you're going to purse this active investment strategy. It's hard work."

In parallel with an investor's due diligence investigation into the commercial and operational aspects of the fund's business and operation will be the negotiation of the fund documentation with the manager. This is a very crucial step in the process, although too many investors in the past reflexively dismissed their own ability to amend or improve legal documentation.

Of course, the ability of prospective investors to potentially negotiate with fund managers about the terms of the fund's legal documentation does not guarantee that in every case, or in any particular case, the investor will be able to agree to adequate terms.

Such commercial negotiations will necessarily result in final terms that reflect primarily the relative negotiating leverage of each party and the cut-and-thrust of the wider financial markets at the time of such negotiations.

However, the clear assumption underlying the line of demarcation drawn around private equity and hedge funds by both the SEC and the FCA – that is, excluding retail investors and enabling only a small subset of prospective investors to participate in these vehicles – is that such sophisticated, non-retail investors will have the ability to evaluate the risks inherent in unsatisfactory legal documentation and decide not to invest.

Investors who are unable to get fund managers to revise the documents to address the concerns that they have identified must be willing to invoke the last line of defense that they have available to them – to "just say no" to an investment in that fund. Surveys of private equity fund investors, for example, have revealed that this is not an idle threat. Over half (53 percent) of investors interviewed indicated that they had in the past determined not to invest in a fund due to the terms and conditions, and approximately 20 percent stated they reached such decisions frequently.

With this in mind, it is worthwhile to look at several of the key issues that often arise in these negotiations. Since, as a general rule, private equity funds are subject to the most negotiations, while many hedge funds are launched with little direct investor input into the documents, the issues examined below will focus primarily on private equity funds, although many of the points can, and should, be applied more generally.

One way that an investor can alter their overall participation in a fund is by securing the right to invest more money in particular investments that they especially like. They would secure the right in the documents to elect in certain circumstances to provide further capital to invest in a particular portfolio company with the main fund on a more preferable fee basis, which is known as "co-investing."

This can be mutually beneficial in a number of circumstances. Typically, no carried interest is charged to these investors, although they may be charged a share of the management fee. Sometimes, a fund cannot take as much of an investment in a portfolio as it would like because of concentration or other restrictions and looks to investors to help make up the difference. Alternatively, sometimes certain investors just want to pay lower fees!

Two approaches to co-investment predominate in the market today. In the lockstep approach, a co-investment fund must invest in lockstep with the principal fund on a *pari passu* basis. In the pledge approach, investors with co-investment rights have the right – but not the obligation – to co-invest on any particular deal. The purpose of the lockstep approach is to avoid adverse selection (otherwise known as "cherry picking"). In effect, it is simply a fee rebate mechanism. The pledge approach can be formalized as a separate fund vehicle, dealt with as rights to certain investors in the principal fund's constituent documents or merely raised informally with certain investors on an opportunity-by-opportunity basis.

A successful co-investment program can have tremendous positive impact on all-in net returns for a limited partner. However, an important caveat should be made. A great deal of "dumb money" is believed by some critics to have been allocated to co-investment. Best track records appear to go to investors with dedicated private equity transaction teams who, in effect, look at all opportunities freshly and make independent assessments.

Co-invest can also serve narrower political purposes. In October 2012, the Colorado Public Employees Retirement Association, which oversees $40 billion in retirement savings, announced its own dedicated co-investment vehicle, called the Colorado Mile High Fund, which is designed to co-invest alongside private equity and venture capital funds in companies based in their own state in order to boost their local economy. The Indiana Public Retirement System and the Nevada Permanent School Fund have already launched similar co-investment programs in their own states.

For investors keen to improve their protections in a new fund, side letters are an important feature of both private equity and hedge funds. The role of a side letter is simply to customize the fund to the particular needs of an investor in a manner more similar to a segregated account. If a fully customized segregated account is seen as analogous to a bespoke suit, and a fund is the off-the-rack option, a side letter operates as a way of taking up a hemline here or letting out some fabric there.

In many ways, side letters are simply a by-product of the "collective" nature of the funds. As discussed earlier, funds serve primarily as a means of accessing the investment talent of a fund manager, when the sum of money being offered for investment is not significant enough to induce the manager to accept the mandate on a stand alone segregated account basis. Even in the context of a "collective" fund, some investors will be of such importance to the manager, either because of their amount of investment or because of the validation of the fund that their investment conveys, that side letters will be entered.

A fund manager will enter into side letter agreements with certain investors to induce or facilitate their participation in the fund. Common side letter terms include fee rebates, notice of particular changes in the personnel or structure of the fund manager, no in-kind distributions and further representations and warranties. In addition, side letters for hedge funds could include special terms addressing improved liquidity and increased transparency with respect to the fund's investments, which may include specific reporting formats.

Importantly, the first realization that should follow the acceptance by the fund manager of a request for a side letter is that it is quite possible that other side letters have been (or will be) agreed with other investors! As a result, perhaps the most common request in a side letter is the most favored nations (or "MFN") clause, which provides the recipient with the benefits of any other letters entered into by the manager. In effect, this pulls away from the "bespoke" nature of side letters and in practice creates two tiers of investors: those within the MFN regime and those without.

An MFN letter guarantees the recipient the benefit of any side letter given to any other participant in the fund. The acceptance of a request for an MFN letter can potentially expand the legitimate requirements of one investor across a large segment of the fund's other investors, leading to increased costs with little accompanying value to the MFN recipient. MFN provisions are powerful in their effects and are typically agreed to by a fund manager only after a complete analysis on how their replication of rights and duties would operate in practice.

Side letter management has become a crucial, but burdensome, feature of alternative investment fund structuring in recent years. As a result, increasing efforts are made to include in the constituent documents of a fund the most frequently requested side letter provisions. With more common side letter terms included directly in the partnership agreements and articles of incorporation, there is the potential for side letters to play less of a role. However, the underlying negotiating leverage of the parties will remain regardless. To the extent that an important investor requires customization, then any sufficiently motivated fund manager will do whatever he or she can to accommodate that investor.

Another important provision for astute and mindful investors to include in their fund documentation is a "key person" provision. As discussed earlier, the purpose of "key person" provisions is to ensure that the same group of investment professionals who were presented to prospective investors at the time of the private equity fund's launch, as essential to a fund's success, are there when needed.

If certain individuals within the fund manager are particularly important to the fund, provisions can be included in the fund documentation that provide for specific consequences if they leave. These could include the suspension of the investment period, in the case of a private equity fund, or the termination of lock-up provisions, in the case of a hedge fund. The trigger is often when one or more of the key persons cease to be involved with the management of the fund and are not adequately replaced. These provisions can be laid out with great detail, outlining different levels of seniority and establishing elaborate procedures for selecting and approving qualified replacements.

Key person clauses historically limited themselves to the most senior principals within the fund manager. After having witnessed the extensive "brain drain" of talent in 2008 and 2009 from firms managing funds unlikely to earn carried interest or performance fees due to early losses on investments, investors are now keen to see a broader inclusion of mid-level investment professionals within the scope of the key person provisions. Fund managers will frequently demand the inclusion of a cure provision for potentially replacing the departing principals, as a way of enabling them to keep the fund operational.

The mechanics of using these provisions in practice are not without their own problems, both within the investors and within the fund manager. On the one hand, many observers and commentators recognize the prevalence of "investor inertia," which can affect both the ability to receive necessary votes for affirmatively ceasing investments as well as for overriding an automatic suspension. On the otherhand, an individual's designation as a key person can provide that person with significant leverage over other members of the fund manager, should such leverage become necessary during the life of the fund. The effect of key person provisions in fund documentation can also be felt in the internal politics of the fund manager itself, especially where the entity is owned in whole or in part by a large financial institution.

Although the management and control of partnerships, the most common fund vehicle, rests squarely with general partners, limited partners will have some very important voting rights that they can choose to exercise from time to time. For example, upon a trigger event, such as the departure of a key person as described above, the partnership may require a vote to suspend the investment period.

During the global financial crisis, for example, limited partners became much more familiar with the finer workings of these provisions as they considered all options they had when confronting those general partners in whom they had lost faith.

Perhaps no vote cast by a fund investor is more important than whether to remove the fund manager from its role directing the investment activity of a fund, and go in a radically different direction. Private equity funds have typically allowed for many years that upon certain "for cause" events, the general partner can be removed from the partnership and replaced, upon a prescribed vote from the limited partners. Funds can vary in what is considered removal conduct and by what standard such conduct must be demonstrated.

Recently, many partnership agreements have also provided for removal of the general partner without cause at any time (frequently referred to as "no-fault divorce" provisions) by vote of the limited partners. Limits can be placed on this to protect the general partner, such as, for example, establishing that the general partner will be compensated for such removal by payment of management fees for a certain period (e.g. one year) or limiting the ability to use the provision within an initial period after the launch of the private equity fund.

The constituent documentation of the fund will typically set out how investors may terminate the fund manager and on what grounds. The removal of a fund manager will typically be viewed as the remedy of last resort. However, a clear understanding of what circumstances can permit such a remedy benefits all parties. Typically, a distinction is made between fault and no-fault removals. As a general rule, a higher percentage vote of investor is required for the latter.

While in the past many fund documents contained only fault provisions, investors have increasingly demanded the inclusion of a no-fault mechanism to provide the investors, when they feel it necessary, with a means for focusing the attention of underperforming or inadequate fund managers. In practice, however, involving the no-fault option remains rare. Its use is primarily as a backstop to other negotiations between the fund manager and the investors, where amendments or changes to the fund structure are being proposed.

In addition to instances where all limited partners may have a right to vote on a decision, many partnerships establish committees consisting of a small (and exclusive) subset of limited partners who can approve a defined list of actions.

Advisory committees consist of investors selected by the fund manager. They are formed by funds to provide a forum for resolution of certain questions and queries without resorting to canvassing all of the investors generally. Typically, the issues that are put in front of the advisory committees include conflicts of interest between the fund and the fund manager, and the valuation of investments. Where a fund is structured as a limited partnership, care must be taken to ensure that such committees operate within the restraints imposed on a limited partner's involvement in management. The loss of limited liability is not an acceptable price to pay for effective supervision.

Investment committees may also be formed, comprising key individual principals within the fund manager and certain third parties with expertise in the area of the fund's investments. Such third parties may or may not be investors. Expertise in the industries or sectors where the fund intends to invest is crucial. The precise role of such committees in the investment process differs from fund to fund, but typically relates to the investment process itself (e.g. sourcing and evaluating potential investment opportunities).

As alternative investment funds continue to become more mainstream, the demands of informed investors for increased protections, clear language and more closely aligned interests will increase. Fund managers must take adequate steps to ensure that they provide demanding investors with the information and ongoing support they require. The global financial crisis has meant that these investors now have many more questions that need answering in order to justify their investments to their own constituencies.

While formal "investor relations" teams can be built up in larger fund managers, the role of certain key principals within the firm who make the investment decisions and oversee the activities of the funds will remain crucial to many institutional investors. The interface between fund managers and investors, both during the fundraising process and on an ongoing basis, will continue to be a key focus of all parties.

A good example of where this interface comes into play can be seen in private equity funds, where disgruntled investors are contemplating a default on their obligations to wire any further money to the fund in compliance with drawdowns of their capital commitment. Disagreements between fund investors and fund managers continue to be a recurring feature of life since the global financial crisis. Any decision that a fund manager makes to enforce or not to enforce default penalties contained in fund documentation should keep in mind the extent to which those provisions benefit the other investors in the fund and the question this raises about the fund managers' own fiduciary duties.

While many investors are still trying to fully implement the painful lessons they learned in September 2008 and the months that followed, the large role of US public pension plans in alternative investment funds remains a frustratingly under-discussed topic.

Interestingly, in 2012 and 2013, a nationwide debate erupted over the generous pension benefits that many public employees enjoy in the United States, which have led to growing shortfalls in the dedicated pots of money set aside to fund these obligations. Protests and counter-protests were featured on the 24-hour rolling news channels, as opposing sides argued over what to do about pension deficits estimated to be as much as $3 trillion in the aggregate.

The high returns promised by private equity and hedge funds, which are seen by many as the simplest way to cover these deficiencies, come with high price tags. As discussed earlier, the fees charged by alternative funds are much higher than the rates charged on more traditional investments. In addition, the people ultimately paying those fees are often former government employees who retain much political clout in and around the halls of power.

As a result, when the hedge funds and private equity funds then end up having a bad quarter, or a bad year, awkward questions can be raised about the state employees who naively handed over precious public money to smooth-talking Wall Street operators, and paid dearly for the privilege.

As the global financial crisis dragged on, critics of alternative funds were regularly voicing their informed opinion that these funds needed to be curtailed, and that "casino capitalism" had to come to an end. They claimed, "We have a hedge fund problem." They claimed, "We have a private equity problem." The problem, in fact, is that we have a public pension plan problem in the United States. Unfortunately, this is not a problem that can be readily discussed and debated in the state legislatures across the country. This is, in fact, a problem that most politicians would prefer to forget.

PART TWO

ONE STEP AHEAD OF THE MARKET, ONE STEP AHEAD OF THE LAW

6: SIFTING THROUGH
THE RUBBLE

The Role of Private Equity and Hedge Funds in the Recent Global Financial Crisis

My administration is the only thing between you and the pitchforks.
President Barack Obama to Wall Street banker, March 2009

During the financial crisis the old-style investment banking model fell apart.
Steven Davidoff, *The New York Times*

The summer of 2008 was memorable for many reasons.

The Philadelphia Phillies were on their way to a winning season and World Series glory. The Boston Celtics, under the leadership of coach Doc Rivers, had just taken the NBA Championship away from the Los Angeles Lakers and the hot hands of Kobe Bryant. Manchester United's tenth Premier League title did little to prepare the English national team for glory in the European Championships in Austria and Switzerland, since England had not qualified for the tournament, having been edged out in the earlier rounds by Croatia and Russia.

Although the markets had been volatile after the earlier collapse of Bear Sterns and its ultimate acquisition by JP Morgan, the continued murmurings about subprime mortgages and mortgage-backed securities seemed to drift gradually again into the background. A crisis had been averted and that was a good thing. Or at least many people thought at the time.

Few people expected that the vast economic meltdown that was soon to be known as the global financial crisis was only a few months away from being unleashed. The handful of people who knew what was coming were preparing themselves to profit significantly from their beliefs. The rest, unfortunately, were simply weeks away from eye-watering, catastrophic losses.

When we look at a financial disaster, we want to ensure that it does not – that it cannot – happen again. Ever! Unfortunately, knowing what steps to take to allow our financial markets to operate, but only at acceptable levels of risks, is frustratingly difficult. To know what to do next, we need to know what just happened.

There remains a tremendous amount of anger about our current economic situation, especially as the after-effects of the global financial crisis continue to be felt. Some of that anger comes from the large number of questions that still remain unanswered, even with the benefit of accruing hindsight, about what exactly went wrong. But often easy, straightforward answers aren't ever available.

Much has been written about real estate bubbles and the pernicious impact of sub-prime loans that were then securitized and labelled AAA notes. In reality, though, there were hundreds and thousands of decisions that led to the financial crisis. As many impatiently await the prosecutions of high-profile individuals in connection with the financial crisis, it is necessary to distinguish between activities that were uninformed or incompetent, and those that constitute actual crimes.

Did Wall Street cause the financial crisis? What role did private equity and hedge funds play? The answer is not as clear as some critics would like, and many would point their finger more at the decisions made inside the Beltway by Washington politicos than at the investment banks themselves.

Trying to uncover what exactly caused the global financial crisis is not a simple task. In April 2011, the US Senate Sub-committee on Investigations issued its 600-page report on the causes of the recent global financial collapse. The convoluted story told in the report bore more than a passing resemblance to James Joyce's *Finnegans Wake*, but with charts.

Unsurprisingly, two years of investigations and deliberations by a bipartisan group of senators resulted in accusations of excessive risk-taking, conflicts of interest and lack of adequate federal oversight. The foundation of the report was a series of hearings held in April 2010, as well as further evidence that was received by the Subcommittee and included in their considerations. Ample blame was allocated to bankers, regulators and legislators. However, what still remains unclear today is whether the laundry list of recommendations that conclude the report have sufficient traction, post-Dodd-Frank, to meaningfully impact on what remains of the regulatory debate.

To this day, few substantive allegations have been made that would link hedge funds or private equity funds to the real estate bubble. Regardless, alternative funds were quickly swept into the financial reform debate, even though many agreed that they were not a component of the past failures.

For example, further hedge fund regulation after the global financial crisis was actually not a foregone conclusion in the months following the dramatic events of September 2008. As financial reporter Jesse Eisenger of ProPublica.org once observed about the attempts at increased rule-making and oversight directed at the hedge fund industry, "It's all the more surprising since hedge funds were not a cause of the crisis. Banks, especially Wall Street firms, get credit for that. Plenty of hedge funds went out of business, but almost none of them were systemically important enough to stoke fears of a wider panic." Still, proponents of increased regulation had the wind at their back and, following ex-Obama chief of staff Rahm Emanuel's sage advice, didn't let a good crisis go to waste. They took advantage of the opportunity that the unraveling of the financial markets afforded them.

Underlying any discussion of developing a broad-based consensus on financial reform is a simple question, "Where do you get your financial news?" *The Wall Street Journal*? CNBC?

A local newspaper? The daily *Marketplace* broadcast on a listener-supported public radio station?

It obviously requires quite a lot of information and analysis to generate an opinion on what constitutes "too big to fail" or to determine the priorities of risks that savers face when planning for their retirement. These are not viewpoints that evolve naturally and simply from other political beliefs, such as the value of redistributionist spending policies or the role in government in addressing issues of morality. Perhaps, however, the more important question in the years following the 2008 rupture in the global financial markets is actually whether investors and savers are even following the developments closely enough to form an opinion on whether financial reform is actually working.

Given the importance of financial markets to modern life, and the importance of private equity and hedge funds to the operation of modern financial markets, it is necessary and worthwhile to walk through the key issues that arose in the global financial crisis and address, where necessary, how they affected private equity and hedge funds, and vice versa.

Is the financial system simply a row of dominoes sitting awkwardly close to each other? If so, what role do private equity and hedge funds have in causing that first domino to potentially fall over?

Many critics argue that the global financial crisis had its origin in the repeal of the Glass-Steagall Act by President Bill Clinton in 1999, the definitive regulatory contribution of his embattled second term, and in Clinton's earlier decision during his first term to radically expand enforcement activities against banks that were not aggressively providing home loans to applicants who did not otherwise comply with strict underwriting requirements.

The Glass-Steagall Act had been in place since 1933, and enforced a strict divide between high-risk investment banks and commercial banks holding customer deposits. After the game-changing merger of Citicorp and Travelers Insurance, the forces that had long campaigned for the repeal of Glass-Steagall finally won the day when President Clinton signed the Graham-Leach-Biley Act repealing it into law.

This transformation of the organization of large banking and investment firms put traditional investment banking to the test. As Steven Davidoff of *The New York Times* succinctly observed about the impact of the financial crisis on Wall Street, "During the financial crisis the old-style investment banking model fell apart."

The global financial crisis that began in 2008 was still an important event for both private equity and hedge funds, even though the main causes of the crisis lay elsewhere. For example, more than $70 billion was yanked from hedge funds as investors sought liquidity wherever they could find it. However, as the years passed and many hedge funds still demonstrated high returns, investors came back with even more money to put to work in the financial markets. Today, hedge funds are again setting records for new money flowing in from investors.

Before the global financial crisis, when cheap credit was readily available, many came to view private equity as a virtual money machine that spewed out lucrative carried interest with little risk of loss and hedge funds as the short cut to untold riches. Since 2008, however, it became clear again that buying and improving businesses that may be past their prime is hard work, with few guarantees of ultimate success, and that the financial markets are as punishing as they are unpredictable.

It also became painfully clear as the global financial crisis gained traction in late 2008 and early 2009 that hedge funds don't last forever. How things had changed in just a few years!

In the sunny, carefree days of 2006, launching and operating a multi-billion dollar hedge fund seemed a relatively straight-forward thing to do. And having obtained any measure of actual success, there would be ample money available to spend on dark wood panelling, restaurant-quality kitchens, expensive art and jaw-dropping views of the city. Then came the global financial crisis.

A number of high-profile hedge funds began to do very poorly in the early weeks of the crisis. Soon, empty trading floors became a common sight in both New York and London, as fund managers either closed their doors for good, or drastically scaled back their operations. The tides moved against many funds quicker than their managers, their investors and their prime brokers could have imagined. Pressing your face against the glass doors of a number of deserted offices in mid-town Manhattan during 2009, the only evidence of their formerly high-flying occupants were the flat-screen TVs, the rows of empty cubicles, the boardroom tables surrounded by leather lounge chairs collecting dust and the arrays of clocks on the wall solemnly pronouncing the time in various foreign capitals.

Interestingly, statistics are often thrown around by critics that highlight how many hedge funds have closed during a given period, to support the contention that the funds were doomed to failure from day one and the managers unsuited for their jobs. However, there are in fact several simple reasons why a fund might close or a fund manager might walk away. In some instances, a fund may do so poorly that investors lose confidence and no longer back the manager going forward. In many cases, however, the managers have made enough money from their efforts that the day-to-day demands, anxieties and stresses of being continually in investors' cross-hairs is no longer appealing. Competing successfully in the fast-moving financial markets can take a heavy toll on an individual over time. Also, as funds get larger and larger, due to new investors wanting to place their money with successful managers who have proven track records, putting that money to work in a way that still produces the same high returns can become harder and harder.

Estimates are that as many as 20 percent of hedge funds may close in a given year. Although clearly a significant percentage, most of these closures happen at the low-end of the hedge fund market. Typically, this translates into funds with less than $100 million in investors' money. There is, in fact, evidence of a survivorship bias whereby larger funds (i.e. $500 million or more) can benefit from the fact that so many other investors are backing the same manager.

A number of hedge fund blow-ups in recent years have drawn significant criticism and raised concerns over the consequences for the so-called "real economy." Names of now-defunct firms such as Long-Term Capital Management and Amaranth Advisors have become bywords for the possible systemic risks that we could face if a hedge fund is big enough and its bets are wrong enough.

One issue that critics have focused on again in the aftermath of the global financial crisis is the use of borrowed money by funds to amplify their gains. Of course, the borrowed money significantly (and sometimes fatally) amplified losses in late 2008, and the months that followed. This math is simple and therefore powerful. When a fund manager raises a billion dollars from investors, and then convinces a bank to lend it two billion dollars based on the collateral of securities it will purchase, the manager now has control over a $3 billion portfolio.

That leads to a lot of profit when things are going well. But when the markets turn against the highly leveraged hedge funds, the losses can be overwhelming. Importantly, though, what doesn't happen is the tipping over of other dominos and an overall collapse of the financial system.

More than just hedge funds and private equity funds are needed for a disaster of that scale.

Stories about the involvement of hedge funds in the unraveling of the financial markets in 2007 and 2008 have been circulating since shortly after the global financial crisis arrived in full force. Articles and books were quickly written detailing how a handful of funds earned enormous profits by betting against the housing price bubble and the complex mortgage securities generated by ever-increasing amounts of sub-prime loans.

For the handful of funds that saw the writing on the walls, there was an opportunity to earn huge profits for their investors.

For many, many more private equity and hedge funds, however, staggering losses lay ahead.

At the start of the financial crisis, Boston Consulting Group predicted that as many as 40 percent of big buyout shops could go out of business. As the financial crisis lingered, it became clear that the barbarians were no longer "at the gate," at least not with the frenzy and intensity that they showed during the second great private equity boom from 2004–07. Meanwhile, the spectacular losses that a number of hedge funds suffered in 2008 caused many investors and commentators to lose faith in the promise of uncorrelated absolute returns, regardless of which way the market moves.

After these catastrophic losses that many private equity and hedge funds showed in late 2008 and early 2009, doubts inevitably emerged about the continuing viability of the investment model that underlies private equity and hedge funds. It would take a few years for those doubts to slowly fade away.

Keeping fund investors on good terms is essential in a falling market. In the first years of the global financial crisis, there were significant net outflows from hedge funds – over $150 billion in 2008 and over $100 billion in 2009. In 2008, reports circulated that over 1,400 hedge funds had been forced to liquidate. Many of those that limped into 2009 were focusing more on possible mergers and consolidation, in order to keep their operations afloat, than on their next payment of performance fees.

Many investors, worried that a prolonged economic stagnation was on the horizon, continued to turn away from private equity and hedge funds in 2010, although demand for certain strategies, such as mezzanine debt, was strong. The Dodd-Frank reforms that arrived that year came at a time when investors in private equity and hedge funds were increasingly focused on governance, oversight and transparency. Unfortunately, little in the legislative process that produced Dodd-Frank did little to establish any more substantive links between these funds and the causes of the economic wreckage still crowding the financial markets. Despite Dodd-Frank, a number of trends that began in the early days of the financial crisis continued into 2011.

Even when most hedge funds do poorly, some often still thrive. For example, in 2011, large managers such as Bridgewater Associates ran up a return of 23 percent. Although hedge funds as an asset class had a bad year in 2011 due to disappointing performances, new money started to flow in again. Estimates have $70 billion, largely from pension plans and endowments, going into hedge funds that year.

Interestingly, large institutional investors continued to cut back on the number of funds in which they invested. In part, this was driven by a desire of investors to concentrate their attention and oversight across a smaller number of fund manager relationships. In addition, investors willing to write big checks were able to find managers willing to accommodate them with concessions on fees and carried interest, as well as greater flexibility in terms of customized, or "bespoke," structures and arrangements.

Alongside these "GP/LP" negotiations, a growing labyrinth of regulation continued to encircle managers of private equity and hedge funds. Interestingly, this regulatory expansion occurred despite advocates of heightened regulation failing to establish exactly what the concrete benefits being produced by the new rules would be. However, despite the lack of any sustained efforts to establish cause-and-effect between the global financial crisis and alternative investment funds, fund managers have quickly adapted to daily life under the new regime.

In many ways, this should be exactly what impartial observers of private equity and hedge funds would expect. These funds are intended to be one step ahead of the market and, if necessary, one step ahead of the legal and regulatory impediments to profit that might arise from time to time. For example, according to Paul Singer, founder of hedge fund giant, Elliot Management, "Stability is not the way of the world." Singer is a vocal critic of the Obama stimulus plan and Federal Reserve policy under Ben Bernacke. Forecasting dire consequences from structural problems in the US federal budget, Singer brooded in a letter to his investors in 2011 over the prospects of another financial crisis. "There is no way to predict the shape and timing of it, except our guess is that when the next real crisis (and not just a head fake) starts, it will play fast, very fast." Meanwhile, Elliot funds positioned themselves to profit on investment opportunities across a number of sectors around the world.

Importantly, no matter which way the markets are moving, on either side of a trade there is a winner and a loser. No matter how badly a market might move, there will be some way for certain investors to profit. There is even a name that has evolved for funds whose purpose is to imagine, and profit from, the worst-case scenarios. They are called "doomsday funds." Firms such as Universa Investments and 36 South Capital Advisers did well in 2011 by identifying and monetizing bad news. While these funds profited in falling markets, many, many more hedge funds following more traditional equity long-short strategies did poorly.

Of course, not everyone can always be a winner! For every private equity or hedge fund that makes a breathtakingly profitable deal, there are many others that lose money. Little can ever be done, by way of further regulation or increased investor due diligence, to change this fundamental law of financial life. Talent is a rare commodity, whether in finance or in other areas of human endeavor, such as art, sports, literature or politics.

In October 2011, placement agent Triago issued a report on private equity firms, which contained some pessimistic assessments, such as "[i]f current trends continue, one-quarter to one-half of today's GP firms may disappear over the next half-decade or so." Around this time, each of KKR, Blackstone and Apollo announced losses as the industry struggled with undervalued portfolio companies which limited their potential to earn carried interest. Like hedge funds, private equity firms at this time were in the process of sorting out their priorities and re-orienting their businesses to deal with the new realities around them.

The inflow of new money did not foretell a good year for hedge funds in terms of investment returns. In 2011, hedge funds as a group actually did worse than the leading equities index, the S&P 500. Of course, many individual hedge funds did phenomenally well. Regardless of the dip in performance across the industry,

$67 billion flowed into hedge funds during the year, with the overall industry thought to exceed $1.7 trillion.

Some very successful managers, however, found 2011 a year that they would rather forget. These included John Paulson of Paulson & Company, and firms such as Owl Creek Asset Management and Fortress Investment Management. Paulson's dilemma, however, attracted the most attention in the media. His funds lost between ten and 50 percent of their value in 2011. Just a few years earlier, in 2007, he had famously bet against subprime mortgages and earned an estimated $5 billion for his efforts. With investors flowing in, he had $38 billion in assets under management by January 2011. But then the market moved against him. Unusually, Paulson's funds began to lose on their big bets. However, unlike when bad performance hits other managers, Paulson's investors have reportedly stood by him in the hopes that 2011 was an aberration.

During 2011, it appeared to some observers that the tide might finally be turning against hedge fund managers in a permanent way. Critics argued that many of these managers earned their large paychecks by playing fast-and-loose with investors' money and regulatory rules designed to ensure a level playing field. To them, real talent was not at work, only gambling and a form of risk-taking where the profits were shared but the losses were solely the investors'.

Regulators took advantage of these mounting criticisms to significantly alter the regulatory framework. As Jesse Eisenger of the news website ProPublica.org observed at the time, "Investors are punishing funds that have engaged in questionable behavior and balking at ever-escalating fees. Regulators are showing uncharacteristic backbone, insisting that they were not merely fighting the last war when it comes to new rules."

As 2012 opened, many hedge fund managers were worried about how their industry would do in the face of uncertainty in the financial markets, increased regulation and investor reluctance. As investors shunned start-up managers, new funds were often successfully launched only when significant seed investors were identified beforehand.

In reality, though, hedge funds entered 2012 on a strong footing with institutional investors increasingly driving the shape and size of the industry. By some measures, aggregate performance across the industry trailed behind the returns generated by the public stock markets in 2010 and 2011. However, exceptional managers still posted exceptional returns, a useful reminder that it has traditionally been the top echelon of the managers that has driven investor demands, rather than some sort of hypothetical "median."

Private equity firms also faced increased competition in 2012 from operating businesses sitting on large piles of cash and willing to expand by strategic acquisitions. In addition, by some estimates as many as five thousand portfolio companies worth $2 trillion were believed to be sitting in private equity funds waiting to be sold. It was estimated at the end of 2011 that almost $1 billion of uninvested capital (so-called "dry powder") remained idle in private equity funds. Fundraising in 2012 also continued to slow, in part because investment returns continued to decline.

The year appeared to be a tough one for the big private equity firms, with Blackstone reporting significant drops in first quarter earnings. According to Hamilton James, president of Blackstone, in an April 2012 conference call, "Overall, we're seeing more money going to alternatives, but it's pretty tough for private equity in general today." Notably, Blackstone has been a leader in diversifying away from pure private equity into hedge funds as well as M&A advisory services. Regardless, they still sat on large quantities of dry powder, estimated in April 2012 to be almost $40 billion.

Industry surveys published at the start of 2012 revealed that many in the hedge fund industry remained stubbornly pessimistic about future prospects. As the year wore on, hedge funds continued to wrestle with lackluster performance and unenthusiastic investors. Fundraising remained difficult and highly competitive, with funds over $1 billion having a repeated advantage over their smaller competitors.

As discussed earlier, small hedge funds have found it increasingly difficult to raise money since the start of the financial crisis in 2008. As a result, many managers are increasingly following the age-old adage, "Bigger is better." These days, this translates into taking larger fund management firms or Wall Street giants on as strategic partners. For example, in 2010, Goldman Sachs invested in Shumway Capital Partners LLC and Level Global Investors LP, although not all of these partnerships turned out to be roaring successes.

Reports from many quarters of the hedge fund world remained negative as 2012 progressed. Some analysts even went so far as to describe the hedge fund industry as having been in a "perpetual slide" since the summer of 2007. Eventually, and perhaps inevitably, uncomfortable questions about fee structures and alignment of interest arose.

Meanwhile, private equity has also struggled on a number of fronts. Many private equity firms were still anguishing over the lingering impact of the global financial crisis on their portfolio companies. Many of these businesses lost significant value since they were acquired, and effective exit strategies were frustratingly hard to come by. Prior to the global financial crisis, private equity appeared to be at the peak of its powers. David Rubinstein, one of the founders of the Carlyle Group, has since remarked, "By the time the bubble burst in 2007, the industry had over $1 trillion under management and became the face of capitalism to some extent."

For private equity, the financial crisis' principal impact on its business model was an inability to do deals that would permit funds to either realize profits on their current holdings or allow them to put new money to work by buying companies at enviable valuations. According to Blackstone's president, Tony James, "The industry will become smaller. We will have bigger organizations but we will have less capital that we can put out. The economics of the business will be much worse." Before the financial crisis, the top tier of private equity firms, such as Blackstone and TPG, were able to raise $20 billion funds. Today, aspirations have returned to more modest levels.

Ultimately, any attempt to construct a picture of the global financial crisis and its after-effects will need to make at least a passing reference to the Bernard Madoff debacle. This is particularly true when discussing private equity and hedge funds, even though the Madoff Ponzi scheme had nothing to do with either.

Much has been written about Madoff, so the discussion here will only cover those points of particular relevance to the issues related to the attempts at financial reform that soon followed, sweeping up private equity and hedge funds along the way. But it is important to note that the Madoff debacle has had a continuing impact on how fund investors now view risk, oversight and control in unregulated alternative investment funds. Perhaps more importantly, as the policy debates have unfolded around what is the best legislative and regulatory response to the global financial crisis, the Madoff story contains within it a "teachable moment" on the limits of the SEC, and regulators generally, to oversee and investigate complex financial firms which they do not actually understand. These issues will be discussed in more detail in following chapters.

To begin with, a quick refresher might be helpful.

An already eventful 2008 ended with the arrest of Bernard Madoff, and concurrent regulatory and criminal actions instigated against his firm, Bernard L. Madoff Investment Securities, in connection with what is generally reported as perhaps the largest investment fraud in history. The SEC's complaint alleged that Madoff informed two senior employees that his investment advisory business was a fraud and that he had for some time been paying returns to certain investors with principal received from other investors, estimating his losses to be at least $50 billion. The complaint charged Madoff and his firm with violations of the anti-fraud provisions of the Securities Act, the Exchange Act and the Investment Advisers Act. In the words of Andrew M. Calamari, Associate Director of Enforcement in the SEC's New York Regional Office, "Our complaint alleges a stunning fraud that appears to be of epic proportions."

Madoff is currently serving a 150-year sentence for his part in orchestrating the largest Ponzi scheme ever. It is estimated that defrauded investors funneled at least $17 billion into the pyramid scheme over the years. Unfortunately, reports of fraud and other malfeasances involving alternative investment funds (especially hedge funds) have become increasingly common. Underlying these incidents is the fundamental question of whether more effective governance mechanisms within the fund would have served to better protect investors over time. The Madoff case provides a useful meter stick against which these concerns about the internal governance of alternative investment funds – e.g. lack of adequate information about the nature and operation of the fund's activities and an inability to effect change in those activities going forward (either directly or indirectly through duly appointed agents) – can be analyzed and improved.

At a time when "increased regulation" is a frequent battle cry for financial market reformers who wish to prevent rampant fraud on investors, the SEC has admitted that it received numerous reports of concern about Madoff and his firm. Despite such warnings, the SEC failed to take necessary action. Any claims that further rules and regulations can, in themselves, serve as an adequate deterrent to the repeat of such incidents must be thoroughly reflected upon in light of the systemic failure of SEC personnel to take heed of any one of the early indicators it received of Madoff's pyramid scheme.

Although well reported in the mainstream and financial press since the story first broke in December 2008, the Madoff affair is not the only case of fraud or malfeasance in the alternative investment funds arena that has unfolded recently. The SEC and other international regulators have pursued a growing number of enforcement actions against hedge funds that involved theft of assets, fraudulent violations of securities held by the fund and false information provided to investors. Civil lawsuits by investors are also becoming a recurring feature in US courts, and include claims involving misrepresentations of performance, misleading disclosures and improper valuations. Importantly, neither the private equity industry nor the UK hedge fund sector has been immune to such incidents.

However, the global reach of the Madoff affair is exceptional and staggering, both in terms of the amounts of money at issue and the breadth of individuals and institutions involved. The question of whether effective multi-national coordination of financial regulators is possible is still an open one, despite frantic attempts at regulatory reform on both sides of the Atlantic. Nonetheless, the absence of any substantive role by the SEC or any sister regulatory organizations in either the prevention or detection of the Madoff scheme serves as an unfortunate reminder of the practical limitations of imposed regulation.

The Madoff affair is particularly instructive because its scale and its scope provide ample examples of alleged failures in reporting, oversight and governance mechanisms which investors should be mindful of in connection with any participation in such vehicles, whether hedge funds, private equity funds, real estate opportunities funds or other more esoteric investment pools.

Often, liability and recovery in an alternative investment fund is viewed as between the fund manager and the participants in the fund. However, fund participants who benefited from fraudulent activity and are able to withdraw money from the fund before the fraud was detected can also be liable to return some or all of their gains, even in the absence of any knowledge of, or a role in, the fraudulent activity. For example, a US bankruptcy court has held that fund investors who received withdrawal proceeds from the fund prior to its collapse could be required to return such proceeds as part of the bankruptcy liquidation. As the Madoff affair unfolded, the issues of whether "winners" should be required to give up their gains to "losers" was clearly on the table. Importantly, not all victims of fraud, either generally or specifically in the context of alternative investment funds, necessarily suffer losses equally.

In addition, the Madoff affair has also demonstrated that many investors who ended up exposed to Madoff, whether with their knowledge or without, by way of various feeder funds or funds of funds, actually believed that, in exchange for the fees they were paying their intermediary fund manager, they were receiving from these agents a service, provided by a competent professional in fulfillment of the fund manager's various legal and equitable duties. In hindsight, this was not the case. In one example that came to light as a result of the Madoff scandal, a Swiss private bank acted as investment manager, custodian and leverage provider to one of the largest feeder funds into the Madoff scheme, earning separate fees for each service, while allegedly failing to conduct vigorous independent due diligence and instead relied on Madoff's reputation on Wall Street and his status as a registered firm with the SEC.

Following Madoff's confession to his crimes, the SEC was forced by the weight of evidence of incompetence to confess to their shortcomings as well. A close inspection of the SEC's repeated failures during the Madoff affair makes for discouraging reading. In a statement issued on December 16, 2008, the SEC admitted that it had missed repeated opportunities to uncover the Madoff Ponzi scheme. SEC Chairman Christopher Cox stated, "Our initial findings have been deeply troubling. The Commission has learned that credible and specific allegations regarding Mr. Madoff's financial wrongdoing, going back to at least 1999, were repeatedly brought to the attention of the SEC staff, but were never recommended to the Commission for action. I am gravely concerned by the apparent multiple failures over at least a decade to thoroughly investigate these allegations or at any point to seek formal authority to pursue them." As a result of these perceived failings, Chairman Cox authorized a full and immediate review of the past allegations regarding Madoff, including the internal policies at the SEC during this time and all staff contact and relationships with the Madoff family.

Some of the potential omissions by the SEC are particularly notable. For example, Madoff's firm appeared to possess far fewer assets than the $17 billion he publicly claimed to be managing. Also, it appears to be impossible in practice for the sums of money involved here to actually be invested pursuant to his claimed investment strategies because the underlying market for such investments was insufficient to handle the necessary trades.

These admissions demonstrate the natural incompleteness of financial regulation as the sole means to address the numerous complex issues involved in alternative investment funds. Madoff was well known to the SEC, and his brokerage firm and investment advisory firm were registered with the SEC and subject to their oversight. The SEC had been informed over the past decade of concerns and allegations involving Madoff. He was a known quantity to the SEC and yet the SEC failed to uncover that he was engaged in one of the most basic of investor frauds – the classic Ponzi scheme.

The global casualty list from the Madoff affair is also very informative. With victims as far afield from New York and Palm Beach as London, Geneva, Dubai and Hong Kong, the ability of one national financial regulator to adequately monitor the interwoven web of vehicles, bank accounts and agreements is questionable.

Importantly, and perhaps more encouraging for the industry than the many tales of slipshod research and non-existent oversight that accompanied the Madoff debacle, many potential investors approached in connection with possibly investing in the Madoff scheme actually declined to participate in his scheme. When due diligence requests and follow-up questions were not satisfactorily answered, they decided not to move forward. The failure of the SEC to act upon the clear and detailed information with which it was presented in connection with Madoff raises significant concerns about any presumptions that financial regulators are better placed than investors in alternative investment funds to monitor the activities of fund managers.

The parties with the most direct interest in seeing that the behavior of the fund manager is adequately monitored are, without question, the investors themselves. Providing effective means for them to actually police their own investments – first, by ensuring that the fund manager provides participants with timely, complete and accurate information on the status of the fund, and second, by giving participants the means to initiate changes to the operation and course of action of the fund – may be the best way to enable them to better protect their rights and help avoid outcomes similar to the Madoff affair.

The reputation of the fund of funds business was not greatly enhanced by the Madoff debacle. Investors who thought that paying a second level of fees to a manager to oversee their fund investments would deliver meaningful safeguards against fraud were disappointed when leading funds of funds, such as Fairfield Greenwich Group, were revealed to be lax and unreliable in the oversight of their portfolio funds.

Many fund of funds managers go to great lengths to emphasize the large amount of work that they do, both pre- and post-investment, in order to secure access to only the best fund managers and to ensure that the performance ultimately delivered meets (or exceeds) original expectations. Implicitly, these claims are necessary to justify the additional 1 percent management fee and 10 percent performance fee that many of these funds typically charge. When layered on top of the 2/20 fees charged by each manager, the overall performance will need to be exceptional in order to ensure that investors have a return that compensates them for the risks they are taking.

The promises made by a fund of funds to a nervous, would-be investor in hedge funds are elaborate and extensive. They may undertake to reconcile trades conducted by each manager and independently calculate the current value of the investments made, either on a weekly or monthly basis. They may stress the periodic meetings they have with the underlying portfolio managers, as well as additional analytics that they will apply to the trading actually done. The value of these services can be significant, but only if they are actually done in a regular and consistent way. If not, their value is dubious at best.

As is often the case, shortly after Fairfield Greenwich's role in the Madoff debacle was fully revealed in December 2008, a story emerged of a would-be buyer who walked away from a possible deal with the fund of funds firm. The potential purchaser broke off negotiations when Fairfield Greenwich refused to give detailed and comprehensive answers to their due diligence questions. In response to the vague and unsatisfactory answers that were offered by Fairfield Greenwich, the investor decided he could not proceed.

In the aftermath of the financial crisis, the future of fund of funds, especially in the hedge fund space, remains uncertain. The business proposition was always a challenge. Fund of funds managers must justify a second level of fees (both annual management fees and performance fees) with promises of the benefits of diversification and ongoing oversight. Failures by firms such as Fairfield Greenwich to deliver such services cast a shadow over much of the rest of the industry.

The amount of money in funds-of-hedge-funds appears to have peaked in 2007 before the crisis. Based on current trends, these funds are not on track to return to prior levels for some time, even as the overall hedge fund industry has set new records for total assets in recent years. Post-financial crisis, with the memory of Madoff still at the forefront of investors' minds, the desire to outsource diligence and oversight over a portfolio of hedge fund investments has declined, especially in light of the failure of fund of funds, such as Fairfield Greenwich and Tremont Group Holdings to detect any wrongdoing before the colossal Ponzi scheme was revealed. Notably, in July 2011, Tremont agreed to a settlement in excess of $1 billion with the trustee that oversaw the recovery efforts for Madoff's victims. Tremont allegedly missed warning signs and red flags that should have alerted it to the fraud that Madoff was perpetrating.

After a financial crisis, legislators and regulators have an opportunity to adopt significant and potentially far-reaching reforms, regardless of whether the reforms actually address the real causes of the immediate crisis.

Although the recent global financial meltdown was not a "hedge fund crisis" or a "private equity crisis," in 2010 both the United States and the European Union adopted significant expansions of their regulatory regimes to address perceived shortcomings in how alternative investment funds and their managers are regulated. As Daniel Awrey of Oxford University noted, "The financial crisis that began in 2007 did not involve systematically important hedge fund collapses or private equity-backed corporate failures." The concerns underlying the new rules significantly pre-date the financial crisis and have been debated by industry members and commentators for some time.

The growth of alternative investment funds, and the debate over the appropriate response by financial regulators, had been a common feature of consultation papers and articles in the financial press for over a decade prior to the global financial crisis. However, the regulatory regime on both sides of the Atlantic remained largely static during these years, despite regular pronouncements from international organizations such as International Organization of Securities Commission (IOSCO) and the Financial Stability Forum.

Only in the aftermath of the global financial crisis was momentum permitted to build in favor of new rules which would materially increase the ability of US and EU regulators to monitor and discipline private fund managers. As Cristie Ford of the University of British Columbia observed, "For students of financial market regulation, the global financial crisis of 2007–2009 (GFC) has been a sobering illustration of human greed and short-sightedness, and regulatory failure."

Ultimately, persistent concerns that alternative investment funds might comprise a "shadow banking system," as well as the ramifications of the Madoff debacle, were sufficient to see the passage of Dodd-Frank in the United States and the Alternative Investment Fund Managers Directive (AIFMD) in the European Union. Interestingly, the desire to "rein in" private funds, however, sits somewhat awkwardly in the academic debate over corporate governance. As Dale Osterle of the Ohio State University has argued, "The irony of the hedge fund regulation movement is that financial economists have, for over seventy years, been decrying, first, the lack of independent shareholder involvement in the management of public firms and, second, the lack of swift capital reallocation in American industry. Hedge funds do both, more effectively, than any financial institutions in American history perhaps, and we should not recoil in fear over the innovation."

Sifting through the wreckage of the global financial crisis, a number of important questions still remain unanswered.

Is the world still on the brink of financial ruin? If so, have private equity and hedge funds either caused the global financial markets to languish or impeded their recovery?

Is the only serious allegation that can be made against them is that they profited from events in the market that they identified and evaluated?

How much cynicism and suspicion should color an analysis of how the financial markets operate?

It is not very clear where the public, or even the informed layperson, can find answers to these pressing questions. The 24-hour rolling news tends to be shrill, while business news channels are often so focused on short-term gyrations and mini-trends that there is little room for thinking the big thoughts. Most newspapers prefer stories focused on either abstract statistics or personality-driven pieces that idealize the entrepreneur and omit much of the boring details that would otherwise distract from the narrative of self-belief and overcoming adversity.

Even if Hollywood has not provided comprehensive answers, at least it has demonstrated a willingness to turn its attention to the global financial crisis and the collateral damage it has left in its wake. *Margin Call* (2011) and *Arbitrage* (2012) each attempted to shine a light on the insularity and self-rationalization that develops in the esoteric world of high finance. For the rest of us, the answers to these questions will drive our views on a long list of topics, including the appropriate scope of financial reform necessary to address the concerns and shortcomings that were laid bare by the global financial crisis.

The lack of consensus on many of the above points has made the process of responding to the crisis even more difficult and contentious than it needs to be. As a result, attempting to map the effectiveness of the legislative and regulatory response constructed to address the perceived risks of private equity and hedge funds is particularly frustrating.

7: THE NEW RULES OF THE ROAD

How Do We Fix a Problem that We Might Not Even Have?

The US securities laws have not kept pace with the growth and market significance of hedge funds and other private funds and, as a result, the Commission has very limited oversight authority over these vehicles.
Andrew J. Donohue, Director of the Division of Investment Management, Securities and Exchange Commission

To some, the emerging roadblocks reinforce a feature that Dodd-Frank, which was intended to touch on almost every aspect of the American financial system, may never provide the sweeping reform it promised.
Jesse Eisenger and Jake Bernstein of ProPublica.org, June 2011

An old adage about government is particular resonant when considering financial regulatory reform in the United States, "There are two things that Congress does well – nothing, and overreact."

The Dodd-Frank Act is quite simply a messy, ungainly compromise over how to deal with the regulation of US financial markets in the twenty-first century. It lacks the clarity and simplicity that many reformers wanted, while at the same time striking many of its opponents as an unnecessary and self-defeating extension of government authority, which will do more harm than good. Ultimately, its ambiguity may be its Achilles' heel.

The demise of Bear Sterns in 2008 demonstrated that there were real gaps in the regulatory regime. The question remained open, however, whether those gaps existed in the black-letter rules themselves or in the manner in which they were enforced. If Bear Sterns had been an isolated event, then perhaps the issue of reform could have been brushed aside quietly, after a suitable mourning period had passed. Bear Sterns was not a popular firm, well-liked by its Wall Street brethren. For those familiar with the vibrant and deep-seated rivalries with English football, Bear Sterns could be readily referred to as the "Millwall of investment banks." The subsequent collapse of Lehman Brothers and the granting of commercial banking licenses to Goldman Sachs and Morgan Stanley by the Federal Reserve, however, demonstrated to many that the then-existing approach for policing Wall Street was no longer fit-for-purpose.

But what should be done – more rules or just better enforcement of the existing rules?

Treasury white papers, industry reports and academic postulations circulated rapidly after President Obama was sworn in to office in January 2009. There were many potential paths that American officials could have taken at this time to begin to address these mounting concerns. As the effects of the global financial crisis spread out across borders and impacted economies around the world, many countries struggled to negotiate their own financial challenges while responding to the after-shocks emanating out of the United States. During these dark days, the markets waited for the promise of a new financial regulatory super structure to be actioned.

With attempts at comprehensive change occurring on both sides of the Atlantic during 2010 and 2011, it is now possible to examine and evaluate the new rules and begin to understand how they will impact the future prospects of private equity and hedge funds in the years to come.

As a result of the recent global financial crisis, widespread attention is now being paid to the nature and scope of financial regulation.

As Charles Whitehead of Cornell University observed, "Financial regulation is often reactive. New regulation seals up leaks in the financial system – usually following a crisis, a shift in markets or other change that threatens financial stability."

In the United States, for example, the modern financial regulatory system was created as a direct result of the Great Depression. From crisis comes the blueprint for the next set of stop-gaps and solutions. The Dodd-Frank reforms, like numerous reforms preceding it, was born from the aftermath of the 2008 financial meltdown. Changes over the preceding decades in the structure and operation of financial markets created perceived gaps in financial regulation, which were highlighted in the autumn of 2008.

The United States was not alone in critically re-evaluating its approach to overseeing investment firms and banks. Wide-ranging reforms were proposed and adopted in numerous countries around the world. They attempted, after the fact, to correct the shortcomings and omissions that critics identified in their regulatory regimes. How far should reform go? Regardless of the financial regulatory model that a particular country follows, there is always a tension during a period of reform between making a fundamental change to a country's regulatory model, and simply making incremental changes within the current financial model.

Importantly, neither Dodd-Frank nor AIFMD directly address many of the inherent problems in private equity and hedge fund structures, such as governance deficiencies, or shifted their regime away from the traditional "we regulate the managers, not the fund" approach. This is an important, and somewhat surprising, observation. Although each regulatory reform package in the United States and Europe made significant changes to the scope and detail of existing rules, the focus was predominately on very different regulatory priorities, such as systemic risk. Even where concerns about investor protection were addressed in the United States or in Europe, the new rules do so in an established and customary manner, in line with past approaches.

Radical changes were not the order of the day. Instead, the recent reforms have introduced some incremental improvements in the regulatory regime, although the extent to which they provide for greater protection of fund investors beyond that which would be provided by good market practice remains unclear.

As discussed earlier, private funds are global phenomena. They carry with them inherently complex questions about jurisdictional reach and the effectiveness of regulation outside the country of origin. Importantly, even with increased coordination and harmonization at the international level, government regulators are subject to *de jure* or *de facto* jurisdictional limitations on their effectiveness. By contrast, private actors (such as the actual investors in these funds themselves) can pursue their interests across national boundaries as the need arises. As Julia Black of the London School of Economics has noted, "private economic actors – financial institutions and investors – are not constrained by jurisdictional considerations and are able to oversee and manage their business affairs across national borders much more seamlessly than any government agency."

The most pernicious limitation on the effective enforcement of centralized, top-down rules survived the recent wave of reform and still reveals a systemic disadvantage that the SEC, the FCA and all financial regulators face – namely, hiring and retaining adequate talent. Regulators continue to struggle to lure experienced people away from potentially lucrative employment on Wall Street or in the City of London. Private firms, of course, have a distinct and sustained advantage on this front.

Despite much sabre-rattling, US and EU legislators and regulators eventually opted for the realistic over the revolutionary. They decided to limit their reform efforts to a number of narrow changes involving the regulatory status of the fund manager and some potentially significant other changes in the applicable marketing restrictions. In doing so, they ultimately favored reforms in line with the traditional regulatory approach that they have historically followed in this area.

In order to fully grasp the inherent shortcomings of the regulatory reforms on both sides of the Atlantic, it is necessary to acknowledge that the new laws were not simply a product of a policy debate, but also a product of a political debate. Unfortunately, this political debate did little to further the cause for meaningful and effective reform. By default, legislators and regulators have sent a clear message to all investors in alternative investment funds – responsibility for establishing appropriate governance mechanisms within your funds rests with you, the investors.

Investors ignore this warning going forward at their own peril!

In the summer of 2010, President Barack Obama signed into law the Dodd-Frank Act, the comprehensive Wall Street reform package. Only one year earlier, Obama had infamously remarked to a banker, "My administration is the only thing between you and the pitchforks."

However, the Dodd-Frank Act was not in itself the final conclusion of the hard-fought legislative and lobbying battle that preceded it. In many ways, the statute was simply the beginning of a longer war of attrition now focused on effectively implementing the numerous rules and regulations necessary to give substance and life to the new law.

Even its champions concede that much work still remains to be done to make sure that Dodd-Frank's passage does not end up as a false dawn. Extensive rule making by the SEC, Commodities Futures Trading Commission (CFTC) and Federal Depository Insurance Corporation (FDIC), among others, is still necessary. By some estimates, over five hundred rules must be adopted by various agencies in order to bring the limp body of the Dodd-Frank Act, in its voluminous two thousand pages, to life. And these rules are in addition to the numerous reports and studies that Dodd-Frank also commissioned.

The opportunities for further lobbying and substantial delays are, therefore, plentiful.

Coordinating the efforts of these various governmental agencies, and making sure that they "play well together," continues to be a serious challenge. Many of the turf battles and controversial standoffs that occurred in Congress during the weeks leading up to the passage of Dodd-Frank eventually broke out again in the months and years that followed. However, these contests were now unfolding outside the bright light of mainstream media attention and Capitol Hill dramatics. Instead, they occurred in the corridors and conference rooms of bureaucratic agencies, where the public's attention will not be so directly engaged.

Perhaps more problematically, Congress did not commit to how the implementation of these reforms would actually be paid for on an ongoing basis. The overall ability of the Obama administration to achieve its public policy goals in this area will be seriously hampered if insufficient funding is provided to follow through on the promises made by Dodd-Frank to American savers and investors. The "fiscal cliff" theatrics that played out over New Year 2013 demonstrated yet again the brinkmanship and leadership failure that remains a central feature of contemporary US political practices.

In fact, a decision to deny these agencies the necessary money and headcount to perform the new tasks now assigned to them could lead to, in effect, a "silent repeal" of some key sections of Dodd-Frank. Those who believe that comprehensive Wall Street reform has already been accomplished should be aware that much of the promise has not yet been turned into reality. The blueprints contained in Dodd-Frank may have been agreed, but the new foundation, walls and support structure must still be laid brick by brick.

In many ways, therefore, US investors and savers are perhaps at their most vulnerable today. They are being asked to invest in financial markets where the ultimate rules of the game are still up in the air, and in the process of being finalized. They may be tempted to think that they are being looked after and protected, but as always has been the case with private equity and hedge funds, the real rule of the game is one of the oldest – "caveat emptor."

As Andrew J. Donohue, Director of the Division of Investment Management of the SEC, observed in 2010, "The US securities laws have not kept pace with the growth and market significance of hedge funds and other private funds and, as a result, the Commission has very limited oversight authority over these vehicles ... Consequently, advisers to private funds can 'opt out' of Commission oversight. This presents a significant regulatory gap in need of closing."

According to Donohue, requiring the managers of private equity and hedge funds to be registered with the SEC would provide the regulator with the tools necessary to oversee the industry and protect investors. This would be accomplished by the managers providing the SEC with reliable and complete data about the operations of alternative investment funds and their impact on US securities markets, while allowing the funds to maintain flexibility with regard to their investment objectives and strategies. The analysis is simple, straightforward and, at times, actually somewhat compelling.

Dodd-Frank, therefore, can be seen as simply the movement of the United States toward the international consensus that private fund managers should be directly regulated by the national financial regulator. This had already been the regulatory position in the United Kingdom, Europe and across the developed world for many, many years. The historic American position that "private" investment advisers who had only a limited number of clients were best left outside the supervision of the SEC had clearly become an anomaly, especially in light of the billions of dollars in assets under management that such "private" advisers were able to amass.

The reform directed at private equity and hedge funds operates by repealing in its entirety the so-called "private adviser exemption" previously found in the Investment Advisers Act. Under this exemption, any investment adviser that had fewer than fifteen clients during the preceding twelve-month period and did not hold itself out to the public as an investment adviser was exempt from licensing requirements in the United States. Managers of alternative funds historically relied on this exemption in order to avoid registration with the SEC. Today, many of these advisers must now register with the SEC and adopt appropriate compliance programs.

Domestic investment advisers with assets under management of $100 million or more fall within the new regime under Dodd-Frank. However, if such advisers manage only "private funds," the threshold is raised to $150 million or more of assets. "Private funds" are defined as entities that would be an "investment company" under the Investment Company Act, but for the exceptions discussed earlier under Sections 3(c)(1) and 3(c)(7).

Advisers which pass these thresholds are required to register under the Investment Advisers Act. The relatively low threshold of $150 million will ensnare many previously unregistered investment advisers to private equity and hedge funds that benefited from the fourteen-or-fewer clients exemption now eliminated by Dodd-Frank. Domestic advisers falling below these thresholds now have to register under state "blue sky laws" rather than being able to register with the SEC under the Investment Advisers Act. As a result, greater pressure is being placed on states to monitor these smaller investment firms that fall outside of the SEC's purview.

Extraterritoriality, of course, remains a key feature of the US approach to financial regulation, and Dodd-Frank is no exception. Acknowledging some discernible limit on the SEC's jurisdiction, Dodd-Frank exempts from registration any investment adviser that is a "foreign private adviser." This is defined as any investment adviser that has no place of business in the United States, has fewer than fifteen clients and investors domiciled in the United States in private funds advised by the investment adviser, has aggregate assets under management attributable to clients in the United

States and investors in the United States in private funds advised by the investment adviser of less than $25 million; and neither holds itself out generally to the public in the United States as an investment adviser, nor acts as an investment adviser to any registered investment company (also known as a mutual fund).

As a result of Dodd-Frank's reallocation of regulatory responsibility, the number of potential SEC registrants has increased significantly. One aspect of the Dodd-Frank financial services reform law that attracted little notice in the mainstream press is the fact that each individual state is now responsible for licensing, monitoring and overseeing all hedge funds and other alternative investment management firms with assets under $100 million.

Simply put, the responsibility of the various states for licensing, monitoring and overseeing all domestic investment management firms has also been increased significantly from firms having less than $25 million in assets to firms having under $100 million in assets. Of course, no additional funding was allocated or apportioned to the states under Dodd-Frank to perform these duties. Where the extra money for personnel and supervisory infrastructure will ultimately come from is unclear. If money is not forthcoming, an inconsistent and largely nominal oversight of a large number of domestic advisers may result.

This represents a substantial increase in the responsibility (and jurisdiction) of state securities departments and law enforcement officials. Unfortunately, states are taking on this increased responsibility at a time when many state coffers are empty and budgets are far from balanced. The extent to which these state budgets are in the red due to unfunded pension obligations has not been calculated, although the awkwardness of this line of analysis is more than readily apparent.

At first glance, such a significant retreat by the SEC would seem out of place in a statute that seeks elsewhere to expand the authority and scope of the agency. However, under the new Dodd-Frank regime, the number of SEC registrants increased significantly and steps needed to be taken to rebalance the role that states must play in day-to-day oversight and enforcement. Without significant investment at the state level underfunded in capitals such as Albany, Sacramento, Springfield, Harrisburg and Tallahassee, the public risk the worst of all possible worlds: the expectation that there will be a cop-on-the-beat, policing managers and their funds, without there actually being one.

In October 2012, the SEC announced that 1,504 advisers to hedge funds and other private funds have registered with the regulator since the Dodd-Frank reforms made registration a requirement, rather than simply an option. This brings the total number of advisers to private funds that are registered under the Investment Advisers Act of 1940 to 4,061, out of a total of 11,002 advisers across asset classes and investment styles. US-registered advisers as a group are believed to oversee approximately $5.7 trillion in assets.

The pressing question must be what to do with them all!

The SEC announced at the same time the launch of its National Examination Program, which provided for risk-based examinations of private fund advisers over the next two years. With registration comes a long list of obligations, including conflicts of interest and record-keeping, and the SEC was keen to ensure that each firm is up to speed on and compliant with the full suite of rules and regulations.

Much has also been happening at the state level as well. Over 2,300 so-called "mid-sized advisers," who manage less than $100 million of assets, have made the transition from the bright lights of federal regulation to the local charm of state regulation. It is believed that a further three hundred advisers still on the SEC's books may eventually be dropped down to state oversight as well, clearing room for the national regulator to focus on the largest advisers in the country.

Regulatory reform inevitably entails wrestling with long-standing definitional categories and the impact of new rules on different constituencies. The financial services industry has many organizations and individuals who have mixed responsibilities, and often different parts of the same organization could be seen as doing similar things, even if the terminology used is different.

For example, what is the difference between a broker, executing your trades, and an investment adviser, counselling you on the composition of your portfolio? Should the duties and obligations of one be higher or lower than the duties and obligations of the other?

In August 2010, the SEC began asking the American public for their thoughts on these important questions. Under Dodd-Frank, the SEC had been tasked with producing a comprehensive study on whether the standards to which a broker is held should be raised to the higher level historically expected from an investment adviser.

Under current law, investment advisers are subject to a fiduciary duty – the "f word" – toward their clients. When they provide them with advice, those recommendations must be in the best interests of the client. Other considerations, such as compensation, are not permitted to drive their decisions. Brokers, however, are not subject to this higher standard. They can recommend securities or other financial products that, for example, provide them with higher commissions. As a result, the potential legal recourse available to an aggrieved client varies greatly depending on whether Uncle Edgar or Aunt Edna made use of an adviser or a broker.

The SEC's public comment period was a means for investors to give their own views on whether there is confusion on the different services that brokers and advisers provide, and an investor's potential legal recourse against each. Investors' confidence is critical to the continued success of the financial markets. Where such confidence is lacking, liquidity will be sacrificed and returns lowered. Unfortunately, as with much of Dodd-Frank awaiting full implementation, it is unclear where the SEC will ultimately go in this area. A long and storied tradition on Wall Street historically separates advisers and brokers, and successful efforts to fundamentally reallocate regulatory oversight in a way that increases the liability profile for financial firms are, in fact, quite rare.

As discussed earlier, fiduciary duty is a key component of any relationship of trust. If there is trust, the heightened requirements of a fiduciary should apply to parties. If such duties are not there, then both parties should be clear that the element of trust, and the reliance that trust often produces, should not be on the table. Although complex factors differentiate brokers from advisers in many instances, clients of each still have a right to clearly understand the obligations and duties that the firm they are dealing with owes them. Otherwise, a client's ability to adequately protect him or herself is significantly compromised.

In order to better police the financial markets, generally and private equity and hedge funds specifically, scriveners within the SEC still remain hard at work drafting the further rules and regulations mandated by Dodd-Frank, in addition to pursuing an increased barrage of litigation and enforcement actions. The scope and breadth of the subject matter and industry practices covered by these new rules provide a compelling view on how seriously Congress viewed the shortcomings of the pre-crisis regulatory system.

For example, in July 2010, the SEC adopted a new rule that limits who can be charged a performance fee or carried interest by SEC-registered investment advisers, including those who manage private equity and hedge funds. The rule, which was mandated by Dodd-Frank, raises the thresholds that determine whether an investment adviser can charge its clients performance fees.

Rule 205-3 under the Investment Advisers Act allows an investment adviser to charge a client performance fees if the client meets certain dollar amount thresholds. Previously, Rule 205-3 permitted performance fees in only a limited number of circumstances, including where either the client has at least $750,000 under management with the adviser; or the adviser reasonably believes the client has a net worth of more than $1.5 million. In the context of private equity and hedge funds, "clients" would refer to the prospective investors in these funds.

The new rule means that an investment adviser is now able to charge performance fees only if the client has at least $1 million under the management of the adviser, or if the client has a net worth of more than $2 million. These requirements are measured at the time the prospective client enters the advisory contract or purchases the fund interests. The SEC is also now required under Dodd-Frank to adjust for inflation these dollar amount thresholds every five years.

The SEC also went on to propose further amendments to Rule 205-3 that would provide the method for calculating future inflation adjustments of the dollar amount tests, exclude the value of a person's primary residence from the determination of whether a person meets the net worth standard, and modify the transition provisions of the rule to take into account performance fee arrangements that were permissible at the time the adviser and client entered into their advisory contract. As a result, a significant number of individual investors who may previously have been eligible to invest in these alternative funds were eventually excluded.

A few months later, in May 2011, the SEC also adopted rules under Section 922 of Dodd-Frank to create a formal whistleblower program. The goal was to reward individuals who provide the agency with tips that lead to successful enforcement actions. The new program is an attempt by the SEC to overcome the constraints on its effectiveness that result from its limited staffing and financial resources.

"Whistleblower" is an evocative term. It reinforces the image of the person providing the necessary information about the illegal or illicit conduct as someone who is calling attention to criminals and their activities, hopefully preventing them from harming any other innocent victims. This image is heroic and admirable.

The SEC program rewards individuals who act early to expose violations and who provide significant evidence that helps the

SEC bring successful cases. Prospective whistleblowers must voluntarily provide the SEC with original information that leads to the successful enforcement by the SEC of a federal court or administrative action in which the SEC obtains monetary sanctions totalling more than $1 million.

In passing Dodd-Frank, Congress substantially expanded the SEC's authority to compensate individuals who provide the SEC with information about violations of the federal securities laws. Prior to Dodd-Frank, the SEC's bounty program was limited to insider trading cases and the amount of an award was capped at 10 percent of the penalties collected in the action.

In general, a whistleblower will be deemed to have provided information voluntarily if he or she has provided information before the government or a self-regulatory organization asks for it directly from the whistleblower. Original information must be based upon the whistleblower's independent knowledge or independent analysis, and not already known to the SEC. Dodd-Frank required the SEC to create an Office of the Whistleblower, which works with whistleblowers, handles their tips and complaints, and helps the SEC determine the awards for each whistleblower.

Several categories of individuals are categorically prevented from benefiting from the program, including individuals themselves culpable for the violation upon which they are informing to the SEC, as well as foreign government officials. Unfortunately, attorneys who might attempt to use information obtained from client engagements to make whistleblower claims for them are also prohibited from participating in the program.

In August 2012, the SEC announced that it had finally managed to find a worthy recipient for its first bounty payment under the Dodd-Frank whistleblower program. The SEC had issued an award of $50,000 to a whistleblower who helped stop a multi-million dollar fraud. Robert Khuzami, Director of the SEC's Division of Enforcement, noted that "had this whistleblower not helped to uncover the full dimensions of the scheme, it is very likely that many more investors would have been victimized."

Unfortunately, the SEC did not disclose much in the way of personal information about the whistleblower, so it is difficult to take a full measure of what the individual may have contributed to any SEC investigations. The payment of the bounty, however, signalled that the SEC is committed to rewarding individuals who are willing to step forward and inform them about wrongdoings at financial firms and public companies. Dodd-Frank recognized that the SEC has had, in the past, great difficulty identifying significant frauds and malfeasances at an early enough stage to protect investors from serious harm.

To correct this, the whistleblower program mandates that the SEC must pay individuals bounties if and when they come forward to report violations of federal securities laws. Payments can range from 10 to 30 percent of the money ultimately collected in the SEC enforcement action. To receive payment, however, the information passed on to the SEC must be original, timely, high quality and lead to the recovery of at least $1 million in an enforcement action. Most importantly, it must be voluntary, which means the information must be given to the SEC before the SEC requests it as part of an investigation.

You can't get paid simply for answering questions put to you by SEC staff!

The following month, in June 2011, the SEC adopted rules designed to implement further provisions of Dodd-Frank regarding investment advisers, including those that advise private equity and hedge funds, by establishing new exemptions from SEC registration and reporting requirements for certain advisers, and reallocating regulatory responsibility for advisers between the SEC and states. In addition, the SEC amended rules to expand disclosure by investment advisers, particularly about the private funds they manage. The information obtained as a result of these amendments was meant to assist the SEC in fulfilling its increased responsibilities arising under Dodd-Frank.

Under the new requirements, private fund managers must provide basic organizational and operational information about each fund they manage. This includes general information about the size and ownership of the fund and the adviser's services to the fund; and identification of five categories of "gatekeepers," including auditors, prime brokers, custodians, administrators and marketers, that perform critical roles for advisers and the private funds they manage.

These new disclosure requirements are intended to facilitate earlier discovery of fraud and potential misconduct. In addition, the SEC adopted further amendments that require all registered advisers to provide more information about their advisory business, including the types of clients they advise, their employees and their advisory activities; and their business practices that may present significant conflicts of interest (such as the use of affiliated brokers, soft dollar arrangements and compensation for client referrals).

The shadow of Bernard Madoff still hangs darkly across the SEC offices!

The clear trend here is toward more disclosure from fund sponsors and managers on the products that they create and market to investors. The form used by all investment advisers to register with the SEC – "Form ADV" – was also revised and expanded, with more information on fee arrangements and conflicts of interests being mandated. The information on these registration forms is publicly available at the SEC's website.

In addition to registration with the SEC, a new "Form PF" was created that many large hedge fund managers and private equity general partners must now submit, detailing sensitive and proprietary facts about the funds they manage. Form PF, which will be discussed more fully below, contains even more sensitive information than Form ADV. Such data, in the hands of competitors or customers, could undermine a fund's investment strategy and subject investors to significant losses. SEC officials point to powerful exemptions within the Freedom of Information Act, which should provide fund managers with comfort. However, many sceptics remain unconvinced and uncertain.

In July 2011, in response to rapid trading of public securities by a number of hedge funds and other aggressive traders, the SEC adopted yet another new rule. Large trader reporting requirements were implemented, in an effort to improve their ability to identify high-frequency trading by large market participants. Large traders must now identify themselves to the SEC, and each trader will be given a unique identification number, which needs to be provided to each broker-dealer that they use. The broker-dealers are required to maintain transaction records for each large trader and report that information to the SEC upon request. The new rule enables the SEC to promptly and efficiently identify significant market participants and collect data on their trading activity so that the regulator can reconstruct market events and conduct investigations.

The large trader rule has two primary components. First, it requires large traders to register with the SEC through a new form, Form 13H. Second, it imposes recordkeeping, reporting and limited monitoring requirements on certain registered broker-dealers through whom large traders execute their transactions. The need for the SEC to have better access to information is heightened by the fact that large traders, including high-frequency traders, are believed to be playing an increasingly prominent role in the securities markets.

A "large trader" is defined as a person whose transactions in exchange-listed securities equal or exceed two million shares or $20 million during any calendar day, or twenty million shares or $200 million during any calendar month. After Form 13H is filed, the SEC will then assign each large trader a unique large trader identification number, which will allow the SEC to efficiently identify and analyze trading activity by the large trader. A large trader will be required to disclose to its broker-dealers its identification number and highlight all of the accounts at the broker-dealer through which the large trader trades.

The SEC hopes that the large trader reporting rule will bolster their ability to oversee the US securities markets in a time when trades can now be transacted in milliseconds. Such changes have allowed large market participants to employ sophisticated trading methods to trade electronically on multiple venues in huge volumes at very fast speeds.

In October 2011, the SEC finally approved proposed Rule 204(b)-1 under the Investment Advisers Act, which implemented Sections 404 and 406 of Dodd-Frank. The rule mandates reporting by certain private fund advisers to assist the Financial Stability Oversight Commission in assessing systemic risk in the US financial system. The rule affects managers of private equity and hedge funds, as well as other private investment vehicles such as real estate funds and liquidity funds.

Under the rule, any investment adviser required to register with the SEC that advises one or more private funds with at least $150 million in private fund assets under management must file Form PF, as first mentioned above. The rule places additional requirements on large private fund advisers, which would include advisers managing hedge funds with $1.5 billion in assets and advisers managing private equity funds that collectively have at least $2 billion in assets

All private fund advisers are required to provide a number of key metrics annually. These include gross and net asset value of each private fund, detailed performance data, investor concentration, notional value of derivative positions, total borrowings, and monthly and quarterly performance data of each private fund. Private fund advisers that manage hedge funds would also be required to report investment strategies; the percentage of the fund's assets managed using computer-driven trading algorithms; significant counterparty exposure (including the identity of the counterparty); and trading and clearing practices. More detailed information is required to be reported by a large private fund adviser depending on what types of assets are managed by the adviser.

In the case of hedge funds, a large private fund adviser must provide aggregate information about the hedge funds it advises, including aggregate market value of investments held, duration of fixed income portfolio holdings, assets' interest rate sensitivity, portfolio turnover rate and geographical breakdown of investments. Large private fund advisers to hedge funds would be required to file Form PF within sixty days of the end of each fiscal quarter.

In the case of private equity funds, a large private fund adviser must provide information on borrowings and guarantees, disclosure on each fund's portfolio companies, including increased disclosure for financial industry portfolio companies, and a breakdown of investments by industry and geography. Large private fund advisers to private equity funds would be required to file Form PF within 120 days of the end of each fiscal year.

The Dodd-Frank Act requires that the SEC and CFTC share information reported on Form PF with the Financial Stability Oversight Council. The SEC has implemented certain safeguards to insure that the information contained in Form PF is provided to other parties on a need-to-know basis and for regulatory purposes.

It remains to be seen, however, to what practical uses this information will be put by the regulators. Simply providing data does not, in itself, assure that it will be dutifully reviewed and analyzed. That was a lesson painfully demonstrated in the Madoff debacle.

Unfortunately, soon after Obama signed the Dodd-Frank Act into law in 2010 and the SEC was compelled to begin its hard and thankless task of promulgating the long list of further rules and regulations, senior SEC staff began to make trips up to Capitol Hill, hat in hand, to plead its case that it needs money to implement and oversee compliance with Dodd-Frank. Congress, however, seems to disagree.

As the federal securities regulator slogged through its growing list of newly imposed requirements and mandates left peremptorily at its doorstep, questions surrounding the adequacy of its funding and its future budget remained unanswered. The SEC eventually issued a study focusing attention on its need for adequate resources in order to adequately police investment advisers and hedge fund managers. Previous requests for additional money to fund eight hundred new professional staff hires, as well as new technology, had been rebuffed by the Republican-controlled House of Representatives, citing a need to cut back government expenditures across the board.

Apparently, things were tough all over!

Difficult questions were soon trotted out as a way of putting the SEC's budget requests into context. For example, will a cash-strapped and understaffed SEC miss the next Madoff-style Ponzi scheme? One could point out that since they missed the last one, anything is possible.

However, the fundamental driver behind this round of Wall Street reform was to ensure that precisely such frauds are either prevented or detected at a much earlier stage. With departing SEC employees not being replaced and new recruitment frozen, this remains a particularly difficult question to answer.

Despite authorization in Dodd-Frank to double the SEC's budget over the course of the next five years, their funding level in 2011 was frozen at 2010 levels. Was the failure to increase funding a stealth attack on Wall Street by the new Congress, which had seen Republicans take control of the House of Representatives from the Democrats, as some critics allege?

Lack of funds soon began to have undeniable real-world effects. Several deadlines to provide the new rules and regulations mandated by Dodd-Frank were awkwardly postponed. Strain quickly began to show in both the SEC and its sister regulator, the CFTC. The most significant change to American financial services regulation since the 1930s still required in 2011 over one hundred regulations or market studies to be prepared in order to complete the broad-brush sketch of the new regime that Congress passed in 2010. Agency staff were said to be working around the clock to get these tasks completed as quickly as practicable.

Even after the new "rule book" was written, however, these agencies were still left with the daunting and largely thankless task of implementation and enforcement. Even if defunding is not meant to be the functional equivalent of repeal, at the very least it is an effective means for pushing down the brake on the speed of Wall Street reform.

Both the SEC and the CFTC repeatedly requested significant budget increases to ensure that they are not forced to compromise existing services. Unfortunately, Congress refused to heed their requests. Lobbying efforts of the chairmen of both regulatory agencies yielded little in new money. "Do more with less" is a recurring mantra in any recession, and the Great Recession has been no different.

In April 2011, however, the SEC and CFTC did manage a modest victory in the budget brinkmanship. Although a number of federal agencies were the subject of approximately $40 billion in cuts, the SEC received $75 million in extra funding for 2011. The SEC's annual budget exceeds $1 billion. Given the vastly expanded oversight responsibilities which have been set at the agency's doorstep by Dodd-Frank, the securities regulator no doubt needed every penny. Interestingly, though, the SEC was still receiving less funding than what was originally allocated to it by Dodd-Frank. The CFTC received an additional $30 million, pushing its annual budget through the $200 million mark.

These increases had as much symbolic value as they did concrete fiscal benefits. Republicans and Democrats are still arguing over the benefits of Dodd-Frank, with many in Congress campaigning openly for its repeal. Despite the dramatic increase in responsibilities brought about by the passage of the Dodd-Frank Act in 2010, US financial regulators still lack much needed increases in funding.

One final observation on SEC funding warrants special attention. Despite the large sums of money paid into the SEC each year by

Wall Street and the companies who make use of the US financial markets, the regulator is intentionally not self-funding. As a result, the SEC is dependent on Congressional benevolence in each budget. Efforts to correct this and give the SEC the independence that critics believe it needs have regularly failed, including during the most recent Dodd-Frank reforms. The need of Congressional incumbents to receive lucrative campaign contributions from firms impacted by SEC rules and enforcement priorities appears to be too powerful a force to allow the SEC a full measure of self-sufficiency.

As mentioned above, with Republicans taking control of the House of Representatives in January 2011, the future of Dodd-Frank quickly began to look uncertain. Some pessimistic critics began to openly worry about the effective repeal of significant portions of Dodd-Frank in the months to come, if adequate funding were denied. In April 2011, Senator Jim DeMint, a Republican from South Carolina, introduced a bill pithily titled the Financial Takeover Repeal Act of 2011. Its purpose was to unwind the Dodd-Frank Act. Critics argued at the time that the bill had little chance of actually passing, as the Democrats maintained control of the Senate. However, the bill did have important symbolic meaning by demonstrating how significant the Republican opposition to the controversial law remains.

Interestingly, the same month, the SEC failed an audit conducted by the Government Accountability Office (GAO). The verdict was a damning indictment of an agency that is notionally responsible for overseeing the compliance by thousands of public companies and financial institutions with the detailed requirements of financial disclosure. The SEC went so far as to hand over responsibility for its own bookkeeping to another government department. SEC Chair Mary Shapiro admitted that there has been a pattern of underinvestment over the years, leaving them unable to maintain their own financial records adequately.

The GAO, as part of their audit, identified numerous mistakes that amounted to hundreds of millions of dollars. For example, the SEC still has on its books over $600 million in fines and penalties owed to it by rule-breakers, even though only a tiny fraction of this amount will ever be collected. If a technology company or a brokerage firm were to engage in such misstatements, the SEC would quickly pass harsh and unforgiving judgment on these shortcomings. Many supporters of the SEC and its mission of protecting investors expressed their hope that the agency would eventually take its own failures equally seriously.

As noted earlier, both the SEC and the CFTC have been charged with writing and implementing numerous new rules and regulations. Without adequate staffing and infrastructure, the risk will be that elements of the reform package will be either postponed or adopted in a cursory manner, with no meaningful ability to monitor compliance and enforce against rule-breakers.

Unremedied, this dilemma could lead the SEC and the CFTC, as well as the country's financial markets, into the worst of all possible worlds – pages and pages of further rules and red tape are on the books, but without a cop-on-the-beat who is ready, willing and able to oversee full compliance. Lacking the specialist expertise to ferret out the next fraud or impropriety, these agencies will risk facing the wrath of disgruntled investors when the next financial crisis begins to unfold.

Investors and savers are therefore left exposed. Comprehensive reforms promised to them in 2010 are still a long way away from being fully implemented. The consequences of their actions, or inactions, especially in the realm of private equity and hedge funds, are still largely left with these investors and savers themselves.

Passing pages and pages of new rules is only one club in a regulator's golf bag. Regulators could, if they chose to, address some of the concerns identified above by regularly conducting a small number of very well-publicized enforcement actions in order to address the more serious malfeasances that could result from governance failure, under the exceptional broad scope of either Section 206 or Rule 206(4)-8 of the Investment Advisers Act. Both are incredibly powerful tools for prosecuting fraud.

According to internationally-renowned funds regulation expert Barry Barbash, a partner at the leading Wall Street law firm Willkie Farr & Gallagher LLP, "Armed with Section 206, the SEC over time has used its enforcement authority to bring a wide array of cases against investment advisers and in the process has set substantive standards for advisers generally." Barbash also noted that "[t]he relative simplicity of Rule 206(4)-8 belies its potential scope. The Rule's reach appears to be virtually unlimited in terms of the written materials prepared by, and conduct engaged in by, advisers that could be prohibited under the Rule."

However, there are significant practical limitations to "rule-making" by enforcement actions that must be acknowledged and addressed. Since the cases that end up becoming the subject of prosecution by the SEC typically involve outlandish or egregious conduct, the remedies dispensed may be more onerous and inflexible than in cases of less extreme conduct.

Also, since each enforcement action is tied to a very particular set of facts, any "rules" that are produced will often be incomplete or difficult to apply in other circumstances. Moreover, where the decisions are made by regulators rather than courts, they can be of limited precedential value, since regulators are not bound by the strict rules of precedent which apply to courts.

Sometimes, passing new rules is simply the most effective way forward.

In the summer of 2011, despite a flurry of studies, rules and supplemental regulations – or perhaps because of it – life appeared to have returned to normal, or at least what passes for the "new normal," on Wall Street in the twelve months since Dodd-Frank was passed.

The Obama administration credited themselves, and their adoption of comprehensive financial regulatory reform, for this mostly positive state of affairs. For those who believed excessive risk-taking on Wall Street was at the heart of the global financial crisis, sweeping reform on a scale not seen in eighty years was the necessary remedy to insure that a similar financial meltdown does not occur any time soon. However, this was not a view uniformly held in Washington DC, let alone across the country. In fact, numerous bills began to float around Capitol Hill with one shared goal: the effective dismantling of Dodd-Frank. Inevitably, a backlash began to build against further rules and further red tape.

In May 2011, with only weeks to go before the scheduled launch of the Consumer Financial Protection Bureau (CFPB), the Wall Street watchdog established by Dodd-Frank, forty-four Republican senators vowed to block any nominee put forward to run the new regulator. They expressed concern in a letter to President Obama about the lack of adequate checks-and-balances for the CFPB.

In particular, they proposed that the CFPB be headed by a board of directors, rather than by a single "czar," and that the agency be funded directly by Congress, rather than receiving its budget from the Federal Reserve. Unsurprisingly, consumer groups began to rally around the CFPB, claiming that the net effect of the Republican proposals would be to strip the agency of its independence.

Elizabeth Warren, a law professor at Harvard, was widely rumored to be the Administration's choice for this important role, and she initially oversaw the agency's initial roll-out. But Warren was a highly controversial figure, and a painful confirmation process in the Senate would have awaited her. President Obama ultimately abandoned Warren in favor of Richard Codray to chair the CFPB.

Warren didn't wallow in despair for too long, however. Shortly after being set aside by Obama, she launched a successful run for the US Senate, where she has been able to put her encyclopaedic knowledge of the financial markets to good use. There is, no doubt, more than one Republican senator who perhaps feels in hindsight it would have been better to have Warren as an agency figurehead, rather than as a colleague on the floor of the Senate!

Obama publically pledged to defend Dodd-Frank from these mounting attacks. Unfortunately, the incredible vastness and complexity of the law was proving to be its Achilles' heel. The various government agencies (such as the SEC and the CFTC) entrusted with bringing Dodd-Frank to life, by way of numerous new rules and regulations, were beavering away at their "to do" lists, but they still had much work left to be done. At the same time, millions of dollars were being spent each week by lobbyists to influence the law's implementation.

Much of Dodd-Frank is just as far from implementation in 2013 as it was when the controversial legislation was first passed. As a result, investors are left with uncertainty over how much of Dodd-Frank will withstand overt and covert attempts at repeal, and uncertainty over how the implementation of what is left of the new law will actually impact on day-to-day life on Wall Street.

Is this uncertainty impacting the overall economic recovery in the United States today?

To the extent that investment capital remains undeployed because of such concerns, the US economy will continue to stutter and stall. Perhaps if the economic recovery had been stronger since Dodd-Frank's adoption, the comprehensive regulatory reform would have quietly assumed its place in the regulatory firmament and Wall Street would have reluctantly grumbled its way into compliance with the new rules of the road.

However, a lingering recession and stubbornly high unemployment means that the battle over Dodd-Frank, and the future regulation of our financial markets, is still being fought, in the open and behind closed doors, and may continue to be fought for years to come.

Finally, no survey of the US government's response to the global financial crisis would be complete without a short discussion of the so-called "Volker Rule." In many ways, this attempt to simplify banking structures and operations has developed a life of its own. The gravitas and drive of its namesake has more than a little to do with the rules stamina, in the face of a reluctant Wall Street and an uncertain Congress.

Paul Volker previously served as chairman of the Federal Reserve, retiring in 1987. He was succeeded by Alan Greenspan, who oversaw the "Long Boom" that ran under the credit crunch which began in 2008. Recently, Volker served as an economics adviser to President Obama. In years past, he had been a vocal opponent of President Reagan's plan to deregulate banks.

His greatest legacy, however, may eventually be his more recent contribution to the restructuring of banks, and the curtailment of ancillary investment activities in these banks. Interestingly, the rule that bears his name also may drive the formation of a whole new generation of hedge funds. Few of the rule's most ardent supporters may have seen that coming.

Simply put, his eponymous "Volker Rule" will reinstate in part the boundary line between investment banking and commercial banking that existed until the Glass-Steagall Act was finally repealed in 1999. The highly controversial rule attempts to prevent banks from engaging in proprietary trading, as well as limiting the type of relationships that they may have with private equity and hedge funds. In order to accomplish this gargantuan feat, the October 2011 proposal for the rule was almost three hundred pages long. Needless to say, there has been strong opposition to the rule from many parts of the financial world.

If fully implemented, the Volker Rule would prevent banks from operating proprietary trading desks in order to speculate in the market. In addition, banks would be unable to be operators of, or investors in, alternative investment vehicles, such as private equity and hedge funds. Underlying this rule is the belief that, since commercial banks provide credit to the real economy, they deserve to be protected, while investment banks that engage in risky activities should not.

Lobbyists have been working hard in 2011 and 2012 trying to water down the effects of the Volker Rule. Compromises have inevitably been made in order to get the necessary buy-in from the large financial conglomerates. Volker himself casts a great shadow over the current debate about regulatory reform, and not simply because of his considerable height. Greenspan's reputation remains under a cloud, and it is unclear how history will treat him. By contrast, although controversial during his tenure as Fed chairman, Volker retains a principled credibility when commenting today on the causes and effects of the global financial crisis.

The Volker Rule is not, and could never be, a silver bullet. At best, it is one part of a larger reform of financial regulation. The question that now must be addressed is how the Dodd-Frank reforms will be implemented and enforced on a day-to-day basis. As discussed earlier, given the track record of individual regulators in the period leading up to the crisis, it is hard to maintain an unqualified optimism.

Will the implementation of the Volker Rule, in some form or other, lead to a vast exodus of proprietary Wall Street investment banks and a resulting surge in new hedge fund launches?

Even as implementation of the Volker Rule remained some distance in the future, many bankers were reading the writing on the walls and moving on to greener pastures. In 2010, the Goldman Sach's prop desk "lateralled" over to KKR, while Morgan Stanley's team announced plans to close its prop desk as well. In January 2012, Citibank announced that it was closing its equity principal strategies desk, which trades the firm's own money. Two months later, Mike Stewart, JP Morgan Chase's global head of proprietary trading, decided the time was right to set up his own hedge fund. JP Morgan was already closing its proprietary trading business, despite uncertainty over the shape and scope of the rule.

In March 2013, Napier Park Global Capital emerged from Citibank's specialist hedge fund team, known as Citi Capital

Advisors, and took its place as a $6.8 billion independent hedge fund. Jim O'Brien and Jonathan Dorfman traded in their careers in Citi to head up Napier Park as co-chief executives, leading over 100 employees that left the bank with them. Like many other US banks, Citi is divesting itself of business units that potentially run afoul of the Volker Rule's prohibition on owning more than 3 percent of a private equity or hedge fund firm.

In the past, prop trading was a significant part of the revenue earned by large Wall Street banks. With the arrival of Dodd-Frank, this would no longer be possible.

Steven Davidoff of *The New York Times* correctly identified the potential benefits of the Volker Rule to entrepreneurial non-bank entities. "If the Volker Rule truly makes the cost of markets higher, then it will reduce the profits of the big banks. But the Volker Rule does not apply to private equity funds, hedge funds and smaller investment banks that do not themselves own banks. So if the Volker Rule is really a drag on the economy, hedge funds and small investment banks that are not subject to it may try to interject themselves and bridge the gap that the investment banks can no longer fill."

Private equity and hedge funds that historically pride themselves on being one step ahead of the market are also demonstrating that they are also quite willing and able to stay one step ahead of the law. As the Volker Rule attempts to draw boundary lines around what investment banks and commercial banks can do, these precautions only reinforce the position of private equity and hedge funds as separate from the traditional cut-and-thrust of life on Wall Street and in the City of London. However, the entire process of implementing comprehensive reform of financial services regulation has again been shown to be very difficult and subject to frequent delays and postponement.

As Jesse Eisenger and Jake Bernstein of ProPublica.org observed in June 2011 when delays to Dodd-Frank implementation were becoming widely evident, "To some, the emerging roadblocks reinforce a feature that Dodd-Frank, which was intended to touch on almost every aspect of the American financial system, may never provide the sweeping reform it promised."

The aspirations of Dodd-Frank were jaw-dropping in their scope and breadth. While fundamentally altering little in the existing US regime, Dodd-Frank contained many extensions, updates and tweaks which were required to bring the system of regulation into the twenty-first century. With this single piece of legislation, which eventually grew to two thousand pages, its champions hoped to fundamentally alter the US's approach to bank bailouts, derivatives, credit rating agencies and the line between investment banking and proprietary trading.

By attempting to cover so much, Congress left many of the more contentious details to be hashed out by appointed regulators rather than elected politicians. As will be discussed in later chapters, the tiered approach to rolling out financial regulation has become standard operating procedure in the European Union under the so-called "Lamfalussy process." On both sides of the Atlantic, this "delegate the details" approach is a candid recognition that only a certain portion of detailed financial regulation is suitable for a traditional political process.

Bitterness continues to grow toward these sprawling financial reform efforts, especially as crucial deadlines pass without the required rules being promulgated by the several regulatory agencies charged with implementing Dodd-Frank. No less than the former SEC chairman Arthur Levitt has been unreserved in his condemnation of these reforms. "It was doomed at the outset and nothing can possibly salvage it. We might even have been better off without it."

If the faults of the financial regulatory system, and recent attempts to reform it, are at their heart political problems, then perhaps the next best place to look for answers regarding the appropriate response to private equity and hedge funds in modern economic and financial life is to the partisan political process itself.

8: OF THE PEOPLE, BY THE PEOPLE, FOR THE PEOPLE

The Interwoven Relationships Between Politicians, Fund Managers and Institutional Investors

The battle for Wall Street cash has become a crucial subtext in the 2012 campaign, which is shaping up to focus heavily on federal banking and markets policies and the struggling economy.
Dave Egger and T.W. Farnam, *The Washington Post*

This is good work.
Former President Bill Clinton, on private equity

You can learn a lot about someone by perusing their tax returns, and Mitt Romney is no exception.

In January 2012, after many questions were raised over the size and source of Romney's vast fortune, his campaign team finally released his federal tax returns. Interestingly, information on Romney's personal wealth had never been publicly disclosed before. Even during his tenure as governor of Massachusetts, Romney was not required by law to publish his returns, and he didn't elect to do so voluntarily.

Two key points quickly become evident when paging through these returns. First, Romney is phenomenally wealthy. Not just "wealthy" or "very wealthy," but "phenomenally wealthy." He far outpaces the standard for White House wealth previously set by the Kennedys and the Bushes. These two families seem thoroughly middle class when compared with the Romneys and their estimated $250 million fortune. Second, Romney paid tax at an effective tax rate of approximately 15 percent. By comparison, the Obamas paid an effective tax rate of 26 percent on just $2 million in income in 2010.

As Romney eloquently stated in a debate at this time, "I pay all the taxes that are legally required and not a dollar more. I don't think you want someone as the candidate for president who pays more taxes than he owes."

Of particular relevance to the issues being raised and wrestled with in this book, much of Romney's money was earned during his time with Bain Capital, the private equity firm he co-founded, and was taxed predominately at capital gains rates rather than the significantly higher ordinary income rates. As discussed earlier, debate over whether this beneficial treatment of carried interest should be maintained has been a recurring feature of budget negotiations in recent years. The Romney tax returns, however, pushed this issue to center stage.

For many American voters, as well as for millions of observers around the world, 2012 became the year in which the inner workings of private equity, including the obscure minutiae of carried interest payments and their categorization for tax purposes, became a daily subject of discussion and debate.

Unlike the unifying concept of the 1 percent championed by Occupy Wall Street, much time was eventually spent distinguishing between different types of rich people. For example, billionaire New York Mayor Michael Bloomberg did not hesitate to make his own personal tax position clear in the days that followed Romney's admission in January 2012 that he paid taxes at only a 15 percent rate. Unlike Romney, Bloomberg – who earns only $1 a year for his services as mayor – assured voters that he paid tax on his income from his global media company at the highest personal income tax rates. Bloomberg's personal fortune has been estimated at approximately $20 billion.

Bloomberg went even further to criticize carried interest directly. "If it were up to me, I would end the concept of carried interest. In every industry there are things that were put there perhaps to encourage or discourage certain kinds of economic activity, but that may not be appropriate today."

As discussed in earlier chapters, carried interest is so lucrative specifically because it is taxed on a preferential basis in the same way as an investment in the underlying portfolio company itself. Arguments are routinely made by supporters that carried interest is much more like capital gains and by opponents that it is much more like ordinary income. Since the difference in these two rates can exceed 20 percent, the distinction is not immaterial.

Opponents of the current approach point to the significant rise in tax revenue that would be gained by taxing carried interest at a higher rate, as well as claiming that other financial services businesses, in addition to athletes and actors, all function perfectly well while paying tax at ordinary rates. Proponents of capital gains treatment stress the investment risk to which carried interest is subject before it is finally earned. In addition, they raise concerns over how the economy would cope with a significant withdrawal of investment capital at such a delicate time in the recovery.

Finally, in what can best be described as more an indictment of the complexities of the US tax code than the political football of whether private equity professionals should pay more taxes, it turns out that upon closer inspection Romney may have actually paid more taxes to the IRS than he actually needed. Floyd Norris of *The New York Times* was able to identify a number of areas where, should Romney have possessed more astute tax advisers, he could have cut his tax bill even further.

To what extent is that little discovery more an indictment of the mind-boggling complexity of the US income tax system than any meaning criticism of carried interest and the private equity industry that is built around it?

Of course, Americans had to form a view about Mitt Romney and the fact that he is a very, very wealthy man. Elections are choices, both for one candidate and against the other.

Americans like success. Americans want to get rich. America is a country based on the belief that people who want to be successful, and quite possibly rich, should have the opportunity to pursue those goals. However, both Romney's wealth and the manner in which he earned it required voters to make judgments about how the economy functions in the twenty-first century and the pervasive role of the financial markets in creating and allocating wealth for a select group of individuals.

In the 2012 Republican primary contest, rivals of frontrunner Mitt Romney set the tone for the months to come by repeatedly attacking his successful career at private equity firm Bain Capital. Unfortunately, no leading lights of the private equity world stepped up during these early days to defend their industry and its investment practices. As a result, many of these initial allegations quickly solidified into the basis of the narrative that would continue to drive the debate until election day.

The industry's leading trade association, the Private Equity Growth Capital Council, eventually grasped the potentially lethal effect of the fallout from these sustained attacks and began to work diligently to get its positive message out. However, it first had to overcome the "heads down" approach that is fairly typical for private equity professionals. This took some time and was not accomplished simply or easily.

One of the most effective means used to attack Romney and highlight the evils and moral shortcomings of private equity was the mockumentary, "When Mitt Romney Came to Town." Funded with money from the "super PAC" allied with Republican challenger Newt Gingrich, the video attracted some buzz on the internet during the primaries, but also led to allegations that the film was inaccurate and intentionally distorting. Underlying the various incendiary claims made in the film is the belief that the sole means by which private equity firms generate tremendous profits is aptly summarized by the phrase, "buy it, strip it, flip it."

Private equity firms, of course, do not typically target healthy, well-run companies with focused management teams and happy shareholders. There are no problems in such companies to fix, and therefore no opportunities for profit. Instead, these firms look for companies that are in trouble – preferably, serious trouble. Their target company may have good products to sell or services to offer, but the business would be poorly run or underfinanced. Otherwise, it would not be undervalued. Well-run and well-financed businesses are not cheap! The troubled company may have failed to reposition itself for a changing economy, or have yet to apply the same innovations to logistics or international distribution that its more successful competitors in the sector have.

Interestingly, despite the vitriolic rhetoric that frequently gets rolled out by critics of private equity when discussing asset-stripping and mass firings, we are generally quite comfortable with applying the exact same methodology in our daily life. For example, few are offended when a young couple who buy the "fixer-upper" house (with an 80 percent or higher mortgage, even!), and then proceed to remodel and renovate the house, replacing worn-out and out-of-date fixtures and fittings. We do not generally denigrate the profit that they make when the "new" house is sold to a willing buyer a few years later. But when the same logic is applied to "fixer-upper" companies, we are tempted to react differently. It is not at all clear why the same approach for financial profit produces such different emotional results.

Although there are certainly legitimate questions that can be asked about how private equity firms conduct their business, such as the appropriate tax treatment for carried interest, the use of debt in the financial engineering or portfolio companies, and the level of fees that funds charge their limited partners, these enquiries only break through the stereotypes and name-calling at irregular intervals. Far too often they are avoided in favor of theatrical allegations and name-calling.

The unavoidable fact is that companies go bankrupt and downsize their operations with distressing regularity. This occurs, and will continue to occur, with or without the help or involvement of private equity firms. The difficult and politically awkward question is what to do about these failures.

After the Republican primaries left the nomination in the hands of Romney, the Democrats got in on the private equity bashing act in a big way. In May 2012, President Obama released his own campaign ad that compared Bain Capital to vampires. That's right – vampires! The Romney campaign eventually countered with their own ad which focused on a successful private equity-backed company and its happy employees. Great efforts were made to paint two different pictures of how private equity actually operated on the ground.

Which vision of private equity is correct? Or, to put the question a better way, which vision is more relevant to American voters?

Underlying this contest between conflicting views of private equity is an important debate about what the ultimate purpose of private equity actually is. Perhaps that is the best place to start to unravel the rhetoric and buzz words that get tossed back and forth when arguments start boiling over.

The fundamental purpose of private equity, quite simply, is not to create jobs, but instead to save faltering companies. This is a crucial distinction to bear in mind when evaluating private equity's impact on the economy. As part of those rescue efforts, some of the jobs at these faltering companies, but not all, may be cut. The alternative, however, is to allow the company to fail and then lose all the jobs. When a company needs to be rescued, someone must step up to rescue it and be given the tools, opportunities and incentives to rescue it. Otherwise, all jobs will eventually be lost. In that regard, private equity can be seen as a job preservation endeavor.

Clearly, private equity plays an important role in modern economies. In the United States alone, 2,600 private equity firms have invested in over 15,000 portfolio companies. In 2012, approximately eight million people in the United States were working for private equity-backed companies. As Steven Rattner, a former Obama Administration Treasury official, observed in 2012, "Whatever its flaws, private equity has made a material contribution to sharpening management. But don't confuse a leveraged buyout with job creation."

When Hostess failed and a new backer was needed to ensure that Twinkies and Ding Dongs would be readily available for a new generation of snack food aficionados, it was private equity funds, led by Apollo, who stepped up to rescue this American treasure. Jobs were no doubt lost, but those delicious confectionaries were saved!

Inevitably, though, the partisan battle lines that are a recurring feature of Washington politics today impact on almost all discussions of private equity by elected officials. On occasion, though, candid and balanced assessments do slip out. For example, the mayor of Newark, New Jersey, Cory Booker, created significant controversy in May 2012 when in a long defense of Obama's record on the economy, he let slip his unqualified support for private equity. "I know I live in a state where pension funds, unions and other people are investing in companies like Bain Capital. If you look at the totality of Bain Capital's record they've done a lot to support business, to grow businesses."

Many who are familiar with the full range of private equity's activities, as well as the financial benefits that overwhelmingly accrue to the public pension plans, university endowments and other investors, readily agree with Booker's conclusion. Unfortunately, as concern over these remarks built up among Democratic Party electioneers, Booker was eventually forced to go on YouTube to "clarify" his position.

Even former president (and occasional Obama campaign surrogate) Bill Clinton was willing to go on the record and made clear his own favorable views about private equity. While a guest on Piers Morgan's CNN talk show, Clinton stated enthusiastically about private equity, "This is good work."

It would be a mistake to misconstrue the cut-and-thrust of American politics as a battle between the party of capital (Republicans) and the party of workers (Democrats). In fact, unlike European political parties, the constituencies that form the base of each party have been derived much more by geography and history than by economic class. As a result, a number of prominent Wall Street professionals are committed Democrats, and there are even elected Democratic politicians with gold-plated resumes featuring profitable stints at leading investment banks and financial institutions.

You don't need an original portrait of Hillary Rodham Clinton by contemporary artist Chuck Close hanging on your wall to demonstrate your political leanings, but it doesn't hurt.

One illustrative example is Jim Himes. A Democratic congressman from Connecticut, Himes's district includes the leafy city of Greenwich, the American capital of the hedge fund industry. Before taking office, Himes spent twelve productive years at Goldman Sachs. Once in the House of Representatives, he earned a seat on the House Financial Services Committee and was instrumental in the adoption of the Dodd-Frank reforms. Understandably, his views on controversial topics such as derivatives and carried interest taxation is more considered and moderate than many firebrands on the left of the party, including at times President Obama himself.

Even Himes, though, recognizes that popular sentiment has turned against Wall Street in recent years. "Americans think this is an unproductive sector, and it's a little hard to talk about capital formation in the context of the emotion."

Despite the lingering anger and suspicion that many on the left direct at the financial sector, including alternative investment funds, Obama and his administration have very close ties to private equity and hedge funds, although this could come as a surprise to many who watched as the one-sided attacks on Romney and Bain Capital as the 2012 presidential campaign gained momentum. Those that instinctively categorize private equity professionals and hedge fund managers as dyed-in-the-wool Republicans would be seriously mistaken. Like Wall Street generally, Democrats are well represented in the alternative investment management industry.

For example, despite his boss's high-profile support for Republican challenger Mitt Romney, Blackstone president Hamilton James put his weight behind Obama in the 2012 campaign, while at the same time criticizing the politically motivated attacks on private equity that have been launched by anti-Romney forces. James has gone on record with his own belief that his industry "is not only an important contributor to a healthy economy, but a vital one."

In addition, the Obama administration is no stranger to the revolving door between public service and private equity, although many of its supporters would probably prefer an image of greater distance between Pennsylvania Avenue and Wall Street.

The links between President Obama and private equity continued to tighten in 2011 when Cathy Zei, Obama's undersecretary for energy and assistant secretary for energy efficiency and renewable energy, joined the private equity firm Silver Lake to form a dedicated "clean tech" fund, together with venture capitalist Adam Grosser, an experienced clean tech investor. The new joint venture, called Silver Lake Kraftwerk, takes its name from the idiosyncratic German electronic music band from the 1980s. The previous month, the stalwartly Democratic former senator from Indiana, Evan Bayh, joined Apollo as a senior adviser with a focus on public affairs. Bayh no doubt received a significant step up from his senatorial salary of $174,000 per year, since his new employer has over $50 billion in assets under management.

In December 2011, Jeffrey Goldstein returned to private equity giant Hellman & Friedman after two years serving as undersecretary for domestic finance in Timothy Geithner's Treasury Department. During his time in government, Goldstein oversaw the bailouts of banks and the domestic automobile industry, as well as the implementation of the Dodd-Frank Act. In addition, Sanjay Wagle left Vantage Point Venture Partners for a position in the Energy Department. Over the next three years, over $2 billion of government money was used to fund clean energy companies in which Vantage had investments. A further $2 billion was given to companies linked to five other Obama advisers. Although advisers with ties to particular companies did not make formal decisions related to them, there was a pattern of informal advocacy that took place, even though Obama spokespersons would eventually insist that decisions were made on a merit-only basis.

Another example of the Obama administration's inclusiveness of the private equity world can be seen in the President's selection of Karen Gordon Mills, from the private equity firm Solera Capital, to head the Small Business Administration. Solera's fund had included sizeable checks from both CalPERS and the Oregon Public Employees Retirement Systems, although returns were reportedly not exceptional. Mills spent several years at Solera before leaving for MMP, another private equity firm. Like Obama, Mills is a Harvard graduate, both for her undergraduate degree in economics and her MBA.

No less than Rahm Emanuel, formerly Obama's Chief of Staff and known for his famous political dictum, "Never let a serious crisis go to waste," quickly reached out to a leading hedge fund manager for assistance and advice once he settled into the office of the mayor of the city of Chicago. Michael Sacks, who spent two decades at Grosvenor Capital Management LP, was picked by Mayor Emanuel to be the city's point person for attracting new companies to town. Emanuel first met Sacks during the mayor's short stint as an investment banker. During Sacks's time at Grosvenor, it became one of the premier fund of funds businesses in the industry.

Unfortunately, despite the close ties between Democrats and Wall Street that have developed in recent years, Obama faced a very different reception during his re-election campaign than four years earlier. In January 2008, candidate Obama had raised in excess of $7 million from Wall Street donors. By comparison, in January 2012, President Obama had just a little more than $2 million in hand from Wall Street.

What caused this dramatic turnaround?

Of course, Republican politicians have also been filling similar roles with large private equity and hedge fund firms for some time. Former Vice President Dan Quayle advises Cerberus, as does former Treasury Secretary John Snow. Ken Melman, who previously ran the Republican National Committee, is head of global public affairs at KKR. Alan Greenspan, former head of the Federal Reserve who oversaw the "long boom" that ended with the current financial crisis, has served as a member of Paulson & Company's board.

During the 2008 campaign, Obama surprised many neutral observers by raising twice as much money from venture capital as his opponent John McCain. Obama was a proponent of clean energy and after his election a number of venture capitalists took on key roles in government. As the financial crisis took hold, in the early months of his administration, Obama set aside $80 billion of his $787 billion stimulus package specifically for clean energy projects.

In addition, a number of high-powered and respected private equity and hedge fund figures backed Obama during his first run for the White House, including Hamilton Jones of Blackstone, Paul Tudor Jones of Tudor Investment Corporation and Eric Mindich of Eton Park Capital Management. Greater New York, home to Wall Street generally and private equity and hedge funds specifically, were Obama's biggest donors in 2008. Wall Street provided $25 million to the two candidates in 2008, but Obama earned by far the biggest share, at $16 million. As momentum built behind Obama in the fall of 2008, financial pundit Jim Cramer went so far as to say Obama was the candidate who could "lead us out of the wilderness."

In 2011, as coverage of the first rounds of serious fundraising began to gain momentum, certain segments of the press were still reporting how well Obama was doing at fundraising from the financial industry. In October 2011, *The Washington Post* noted that Obama was actually receiving more money from Bain Capital than Romney, the firm's co-founder. According to Dave Egger and

T.W. Farnam of *The Washington Post*, "The battle for Wall Street cash has become a crucial subtext in the 2012 campaign, which is shaping up to focus heavily on federal banking and markets policies and the struggling economy."

Although the numbers would soon move against Obama, not all Wall Street movers and shakers abandoned him during his second run. Many key figures still supported Obama during his 2012 campaign, including William Daly, who served as Obama's White House Chief of Staff, and was previously JP Morgan Chase's vice chairman. However, as the Occupy Movement gained momentum in the autumn of 2011, Obama increased his direct attacks on Wall Street, which were quite popular with many on the left of his party. As a result, the financial industry began to feel as if the administration was more interested in scoring short-term partisan political points by blaming them and using them as scapegoats, rather than in taking advantage of their experience and insight.

The Dodd-Frank reforms discussed earlier, as well as concerns over the stumbling economic recovery, drove significant numbers of Wall Street men and women away from Obama, including numerous private equity and hedge fund managers. In part, this was due to the feeling that they had been excluded by his administration from having any meaningful influence on the reform efforts. As a result, as the 2012 campaign unfolded, many Wall Street donors quickly turned to one of their own, in the form of Mitt Romney, a founder of Bain Capital. In addition to investment bankers and private equity professionals, Mitt Romney supporters also include senior figures in the hedge fund industry, such as Julian Robertson of Tiger Management, John Paulson of Paulson & Co. and Paul Singer of Elliot Associates, as well as members of SAC Capital Advisors, Caxton Associates and Rosemont Capital.

There was a sense among many in the alternative investment management industry that, having built up both his own firm and his own fortune through private equity, Romney understood their businesses, warts and all!

Given Obama's rhetoric against banks and private equity during his first term, it is unsurprising that when fundraising for his re-election began in earnest, he met with a frosty welcome on Wall Street. In the spring of April 2011, news reports began to trickle out confirming what many in the private equity and hedge fund community had been noticing over the last few months. These once-generous donors, who helped Obama walk into the White House in 2008, were now turning their backs on him. High-profile "bundlers" and fundraisers, who played a crucial role three years ago, were now actively backing Republican candidates. What began as a notable "rebalancing" in the 2010 mid-term elections appeared to be building into a genuine trend.

The question then became, what effect would it have on election day?

As mentioned above, this shift came as little surprise to the Obama camp. Since taking up residence in the White House, the President had consciously and consistently engaged in a series of populist attacks on the financial services industry and to heap blame for the economic crisis on the doorsteps of hedge fund managers. Also, he has made it repeatedly clear that significant increases in taxes are on the horizon. Perhaps the President took Wall Street for granted. Really, who else would they support?

In 2008, investment professionals ranked second – just behind lawyers – as the largest donors to the Obama campaign. But their support decisively turned against him in 2012.

As election day approached, private equity and hedge funds displayed a serious grudge against President Obama and his Democratic Party, despite having contributed so heavily to their electoral success in 2008. Tax increases remained a key element of the Democratic platform. Where would the new taxes come from? Most likely, fund managers feared that attempts would eventually be made to close the so-called "carried interest loophole" and pay tax on their ordinary income at even higher rates. As discussed earlier, carried interest is taxed in the United States at lower capital gains rates, so long as the underlying investments are held for at least one year. Democrats have frequently campaigned to repeal this rule and charge tax on all such revenues at the significantly higher ordinary income rates.

The days of Obama's high-profile courtship of these financial titans quickly began to look like a thing of the past. Concerns over tax hikes and the country's ambivalent economic performance took center stage. Disgruntled murmurings and veiled threats to decamp overseas soon began escalating into a significant reduction in campaign fundraising among the many Democratic Party bundlers on Wall Street who were so successful during the last campaign.

In March 2012, *The New York Times* reported that one anonymous hedge fund manager was quite unreserved in his assessment of the challenges facing the Obama campaign. "What he's done is insulted every guy on Wall Street. I don't take it personally, but a lot of people do. He is going to have a hard time raising money."

As Obama wrestled with dissatisfaction on Wall Street, Romney and the entire private equity industry began to formulate and launch a comprehensive counter-attack against their critics. In January 2012, as the Romney campaign was gaining momentum in the Republican primaries, Steve Judge, interim head of the Private Equity Growth Capital Council, began to position his trade association for a robust defense of itself. "There is a lot of misinformation being spread, purely for political purposes and on both sides of the aisle, as it pertains to private equity." Interestingly, Bain Capital withdrew from the Council in 2011 due to dissatisfaction with the approach being taken by the trade association. The Council is non-partisan and did not officially support Romney in his White House bid. As discussed earlier, many top private equity professionals are, in fact, staunch Democratic supporters and fundraisers, so oversimplifying the partisan nature of the industry is a grave and self-defeating mistake.

The image of "barbarians at the gate," a phrase immortalized in the title of the 1990 account of KKR's takeover of RJR Nabisco, still lingers in many people's minds when considering the merits of private equity. The 2012 campaign brought much of that imagery to the forefront again. The challenge facing Romney, his election team, the Private Equity Growth Capital Council and the entire private equity industry around the world was simple – they had to overcome these stereotypes, prejudices and caricatures.

Unfortunately, much of the initial damage inflicted on Romney was caused by his fellow Republicans. On the 2012 campaign trail, despite Texas pension plans being large investors in private equity, Texas Governor Rick Perry labeled private equity professionals as "vulture capitalists." Even more inconvenient for Perry, while governor he actually approved the leveraged buyout of TXU, the Texas utilities company, which was the biggest private equity deal ever completed, although the results were somewhat less than spectacular.

One of Romney's opponents for the Republican nomination, Newt Gingrich, repeatedly portrayed Bain Capital as a firm that looted companies and fired employees indiscriminately. As mentioned earlier, it was Gingrich's own political action committee that backed a short film entitled "When Mitt Romney Came to Town" which showcased unfavorable coverage of Bain deals. Gingrich once summed up private equity in fairly dark and foreboding terms. "Is capitalism really about the ability of a handful of rich people to manipulate the lives of thousands of other people and walk off with the money? Or is that, somehow, a little bit of a flawed system?" However, Gingrich had not kept private equity at arms' length during his years out of government. In fact, he had served on the advisory board of Forstmann Little, a leading private equity firm in the 1980s and 1990s, and had invested in portfolio companies advised by Forstmann Little.

Needless to say, Romney also undermined his own cause. They say a picture is worth a thousand words, and an unflattering photo of a much younger, less politic, Romney generated many, many more words than that.

The photo of Romney from around the time of the RJR Nabisco takeover first surfaced in 2007, but was eventually unavoidable during the 2012 campaign. The picture, taken back when Bain launched its first fund, showed Romney and several of his Bain colleagues holding wads of cash, smiling with enormous confidence and satisfaction. This reinforced stereotypes of greed, selfishness and disdain for others that had been gaining traction in recent years.

For almost ten years after Romney left Bain for his first crack at public life, which took the form of rescuing the 2002 Winter Olympic Games in Salt Lake City, he received a profit share in the firm and its funds as part of his retirement agreement. Fortunately for the Romneys, this period of time turned out to be the "Golden Age" of private equity. Bain itself grew from $4 billion in assets to $66 billion while Romney collected his retirement payments. Interestingly, federal law prohibits national elected officials from holding investments in private equity or hedge funds. If Romney had been successful in his quest for the White House, his various Bain holdings would have had to be sold. A direct result, therefore, of his defeat was that Romney is now able to maintain his considerable private equity holdings indefinitely.

During his years on the national stage, Romney was repeatedly required to give a defense of private equity that would resonate with men and women far removed from the technicalities of life on Wall Street. For example, in 2007, Romney remarked that "sometimes the medicine is a little bitter, but it is necessary to save the life of the patient." Critics have repeatedly taken issue with this analogy. While private equity's defenders were coordinating their response, a number of independent and aligned organizations, groups and movements continued in their sustained attacks on Romney's wealth specifically, and private equity generally. Perhaps most humorously, a pro-Union Democratic political action group called Americans United for Change went so far as to launch a website – www.romneygekko.com – in an attempt to make the comparison between the Republican challenger and the iconic character, Gordon Gekko, from the Oliver Stone film, *Wall Street*.

It was, of course, inevitable that, with Romney as a candidate for America's highest office, private equity would eventually be subject to constant and unrelenting scrutiny. The only real question was how the industry would respond and what its image in the public imagination would be once the ballots were cast, the balloons dropped and the red-white-and-blue bunting was taken down. As Henry Kravis, co-founder of KKR, reportedly informed a group at a Hong Kong dinner in November 2011, "If [Romney] is a nominee, well, hold your seats. They're going to describe us as asset strippers; we're flippers of assets, we just put on a lot of debt, fire a lot of people and that's how we make money. You know that's not the case. That's absolutely not what we do."

Paul Levy, a co-founder of JLL Partners, a midsized private equity firm, voted for Obama in the 2008 election. When "private equity bashing" began in earnest during the re-election campaign, Levy decided to speak up and defend the industry on his own in January 2012. More concerted efforts by the Private Equity Growth Capital Council were still in the works at this time, and would only begin to bear fruit in the months to come. According to Levy, "There is a tinge of McCarthyism here. I think it's a pretty honorable industry and I don't know why people aren't stepping up and defending the careers that define their lives."

By February 2012, with Romney's continued success at the polls, and the lingering criticism of his tenure at Bain Capital, a few stalwart defenders of the private equity industry began to put their heads up above the parapets and voice their defense of their business model. The Private Equity Growth Council launched an expensive campaign to provide a fuller picture of what it is that buyout firms actually do. "Private Equity at Work" sought to explain who benefits from private equity, and how. According to trade association head Steve Judge, "We wanted to set the record straight."

Supporters of the industry began to point out that the overwhelming majority of profits made by these funds go to pension plans that use the money to fund their retirement benefits, or to charitable organizations, including university endowments, as discussed in detail in earlier chapters. Unfortunately, few in the wider media went out of their way to reflect this fuller description of private equity in their reporting and commentary.

In April 2012, Ken Spain, spokesman for the Private Equity Growth Capital Council, stated resignedly, "We expect the conversation about private equity to increase in the coming months. Therefore, we have a responsibility to tell our side of the story." Private equity's champions argued that their restructuring of businesses made them more competitive in a rapidly changing world, while at the same time producing high returns for the public pension plans and other institutional investors who entrust their money with them. Freed from the demands and pressures of the public securities markets, private equity managers instead can focus on long-term value creation. Armand F. Lauzon, Jr, an executive at several Carlyle portfolio companies, acknowledged that "private equity firms are not perfect, but they can be lifelines when the future of a company is in question and jobs are at stake."

Critics, however, repeatedly contended that the use of excessive leverage to buy companies leads to unacceptably high levels of bankruptcies and job losses. Since this central accusation is made so frequently against private equity, it seems worthwhile to dissect it. As mentioned several times earlier, though, it is only very troubled companies that typically attract the attention of private equity firms and the turnaround experts they employ. These companies are disproportionately stumbling down the path toward failure, bankruptcy and liquidation. Private equity enters the scene to see if its tools, skills and expertise can change the direction in which these companies are headed.

Of course, private equity is not a "no lose" proposition. A portion of private equity-backed deals consistently fail. The ultimate question becomes how do the tools provided to damaged and declining companies by private equity fit into the larger growth strategy for the economy?

As exhausted investors and concerned citizens returned from their New Year's celebrations to begin their methodical assessment of what 2012 held for both the financial markets and the inside-the-Beltway political culture that was charged with overseeing these markets, there seemed little about the New Year to actually be too "happy" about.

2011 ended with nearly three-quarters of the deadlines contained in the massive Dodd-Frank reform package missed. Literally hundreds of required rules had yet to be passed. Although some rule proposals were floating around, waiting to be formally adopted, almost 40 percent of the required rules had not even been proposed in draft form for review and comment. The SEC and the CFTC continued to struggle to keep pace with the schedule that was set for them by Dodd-Frank, as their budgets have remained subject to political horse-trading in Congress. Despite significant increases in their responsibility, Congress had effectively frozen their budgets, leaving them to attempt to execute significantly increased responsibilities at their pre-Dodd-Frank funding levels.

The 2012 presidential elections would take place against a backdrop of incomplete reform of the financial regulatory system and uncertainty regarding whether the US markets were, in fact, more protected or less protected than they were when the financial crisis first began in 2008. Unfortunately, these issues never broke through the pre-packaged partisan white noise to drive the narrative of the campaigns, instead being relegated only to the odd corners of stump speeches and fund-raising appeals.

The spotlight eventually fell on Obama when he again stepped into the partisan fray by naming Richard Cordray as the director of the CFPB, the controversial new watchdog, over the vocal opposition of Senate Republicans. Cordray was the administration's second choice for this appointment after Elizabeth Warren, the Harvard Law professor who laid the groundwork for the Bureau, was deemed too controversial to survive a Senate confirmation hearing. By using his power to make recess appointments when the Senate is not in session, Obama issued a clear and direct challenge to those vocal Republicans who questioned the broad powers of the CFPB. Cordray's appointment had been filibustered previously in the Senate.

With Cordray in place, the CFPB was able to begin implementing numerous new rules and regulations in order to complete the overhaul of how US financial markets and financial institutions are regulated after the global financial crisis. Although Obama made clear with this recess appointment that he refused to take "no" for an answer, House Republicans quickly voiced their displeasure with the President's procedural end-run and vowed to introduce legislation to block the Cordray appointment until a court ruled on whether Obama's actions were unconstitutional.

At a time when the financial markets, and the real economy, needed certainty and stability, the political classes in Washington were still arguing over fundamental questions about the causes and effects of the global financial crisis years after the financial system seized up and nearly sputtered to a halt. What savers and investors need is the confidence to put their money to work in the most effective way possible. How voters reacted to partisan grandstanding on these important issues would significantly influence the election results in November 2012. And rightly so.

In hindsight, few observers in the United States or abroad were surprised by Obama's narrow, but definitive, re-election. Key polling throughout the spring, summer and autumn of 2012 consistently pointed to him as the likely victor. The Democratic constituencies delivered effectively when needed.

The reasons why Romney lost are several. Much has been, and will be, written about why his message and platform were not sufficiently appealing to American voters to win on the day. Importantly, however, he did not fail either solely or primarily because of his professional ties to private equity. Much time was spent as part of campaign coverage by the leading domestic and international news outlets dissecting private equity and, to a lesser extent, hedge funds. Yet again everyday American working men and women were asked to confront and overcome their understandable ignorance of the arcane world of finance.

It is, therefore, notable that as the election reached its conclusion and the enthusiasms of campaigning exhausted themselves, private equity was not in the end convicted in the court of public opinion of high crimes and misdemeanours. Allegations were made and answered. Counter-arguments were laid out and although critics of private equity parsed them and offered their own refutations, most American voters appear to have proceeded with their ultimate ballot-casting without being unduly driven by the potential evil of leveraged buyouts and carried interest.

Private equity can be said to have had its time in the spotlight and has survived it without mortal wounds or fatal injuries, in order to live and thrive another day.

The United States has a long tradition of national politicians building their reputations by wrestling with the leading economic and financial juggernauts of their day. In the 1830s, Andrew Jackson took on the Bank of the United States, against widespread opposition among many top legislators and financiers. In the end, he succeeded in this fierce and prolonged confrontation, although whether the victory was ultimately in the best interests of the country and its citizens is open to academic debate.

As discussed above, both American political parties have maintained strong ties with the burgeoning private equity and hedge fund community in recent years. The intersection of money and politics is an unavoidable feature of the democratic process in the United States, so these ties should not come as a surprise. As the role of finance as a contributor to the US economy has continued to rise in importance, it is unsurprising that the latest evolutionary step in the development of Wall Street – independent, entrepreneurial alternative investment firms – quickly took a position of prominence in both the Republican and Democratic camps.

The larger issues of what role government should have in private equity and hedge funds, and vice versa, remains a subject of discussion and debate today. The prospects of a latter-day Andrew Jackson arriving in the White House with a desire to upend the current Wall Street power structure is highly unlikely. Even at its greatest theoretical breadth, Dodd-Frank settled for pruning the branches of financial institutions, rather than pulling up offending shrubs and trees by the roots.

Any critic of the intersection of finance and politics must recognize there is a natural symbiosis between the two, regardless of which end of the partisan political spectrum a given person, party or government happens to reside. For example, private equity and public funding by governments are, of course, not mutually exclusive. Much of the rebound in private equity portfolio companies that occurred after the darkest weeks of 2008 has been attributed to government interventions in the financial markets and the economy at large.

In March 2011, at the prestigious SuperReturn conference in Berlin, Guy Hands, head of UK private equity powerhouse Terra Firma, laid clear credit at the feet of three controversial government actions: the bailout of European banks, the extra liquidity provided by various central banks and the United State's Troubled Asset Relief Program, known as "TARP." According to Hands, "Because of all these three, our business and our portfolios look a lot better today than they did at the end of 2008. But, in truth, we ourselves didn't have as much to do with this rebound as we sometimes tended to claim."

The focus, therefore, should be on effectively allocating responsibility for overseeing the financial markets generally and private equity and hedge funds specifically between those parties ready and willing to perform a regulatory, or quasi-regulatory, role. By recognizing that private equity and hedge funds are a natural evolution of wider trends within the financial markets, rather than some random mutation or aberration that places them outside the context and history of Wall Street, appropriate and effective steps can be taken to ensure that investors in these funds are adequately pro-tected and that the actions of these funds are adequately policed.

The sprint toward the passage of Dodd-Frank in 2010, motivated by a widespread outrage at the various shortcomings and failings that came to light after the collapse of the housing bubble, seems a very, very long time ago now. The surprise adoption of the JOBS Act in April 2012 signalled an abrupt change in the direction of financial regulation in the United States after a decade of ever expanding rules and prohibitions.

As the JOBS Act attempted to open wider the spigot of investment and capital flows that both Sarbannes-Oxley and Dodd-Frank had significantly restricted, it became clear that the focus inside the Beltway was moving away from legislation and regulation. 2013 was the first year since the financial crisis to begin with the pendulum swinging distinctly in the other direction.

Ultimately, laws on the books do little to ensure that people comply with them, unless there is effective policing when viola-tors are identified. As a result, the next task to be addressed in any comprehensive assessment of private equity and hedge funds is to identify and assess those prosecutors and enforcement agencies whose day-to-day job is to walk their beat and ensure that the laws govern-ing the activities of these funds are being followed to the letter.

9: THE COP WALKING
THE BEAT

Policing Private Equity and Hedge Funds, and Whether Regulators are Up for the Challenge

Investors are sometimes too busy looking for profits to notice where the truth ends and deception begins.
Andrew Ross Sorkin, *The New York Times*

In the past several decades, the financial markets have seen geometric growth in complexity.
Robert J. Rhee, the University of Maryland

Under the leadership of Preet Bharara, the Office of the US Attorney for the Southern District of New York, located at historic One St Andrew's Plaza, has been very busy lately. Nestled in downtown Manhattan, a short walk from City Hall and One Police Plaza, home of New York's Finest, the Southern District is perhaps the most high-profile prosecutorial platform in the English-speaking world. It sets the tone for law enforcement priorities across the United States and enjoys international prestige and notoriety. Taking on a role previously performed by Rudy Giuliani in the 1980s, Bharara's top priorities included looking into allegations of insider trading by hedge funds.

According to Bharara's deputy, Boyd Johnson, "We're fans of business and of Wall Street. But we're called to enforce a series of laws that apply across the entire economy, and across various areas of America. And that's our job."

To the extent that there is fraud and theft occurring, whether in the market, generally or in connection with private equity and hedge funds specifically, there is an important role for prosecutors to play in ensuring that there is a level playing field for all market participants. Markets require trust in order to operate. When the trust is gone, the market inevitably ceases to function.

Bharara has made it clear that his eyes are squarely on Wall Street. As charges were first being laid against Raj Rajaratnam, who would eventually be convicted of insider trading in relation to his hedge fund, Bharara issued a stark, but memorable, warning, "Today, tomorrow, next week, the week after, privileged Wall Street insiders who are considering breaking the law will have to ask themselves one important question: is law enforcement listening?"

The conviction of Rajat Gupta, former Goldman Sachs board member, for insider trading in June 2012, again drew widespread attention back to the trading practices of hedge funds. Gupta provided Galleon boss Raj Rajaratnam, who had previously been convicted of insider trading, with confidential information on certain securities. According to Bharara, "Having fallen from respected insider to convicted inside trader, Mr. Gupta has now exchanged the lofty boardroom for the prospect of a lowly jail cell."

No explanation or defense of private equity and hedge funds could, or should, ever attempt to go so far as to claim that either no one associated with these investment vehicles had ever committed a fraud or a crime, or that frauds and crimes were somehow less important than allowing these funds to continue pursuing their investment objectives and generating potentially high returns for their investors. Acknowledging that these funds have a legitimate role to play in the financial markets and the wider economy doesn't preclude one from insisting that the law be strictly complied with by them while they continue their search for investment performance. Since both the private equity and hedge fund industries are, in fact, large and diverse, these industries themselves have a deep and sincere interest in seeing the rules of the road applied rigorously and consistently.

With the tide pulling out in 2013 on further financial regulatory reform in the United States and Europe, the pressing question becomes how the statutes and rule books currently in effect will be interpreted and enforced when applied to private equity and hedge funds. How will prosecutors and enforcement authorities engage with alternative investment firms who pride themselves on being both one step ahead of the markets, and one step ahead of the law?

Getting an edge over your competitors is vital in almost every industry. In the financial markets, however, even a small advantage can mean the difference between significant profits and punishing losses on a trade. To make the best trade, hedge fund managers (like all investors) seek out the best information, often times going to great lengths to track down and obtain the tiniest morsel of data that could somehow result in their gaining a decisive advantage in their next trade.

For example, in the summer of 2011, a small scandal erupted over whether or not a group of hedge fund managers, including Steve Eisman of FrontPoint Partners (who was featured prominently in Michael Lewis's bestselling book, *The Big Short*), were able to get important information on forthcoming regulations being promulgated by Obama's Department of Education affecting for-profit colleges. Republican Senator Charles Grassley of Iowa launched an investigation into whether Department of Education staffers disclosed information to short sellers prior to that information's formal publication. Email traffic within the Department of Education revealed that Eisman's views on the effect of the regulations on the price of stock in affected companies was forwarded to the top of the government department within minutes. Interestingly, in March 2012, Eisman successfully launched his own independent firm, Emrys Partners LP.

Getting the right information into, or out of, a business can move prices, and from there, money can be made.

In search of their own informational advantage, many traders began turning in recent years to so-called "expert networks" for special insights on an industry, a company or a particular market or economic trend. In exchange for a fee, these independent research firms provide potentially valuable investment information to their clients. Unfortunately, the line between "investment insights" and "inside information" is not always as clear as we would like it to be. In the past few years, a number of hedge funds and other traders have been charged with insider trading on the basis of information obtained from individuals introduced to them by expert network firms.

Current federal insider trading laws are being used to prosecute these cases, but the question remains whether these expert networks require additional regulation. One state quickly stepped forwarded and decided that, in fact, they do. In April 2011, Massachusetts announced plans to indirectly regulate expert-network firms. All investment advisers registered in Massachusetts that pay expert-network firms will be required to obtain written certification that the firms aren't subject to any confidentiality restrictions and won't provide confidential information.

Which is a good thing, because, of course, that is what "confidential" means. Otherwise, the information wouldn't be "confidential."

The shadow of insider trading continues to hang over the hedge fund industry, even the most successful firms. On May 11, 2011, Raj Rajaratnam, founder of Galleon Group, one of the world's largest hedge fund managers, was convicted on charges of insider trading and breaches of securities law. The convictions represent one of the US government's greatest victories in its current attempt to crack down on insider trading on Wall Street, with hedge funds being a particular focus of federal prosecutors. In the eighteen months prior to the Rajaratnam verdict, Bharara and his team at the US Attorney office in Manhattan had obtained thirty-five other convictions for insider trading.

For the government, the conviction of Rajaratnam was a forceful demonstration that there are rules that all participants in the financial market must comply with, including hedge funds. The law must be respected, even by the most highly successful traders and portfolio managers. At its peak, Galleon Group managed more than $7 billion in assets under management. In addition to generating high returns for his investors, Rajaratnam was a lucrative trading partner for many Wall Street investment banks.

Given the frequency with which hedge funds trade in and out of their security positions, it is perhaps inevitable that at least some aspects of their trading activities would attract the attention of prosecutors. Importantly, hedge funds quickly rebounded from the financial crisis that erupted in 2008 with many having either reached or exceeded their prior peak levels. They have not disappeared from the financial landscape, contrary to the prognostications of many of their critics.

In an increasingly decentralized and interconnected global financial market, hedge funds continue to play a crucial role in providing liquidity to support the trading of a growing number of financial instruments, while also attempting to provide their investors with lucrative investment returns. They seem to have become a permanent feature of modern economic life, although that status raises as many questions as it answers.

In March 2013, SAC Capital, the hedge fund manager controlled by Steven A. Cohen, finally reached a settlement with the SEC for allegations of misconduct relating to alleged insider trading. SAC agreed to fines of approximately $616 million, reportedly the largest settlement ever agreed in cases such as this. According to George S. Canellos, the SEC's acting enforcement director, "These settlements call for the imposition of historic penalties."

In many ways, this was a further culmination of many years of work spent by the SEC and other federal prosecutors to ferret out what they believe is an epidemic of insider trading that has infected US financial markets. They were clearly not resting on their laurels after the Rajaratnam case. Despite SAC's solid investment performance, the allegations had cast a shadow over the hedge fund. In February 2013, redemption requests amounting to $1.7 billion reportedly arrived from clients wanting to take their money out, which equals roughly 25 percent of the $6 billion in the fund. Settlement followed shortly thereafter.

Although successful insider trading prosecutions draw attention to criminal activity that should be addressed, hedge funds are not simply a means to commit fraud, or a short-term aberration, or some unique historical phenomenon that will soon pass. It seems abundantly clear now, regardless of one's partisan political beliefs, that they are here to stay.

Importantly, however, the fact that one or more hedge fund managers are convicted of securities fraud does not, and cannot serve, as an indictment of the industry as a whole. It merely demonstrates that, like all human beings faced with difficult moral choices, on occasion some will fail to make the right decision. Clearly, the financial markets must be policed. No champion of private equity or hedge funds, no matter how ardent or enthusiastic, could seriously argue otherwise. The rules are there to be enforced. Like all other market participants, hedge funds and their investors benefit from the trust and certainty that the rule of law can bring.

As the lead regulator of US financial markets, the SEC has received a great deal of criticism for how it operated during the years leading up to the financial crisis. Despite the attention-grabbing headlines that can be obtained from a high-profile insider trading conviction, the factors that led to the near-collapse of the global financial markets in 2008, and the weaknesses that were subsequently revealed in the regulatory infrastructure, are far more complex and far more relevant to overall market stability than simple tipper-tippee scenarios. In light of these concerns and in an attempt to better oversee private equity and hedge funds, and their managers, the SEC's Division of Enforcement established a dedicated Asset Management Unit, initially headed by Robert Kaplan.

The SEC prioritized enforcement in the aftermath of Madoff and a flurry of proceedings were launched against a number of prosaically named hedge funds, such as LeadDog Capital, Solaris Management and ThinkStrategy.

Unfortunately, despite the increase in enforcement actions and rule-making, the SEC continues to have problems dealing with the ramifications of the Madoff debacle to this day. In November 2011, the SEC finally got around to disciplining eight of its own staff members in connection with agency failings relating to the Bernard Madoff Ponzi scheme. Notably, no one was fired. The stiffest punishment handed out was reportedly a thirty-day suspension without pay. Other punishments included demotions and pay cuts. Recommendations that at least one of the eight staff members be fired were overturned by the agency's then-chairman, Mary Schapiro.

As discussed earlier, SEC staff ignored repeated warnings that Madoff, a widely admired and well-known figure, was stealing money from his clients. The SEC's own internal examination into these crimes, which resulted in a detailed 500-page report, determined that the agency had received more than sufficient information over the years to warrant a thorough investigation of Madoff and his companies. However, despite three examinations and two investigations of limited focus being conducted, a thorough and competent investigation was never actually performed.

In the end, Madoff confessed to his crimes of his own volition to federal investigators. The SEC was caught completely off-guard in regard to both the existence and the scope of the fraud. Madoff, possibly the largest embarrassment that the SEC has faced, is now serving a prison sentence of 150 years. While he finally has been made to suffer the consequences of his actions, little has been done to apply the same standard to the regulators who ended up asleep at the wheel.

With large numbers of angry protesters on the streets as part of the Occupy Wall Street protests in the autumn of 2011, the

SEC's refusal to sack any of those responsible for oversight and supervisory functions regarding Madoff sent a disappointing message to Wall Street critics. In this light, Dodd-Frank's extensive reliance on an unreformed SEC to effectuate its numerous policy goals seems either idealistic or simply self-defeating.

To the extent that recent attempts to clean up the financial markets' excess have relied on an increased role for the SEC to play, it is unclear how long it will take the agency to regain its credibility with investors.

The Madoff debacle showed the world that the SEC faced numerous systemic shortcomings. The world is still waiting to see how the overburdened agency fully addresses and overcomes these challenges.

Of course, hedge funds are rarely established as fraudulent endeavors on day one. Much more typically, they are launched with all the hopes of success, until at some point a significant trading loss occurs unexpectedly. Rather than admit to investors this mistake, and risk a loss of faith that quickly leads to massive redemptions, the fund manager lies. The loss is buried under falsified financial reports in the hope that next month, or next quarter, the fund can trade its way into profit again. But when the losses grow, the lies grow, and the fraud gets bigger and bigger. As Andrew Ross Sorkin of *The New York Times* aptly remarked, "Investors are sometimes too busy looking for profits to notice where the truth ends and deception begins."

For example, in May 2012, the SEC charged a Miami-based hedge fund manager for deceiving investors in its hedge fund about whether its senior principals had personally invested in the fund themselves. Quantek Asset Management LLC made various misrepresentations about fund principals having "skin in the game" alongside fund investors. In fact, Quantek's executives never invested their own money in the fund. Quantek's misstatements were made when responding to specific questions posed in due diligence questionnaires that were used to market the funds to new investors.

Quantek also repeatedly failed to follow the robust investment approval process it had described to investors in the fund. They concealed this deficiency by providing investors with backdated and misleading investment approval memoranda. Three individual Quantek executives agreed to pay more than $3.1 million in total disgorgement and penalties to settle the charges.

The SEC made clear that private fund investors are entitled to the unvarnished truth about material information, such as management's investment in the fund or the adviser's handling of related-party transactions. The scope for "puffery" is practically non-existent. What the fund manager says to induce a prospective investor to buy shares or interests in the fund must be the truth, and the complete truth at that.

Frauds come in many shapes and sizes. Many have some element of humor to them. All leave innocent people damaged by their wrongdoings. On occasion, the forces of law and order are embarrassed by their ineffectiveness. In other cases, effective prosecution allows some partial remedy for the losses suffered.

The colorful story of former hedge fund manager Samuel Israel III is, perhaps, one of the more compelling and memorable incidents in recent years, even though it is more a story of elaborate fraud and desperate escape than anything particularly unique to hedge funds.

Now serving a 22-year sentence in the same prison complex in North Carolina as Bernard Madoff, Israel gained international notoriety in 2008 when he faked his own death to avoid going to jail as a result of frauds committed by him at his Bayou Hedge Fund Group. Israel used a fictitious accounting firm to bless fictitious profits in an audacious attempt to steal money from investors. As Israel eventually conceded to *The New York Times* during a 2012 prison interview, "I'm a proven liar. Don't believe anything I say."

In 2005, his fraud was uncovered and eventually Israel pled guilty, receiving a 20-year prison sentence. However, Israel had other plans. He staged his death in 2008 on the day he was to report to prison, leading to a two-month global manhunt. Eventually, Israel turned himself in after his girlfriend was charged with being an accessory to his escape.

As with the Madoff debacle, the SEC came out of the Bayou case looking understaffed and overwhelmed. When the attention of Congress and the mainstream media quickly turned their attention to other priorities, including the ongoing pantomime battle over the fiscal cliff and the debt ceiling, those charged with policing the financial markets and protecting investors were forced to do the best that they can with the resources that they have available.

Dedicated agencies, such as the SEC, must make do with the resources they are given by Congress. As noted earlier, this amount is intentionally limited and repeatedly below requested levels. For agencies with multiple responsibilities such as a US Attorney's office or a state Attorney General's office, priorities must be established that allocate time and headcount to protecting private equity and hedge fund investors and ensuring compliance with applicable law.

Much good work continues to be done to ensure that laws and regulations are being enforced after the financial crisis. With Madoff safely behind bars, the attention of US prosecutors quickly turned to the potential criminal and civil liability of large investors in the Madoff scheme who may have breached duties to their own ultimate beneficiaries. For example, in June 2012, J. Ezra Merkin reached a civil settlement with the New York Attorney General under which he agreed to repay over $400 million to his own clients who had lost money in the Ponzi scheme. Merkin lost over $1 billion when the scheme collapsed.

The attorney general filed a case against Merkin weeks after Madoff confessed to his crimes. The basis of the civil case was that Merkin defrauded his own clients by not conducting any due diligence or oversight on his investments with Madoff. The inaction and ambivalence of Merkin cast a further shadow over the numerous intermediaries who, whether by way of "feeder funds" or "funds of funds," profited by in effect funneling money blindly into a Ponzi scheme. His funds took money from various charities, including the Harlem Children's Zone and Bard College. According to Attorney General Eric Schneiderman, "By holding Mr. Merkin accountable, this settlement will help bring justice for the people and institutions that lost millions of dollars."

To understand how prosecutors and law enforcement officials need to address the violations that frequently occur in and around private equity and hedge funds, it is necessary to acknowledge the larger policy concerns of the current regulatory regime that has evolved around these funds. The priorities of financial regulators in this area include both systemic risks to financial markets and investor protection. Regulatory responses to unforeseen developments tend to seek to correct perceived shortcomings in one or both of these two areas.

Some critics claim that alternative investment funds are particularly vulnerable to fraud. Each business cycle demonstrates, however, that the capability for criminal activity exists throughout the financial markets. The recent financial crisis that began in 2008 has given prosecutors and law enforcement ample examples of these activities. A sufficient desire to defraud will circumvent all regulatory prohibitions regardless of their breadth and detail. No legal system can ever be so completely comprehensive that criminal acts simply no longer occur. Prosecutors will always need to be willing to take steps to enforce the law when necessary.

Of course, the consequences of fraud and malfeasance on alternative fund investors can be severe, especially where fund participants are individuals. The global financial markets have seen a dramatic increase in complexity in recent years. At each step of the way, prosecutors and enforcement officials are among the first within the regulatory regime to confront these complexities. As Robert J. Rhee of the University of Maryland observed, "In the past several decades, the financial markets have seen geometric growth in complexity. The junk bond market matured in the 1980s, the derivatives market saw explosive growth in the 1990s, and the new century witnessed the evolution of ever more exotic derivatives and financial instruments that directly connected Main Street to Wall Street."

Alternative funds have both driven that trend and been directly impacted by the complexity they have helped create. As Rhee has also noted, "Among the many leitmotifs of the financial crisis is the failure of lawyers as regulators and gatekeepers ... The Madoff Ponzi scheme personifies the 'new' era of economic catastrophe ... Importantly, the scandal provides the best documented episode and case study of how lawyers and the SEC, a principal financial market regulatory agency operated mostly by lawyers, failed to understand the market they regulate and the non-legal complexities surrounding their work."

Lawyers perform so many important roles at the forefront of the government's response to private equity and hedge funds. As earlier chapters have laid out in great detail, legal and regulatory decisions sit at the heart of how these funds are established and operated. It is, therefore, important that these key individuals within the SEC and other regulatory and prosecutorial bodies remain informed on the latest developments and techniques being used.

Otherwise, these earnest government officials, despite all the goodwill they deserve, will remain one step behind those whom they are charged with policing.

Even after the media whirlwind that developed after Bernard Madoff turned himself in, Ponzi schemes have continued to surface with frustrating regularity. Not all reach the stratospheric heights that Madoff did with billions of fictional gains, masking massive losses by the participants, but each in their own way reinforced the risks faced by investors and the need for prosecutors and law enforcement to identify and convict those responsible.

Delay in doing so can lead to significant increases in the pain and suffering ultimately meted out to the victims.

Some Ponzi schemes can be relatively modest, such as the $20 million fraud in Florida perpetrated by James Davis Risher and Daniel Joseph Sebastian. Their calmly reassuring funds, which included the Safe Harbor Private Equity Fund and the Preservation of Capital Fund, were found by the SEC to be simple frauds.

On a larger scale, in June 2011, the Allen Stanford case shows the complex web of issues that arise in a large fraud even when the SEC manages to take the initiative and drive an enforcement action. In short, the SEC alleged that Stanford operated a Ponzi scheme in which certain investors were sold certificates of deposit (CDs) issued by Stanford International Bank Ltd. (SIBL) through the Stanford Group Company (SGC). The SEC eventually held that certain individuals who invested money through the SGC, the US broker-dealer that was owned and used by Allen Stanford in connection with his Ponzi scheme, were entitled to the protections of the Securities Investor Protection Act of 1970 (SIPA). The SEC exercised its discretionary authority under SIPA, and requested that the Securities Investor Protection Corporation, of which SGC was a member, initiate a court proceeding under SIPA to liquidate the broker-dealer.

The SEC decided that investors with brokerage accounts at SGC, who purchased the CDs through the broker-dealer, qualified for "customer" status under SIPA. The report of the court-appointed receiver for SGC noted that corporate separateness was not respected by Stanford, and that many of his companies "were operated in a highly interconnected fashion, with a core objective of selling" the CDs.

Yet again, however, the SEC's efforts were found wanting by fleeced investors. Earlier in March 2011, investors in the Stanford Ponzi scheme actually sued the SEC, claiming that the US regulator should have done more to identify and stop the fraud. Suits like this are awkward for the US regulator, since it forces them to defend the decisions that they made, under the punishing glare of hindsight. The investors in the Stanford case alleged that the SEC's negligence and misconduct caused their losses.

A report by the SEC's own inspector general laid blame for the failure at the regulator's Fort Worth office. Despite repeated suspicions of fraud, SEC officials failed to inspect Stanford for several years. Stanford's operations were seized by US officials in 2009. Total losses by investors who purchased CDs from Stanford's bank, based offshore in Antigua, were believed to amount to more than $7 billion. The SEC declined to comment on the lawsuit. Fortunately, Stanford eventually dropped his own $7 billion lawsuit against the US government, which had alleged that regulators and prosecutors had abused their authority and engaged in malicious prosecution.

Again, the SEC was left with unanswered questions about its effectiveness in policing the increasing complexities of modern financial markets.

On either side of the Atlantic, different approaches to enforcement reign when it comes to policing the investment firms. Those differences are particularly clear when it involves private equity and hedge funds.

The FCA (and its predecessor, the Financial Services Authority) to date has limited its enforcement activities involving private funds to isolated cases of market abuse and insider trading. The most high-profile case that the FCA has pursued so far was against Philippe Jabre of GLG who received a fine of £750,000 for insider trading in August 2006. Other cases, such as Steven Harrison of Moore Capital (September 2008), Simon Treacher of Blue Bay Asset Management (February 2010) and Anjam Saeed Ahmad (June 2010), led to lesser fines, but each expressly excluded any criticisms of these individual's employers.

The United Kingdom's approach to financial regulation has been a work-in-progress in recent years. The FCA formally took over from the Financial Services Authority in April 2013. All financial and investment firms, except for the largest banks, are now authorized and supervised by the FCA. Banks are subject to a dual regime under the eyes of the Prudential Regulatory Authority and the FCA. All private equity and hedge fund firms who were previously FSA-regulated were grandfathered into the FCA.

There has been little day-to-day difference for most firms, since the FCA sensibly adopted the existing regulatory handbook and is generally following the prior precedents and procedures of the Financial Services Authority. The FCA may adopt a different approach to regulation and supervision as time passes, but the financial services firms in the United Kingdom will have to wait and see.

While the FCA has historically prided itself on a balanced approach to its responsibilities, the SEC's primary mission (at least on paper) is to protect investors and the integrity of US financial markets through the enforcement of the federal securities laws. A "gung ho" tendency favoring enforcement and prosecution has managed to sit side-by-side with a frustrating tendency to miss catastrophic crimes despite fairly clear evidence of wrongdoing.

Although alternative investment funds in the United States are not subject to the detailed, prescriptive requirements and fiduciary safeguards of retail mutual funds, they remain subject to the numerous anti-fraud provisions of the federal securities laws. The layperson should not forget that each share or partnership interest that is being bought and sold in connection with any fund launch is, quite simply, a security. As a result, the full weight of the federal law can be brought to bear on that transaction if there is any whiff of fraud having taken place. For example, when contemplating a criminal action against an accused party in those circumstances, US authorities have a wide array of statutory bases from which to launch their prosecutions, including Section 10(5) of the Exchange Act and Rule 10(b)-5, Section 17(a) of the Securities Act, and Sections 206(1) and 206(2) of the Investment Advisers Act and Rule 206(4)-8.

In recent years, the SEC has instituted a significant number of enforcement actions against hedge funds. The fraud charged against fund managers has been similar to the types of fraud charged against other types of investment advisers. Potential securities law violations may come to the SEC's attention through complaints from either disgruntled employees or investors. Matters may be referred to the SEC's Enforcement Division by their Office of Compliance, Inspections and Examinations (OCIE), where issues arise as part of a periodic examination. However, OCIE's coverage of alternative investment funds is limited to those with fund managers registered under the Investment Advisers Act. Although OCIE and Enforcement are two separate teams within the SEC with different functions, fortunately there is a growing level of communication and coordination between the two.

"Pick your fraud of the day," noted Robert Plaze, deputy director of the SEC's Division of Investment Management, "and the question is, 'Can we extract information from [our] data system together with other data bases we have access to and home in on problems before they do damage?'"

Since the passage of Dodd-Frank, the SEC has significantly benefited from an increase in the amount of data it now collects on hedge funds. This is primarily a result of both the further 1,400 new fund management businesses that have registered with the SEC since the generous "fourteen or fewer" clients exemption was repealed, and the new reporting requirements simultaneously put in place, both of which were discussed in detail in earlier chapters. The question is now how effectively could the SEC mine this growing mountain of data in order to better identify risks and protect investors? Plaze has referred to his team's ability to comb through this information and identify high-risk situations as "a powerful new tool to police markets."

Traditionally, financial regulations uncovered fraud and malfeasance in hedge funds through either unhappy investors who wanted their money back or former employees who were willing to "tell all" about suspicious activities they witnessed first-hand. Now, the SEC is developing advanced computer systems that mine vast quantities of raw data in order to better detect suspicious activity among hedge funds, including unusually good investment returns that defy explanation. According to Robert Khuzami, director of the SEC's Division of Enforcement, the regulators are "using risk analytics and unconventional methods to help achieve the holy grail of securities law enforcement – early detection and prevention." Khuzami himself, however, will not be there to achieve the holy grail in person. He resigned from the SEC in January 2013, in order to pursue other opportunities.

Of course, fund managers have been making use of cutting edge computer hardware and software for years, including large numbers of the best economists and mathematicians on the planet. These latest efforts by the regulator at making their enforcement activities more robust are a logical reaction to the Madoff scandal and other prosecutorial failures since 2008. Unfortunately, fund managers will still continue their relentless innovations. As a result, the SEC will need to keep pace with each and every new development in the years to come.

Equally important is the increased use that the SEC can now make of whistleblowers. As discussed earlier, whistleblower programs mandated by Dodd-Frank have been up and running since August 2011. On average, the SEC gets ten tips, complaints and referrals each day, although only a handful relate to private equity and hedge funds. Unfortunately, often the tips are not sufficiently clear or precise to allow the SEC to act immediately.

At the end of the day, therefore, on-site inspections by SEC staff remain central to the regulator's approach to ongoing oversight and monitoring. The SEC's Office of Risk Assessment and Surveillance uses Form ADV to evaluate which investment advisers pose the greatest risk to investors and the market at large. Importantly, many of the recent changes to Form ADV pre-date Dodd-Frank and were actually initiated by OCIE, rather than being mandated by Congress.

The number one priority of OCIE in 2012 was the fees and expenses charged by private fund managers, particularly where disclosure is inadequate in the fund's offering documents. These issues can arise in a number of different contexts. One issue that has come up frequently is when an investment manager has said that expenses would be allocated *pro rata* between various fund clients, but in reality the splits are not equal. For example, a fund with significant investments by employees or founders of the investment manager might be allocated a smaller share of these expenses.

Also, where there are particularly complicated fund structures, there can be hidden fees, or relationships with particular service providers that are not obvious and give rise to questions of conflicts of interest. In the case of layered fund of funds or feeder structures, there can also be questions about how much due diligence they are actually doing on the underlying funds, as seen numerous times in the Madoff debacle.

In the spring of 2013, reports began circulating that the SEC had also begun investigating exotic expenses, including those related to travel and entertainment, that private equity and hedge fund managers have been charging to their funds, rather than paying themselves. Fund documents usually have broadly drafted provisions whereby the fund (and therefore its investors) is required to pay for the costs incurred in connection with its investment activities. The fund manager is meant to fund all of its internal expenses out of the generous management fee paid to it on a regular basis by the fund. SEC examiners poring through the books and ledgers of the funds began to come across some highly exceptional invoices. These invoices raised questions about whether certain fund managers were actually taking advantage of their clients, the funds.

Eventually, even private equity made it on the SEC's radar. In February 2012, media outlets began reporting that the Enforcement Division had initiated a root-and-branch examination of the structure and operation of the private equity industry. Previously, the

SEC had spent several years coming to grips with the rapid growth of hedge funds. Now their attention had turned to private equity.

At the end of 2011, the SEC began sending informal inquiry letters to private equity firms. The purpose of the mass mailing was to obtain adequate information from which the regulator could determine if any securities laws may have been violated, either in connection with valuations, performance reporting or otherwise. Over the past decade, private equity firms had used debt financing readily provided by banks to conduct a number of high-profile purchases of well-known companies, such as ClearChannel Communications and Chrysler in the United States, and AA and Saga in the United Kingdom.

The SEC is not alone in its interest in private equity. The US Department of Justice also conducted an investigation into whether private equity firms have been violating anti-trust statutes by colluding on their bids for certain target companies, in an effort to artificially drive down the prices they would otherwise have to pay.

An ongoing civil law suit before Judge Edward Harrington in the Federal District Court in Massachusetts against eleven of the largest private equity firms, including KKR and Blackstone, alleges that these firms engaged in a conspiracy to rig bids of twenty-seven of the largest takeovers over the past decade, including the acquisition of SunGard Data Systems, Freescale Semiconductor, TXU (now known as Energy Future Holdings), ClearChannel, Univision and Toys "R" Us.

Notably, the plaintiffs in this case are former shareholders of these companies. The case was originally filed in 2007. The Justice Department, which had been investigating similar allegations, decided against bringing their own case.

At question in this case is whether the occurrence of so-called "club deals," which involve private equity firms partnering together to jointly acquire a target, constituted an attempt by these firms to drive down asking prices illegally through collusion. Lawyers for the private equity houses have argued to the court that the case against their clients is based upon a "far-fetched theory by doing nothing more than describing routine M&A activity and labeling it anti-competitive." It has been reported that these private equity firms have incurred over $100 million in legal fees in the course of defending themselves in this case over the past several years.

Due to a broad protective order issued by Judge Harrington at the beginning of the case, little of the information discovered by the plaintiffs so far has found its way into the public domain. Notably, however, club deals have fallen out of fashion since the global financial crisis, as reluctant banks unwilling to write large loans have meant that deal sizes have significantly decreased.

The allegations, however, do not appear to be going away. In March 2013, Judge Harrington refused to dismiss the lawsuit accusing private equity firms of colluding to drive down the prices of corporate takeovers during the recent buyout boom. A full trial may be imminent, although Judge Harrington did narrow the scope of the case against eleven leading private equity firms. The case has caused hand-wringing in some quarters of the industry, as accusations of "bid rigging" make for poor public relations.

The SEC's focus has historically been on protecting investors and those aspects of alternative investment funds which raise investor protection issues. It can be very useful in certain contexts to distinguish between public enforcement, which focuses on punishment, and private enforcement, which focuses on compensation.

The private law remedies enable disgruntled investors to pursue damages independently of government enforcement agencies and prosecutors. In a very practical way, the line that is drawn between retail investors, such as Uncle Edgar and Aunt Edna, and non-retail investors, such as large institutions and very wealthy individuals, is placed where it is as an approximation of who can reasonably be expected to pay out-of-pocket for their own lawyer to protect their interests in civil court, and who cannot be.

In recent years, the financial regulatory system has become the primary focus of attention when debating what to do about problems which have arisen in the financial services industry. This may strike the layperson as wholly unsurprising. However, underlying this system of rules and regulations is a much older system of private law that addresses many aspects of the relationship between an investment manager and its clients. These private causes of action, which are hundreds of years old and form the bedrock of Anglo-American jurisprudence, allow individual investors harmed by the malfeasance of a fund manager to pursue remedies directly against that manager, outside of both the regulatory system and the criminal law.

Prior to the development of a more comprehensive system of financial services regulation, the private law provided the primary basis for resolving disputes when they arose. The increased use of intermediary vehicles such as private equity and hedge funds, however, has meant that in many circumstances these potential remedies have ceased to be effective for many fund participants.

For example, investment managers owe general legal duties to their clients arising under contract, tort and as fiduciary duty from the provision of investment management services. Where the client is an alternative investment fund, participants in that vehicle must rely on the governance mechanisms built into the legal entities being used (such as limited partnerships and offshore companies) in order for redress to be sought against a fund manager who has breached such duties.

Private law remedies that might be adequate in a bilateral relationship between a single client and a directly appointed investment manager pursuant to a negotiated agreement between the parties can be undermined by the complexity of the fund structure adopted by the fund manager. In those situations, the savvy investor will need to ensure that extra steps are taken to address those concerns when a prospective investor is negotiating the terms of their investment.

A sample of potential private law causes of action available to disgruntled investors in alternative investment funds can be seen in the various lawsuits emerging from the Madoff affair. At least, when all is said and done, the Madoff debacle was a "teachable moment."

On December 19, 2008, a class action lawsuit was filed in New York State Supreme Court in Manhattan against the fund of funds firm Fairfield Greenwich Group, one of the largest investors in the Madoff scheme. The plaintiff alleged in their complaint that the various defendants breached fiduciary duties and committed negligence in connection with their management of the fund of funds. Specifically, the plaintiffs alleged that the defendants failed to act with loyalty and in good faith toward the plaintiffs, failed to take reasonable steps to oversee and preserve the plaintiff's investments, failed to perform necessary due diligence and maintain oversight and transparency for investments, and failed to exercise generally the required degree of prudence, caution and good business practices.

Notably, litigation involving investment managers has been surprisingly rare in both the United States and the United Kingdom, leading to an unhelpful lack of decided cases involving the question of private law duties of investment managers. Explanations suggested in the past for this anomaly include that the burden of proof is perceived to be high and that the time required litigating such claims means that significant gains and losses could be experienced in the client's portfolio before a final judgment is rendered. Perhaps a (minor) benefit of the Madoff litigation will be a fuller analysis of how the general legal and equitable principles apply to investment managers generally and private fund managers specifically. Of course, few of Madoff's victims will take much comfort in that collateral benefit of their painful losses, unless the damages ultimately awarded are sufficiently lucrative.

The "educational effect" of the global financial crisis is not just limited to onshore jurisdictions. Even in offshore jurisdictions such as the Cayman Islands, there are now many more lawsuits being filed – and ultimately litigated in court – that address questions or concerns of great relevance to alternative investment funds, their investors and their managers. A particularly interesting case was decided in August 2011 by the Grand Court of the Cayman Islands which addressed the proper role of independent directors on the board of an offshore hedge fund.

In the case of *Weavering Macro Fixed Income Fund v. Peterson*, the directors of the fund were found guilty of wilful default in the discharge of their duties. The court ordered them to pay damages to the fund's liquidators in compensation for the losses it suffered. The fund's manager was Weavering Capital, which was headed up by Magnus Peterson, who had been accused of fraud. The fund's directors were Peterson's brother and stepfather.

In punishing the directors, the court held that they were obliged to exercise a "high-level supervisory role." In practice, they should have satisfied themselves on an ongoing basis that the fund manager and other service providers were performing their functions to the standards required under the terms of their contracts. Instead, the Weavering directors consciously chose not to perform their duties to the fund in any meaningful way.

Importantly, alternative investment funds traditionally differed from other financial investments, such as the security of public listed companies, by the relative lack of lawsuits by disgruntled investors on both sides of the Atlantic. In the United States particularly, the dictum "when investors lose money, they sue" has proved reliably constant for corporate shareholders, but surprisingly inapplicable to private fund participants, at least until recently. One theory is that fund investors were afraid of gaining a reputation for being litigious which might lead other fund managers to exclude them from their funds. Recent events following the global financial crisis are changing this anomaly.

Historically, there has also been a noticeable absence of private litigation by disgruntled investors against fund managers in the United Kingdom, especially in comparison to the United States. In addition to being a larger market for alternative investment funds than all other countries (including the United Kingdom) combined, the United States has been the source of the majority of litigation surrounding alternative investment funds in recent years.

As Iain MacNeil of Northwestern University has noted, "Perhaps the most prominent feature of regulatory enforcement in the UK capital markets is its low incidence ... Moreover, from an international perspective, it is well known that the FSA is much less active than its US counterpart, the SEC, in taking enforcement action: even adjusting for different levels of market capitalization, the number of enforcement cases initiated by the SEC and the financial penalties imposed are much greater." The observation, of course, could be made more generally about civil litigation in the United Kingdom.

Since 2008, civil lawsuits by investors and other creditors arising from hedge fund "blow-ups" are now more frequently seen in US courts. Lawsuits involving limited partners of private equity funds have historically been much less common than is the case in the hedge fund arena. In part, this may be driven by the fact that such limited partners have tended to be institutional investors with the sophistication and experience to negotiate the levels of protection they require to address the risks related to the private equity funds within which they invest. However, litigation is now occurring with some regularity since 2008 among limited partners and general partners in private equity.

Similar to enforcement actions brought by a regulator such as the SEC or the FCA, civil cases have covered a range of claims against fund managers, including misrepresentation of performance, misleading disclosures and improper valuations. These cases frequently include charges against the fund manager, although in many cases such firms often lack the necessary assets to make investors and creditors whole for their losses. Alternatively, claims may be pursued against a fund's auditors or administrators, or in certain circumstances against either the independent directors of the fund or the fund's lawyers.

However, even where a hedge fund collapses amid substantial allegations of fraud, the money available for recompensing investors will often not, in many cases, be expanded by litigation. Judgments of courts ordering damages are not typically worth very much when the party against whom they are to be enforced are "judgment proof" because they no longer have any money.

Fortunately, where a hedge fund manager has stepped over the line into criminality, the SEC or the FCA can intervene and appoint a receiver to preserve remaining assets and oversee the orderly unwinding of the fund. The ultimate goal of the receivership is to locate and preserve as much of the estate as possible for investors. Unfortunately, if the fund manager and its principals are all insolvent themselves, as will often be the case in the wake of a sudden fund's collapse, and there were no third parties involved in the fraud, litigation may ultimately prove unsatisfying for the aggrieved fund investors.

Litigation against private equity and hedge funds arises often out of the offering memorandum originally establishing the fund in question. As discussed earlier, the claims in such cases are rooted in allegations of misrepresentations made by the fund, focusing particularly on any divergence between the representations made to induce the original investment in the fund and the manner in which the fund was actually run. Underlying claims may involve allegations that a fund misrepresented the risk that would be involved in pursuing its investment objective, departed from its investment strategy, failed adequately to diversify its investments or failed to invest with prudence. These causes of action may ultimately take the form of claims for fraud, fraudulent inducement, breach of fiduciary duty, negligent misrepresentation or gross negligence.

Although Dodd-Frank represents the most significant attempt to reform US financial services regulation in over seventy years, the law's ultimate effectiveness as a means to better enforcement remains unclear. The SEC is central to the US approach, but its limitations and recent shortcomings are still acknowledged within Dodd-Frank.

According to US securities regulation expert Edward F. Greene, partner at Wall Street law firm Cleary Gottlieb Steen & Hamilton,

"The [Dodd-Frank] Act evidences a love/hate relationship with the SEC. It assigns to the agency more rule makings and studies to be conducted than to any other agency, reflecting the Congress' reluctance to make hard decisions. At the same time, the Act imposes structural changes and controls, which suggests the Congress' lack of trust in the agency partly inspired by the SEC's failure to detect the Madoff scandal."

Even before the recent global financial crisis, questions concerning the adequacy of the SEC's resources to perform its required functions were regularly raised. According to Martin E. Lybecker of the law firm Perkins Coie, looking back to an earlier set of scandals involving mutual funds, "The scandals of 2003–2004 are unique in the history of the SEC's administration of the Investment Company Act but appear to validate the concern that the Commission still has insufficient resources adequately to survive the securities industry and to catch wrongdoers among those that it is responsible for regulating before serious harm has been done."

Since the financial crisis and the increase in SEC responsibilities under Dodd-Frank, these issues are now even more important. Perhaps most disappointing to many observers, Dodd-Frank did not attempt to rationalize or improve the US regulatory infrastructure. An opportunity to categorically reimagine the approach taken to regulating investment activity was dismissed out of hand. As Lybecker also observed, "Critically, the Act fails to reconfigure in any significant way the fragmented US regulatory structure, which currently encompasses fifty state-banking and securities regulators as well as multiple federal agencies."

The many cumulative mistakes that the SEC made in its investigations into Madoff's investment business remain highly disconcerting, especially in light of the further responsibilities being placed on the agency and the heightened expectations of investors today. To the extent that the SEC is mandated to "protect investors" and police the operation of the US financial markets, its failure to conduct a serious investigation into substantial allegations of fraud demonstrated how exposed American investors actually are. To put this into concrete terms, if the SEC investigation in 2006 would have taken adequate steps to issue subpoenas and thoroughly investigate the claims of Harry Markopolos, the Ponzi scheme would only have been a fraction of what it grew to be over the next two years. Inaction and incompetence by regulators can clearly have devastating consequences.

Madoff eventually admitted that his investment business was "just one big lie." Unfortunately, the SEC was unable to make that determination on its own and unaided. In the face of a well-respected Wall Street figure, SEC staff were simply unable to ask the right questions at the right times.

With the 2010 change in the control of the US House of Representatives, reports regularly circulated about attempts by the Republicans to repeal certain elements of Dodd-Frank, as discussed earlier. However, the Democrats retained control of the Senate and the White House in 2010 and again in 2012, leaving several significant hurdles in the way of any attempted amendments. Even if not repealed or significantly scaled back, it is highly unlikely that further reform will be passed in the foreseeable future.

As a result, the wide coalition of prosecutorial authorities, such as US Attorney's offices and state District Attorney's offices across the United States, and the Crown Prosecution Service in the United Kingdom, as well as the enforcement teams within the SEC and the FCA, will be left to make as much sense out of Dodd-Frank and AIFMD as they can, and enforce their provisions to the extent that their funding levels (and other priorities) permit. It is by these individuals walking their beats, along with those investors who elect to pursue their rights directly through civil litigation in the court system, that those individuals who ultimately cross the line and break the law are identified and prosecuted, and their actions measured out against the black letter of the criminal code, the statute book, the regulatory rule book and the common law itself.

PART THREE

THE FUTURE'S SO BRIGHT...

10: IT'S A SMALL WORLD

The Global Nature of Alternative Investment Management in the Twenty-First Century

It is because Britain is so well placed – with the right time zone, language and legal system – to provide financial services that the sector employs hundreds of thousands of people, not all of whom are on stonking bonuses ...
Boris Johnson, London Mayor

We cannot put enough money in China.
David Rubinstein, Carlyle Group

The uniform for private equity and hedge fund professionals in central London is well established by now: a bespoke suit from Savile Row and a colorful open-neck shirt.

Walking the streets of Mayfair, sharply dressed men working for these boutique financial firms populate the office buildings, restaurants, cafes and art galleries. Coming from a variety of countries near and far, the alternative investment community has adapted well to life in this fashionable bit of central London. The neighborhood, bounded by Park Lane, Oxford Street, Piccadilly and Regent Street, has become the international face of this new generation of financiers. Fans of Georgian architecture feel very much at home here. Gourmands are able to break bread at twenty Michelin-starred restaurants.

Nearby St James's is also popular with the hedge fund and private equity set. Located between the world-famous landmarks of Buckingham Palace and Trafalgar Square, buildings that once housed foreign ambassadors have now been divided up into offices that can accommodate trading floors for the new financial elite. Piccadilly (with its tourists) and Pall Mall (with its members-only private clubs) provide contrasting options for a post-lunch stroll. Fortnum & Mason admirably serves as a particularly upmarket corner shop, if you find yourself in dire need of a nice jar of jam.

Although private equity and hedge funds can be based any-where, New York and London play host to a disproportionately high number of them. Both cities have a long tradition of serving as international financial capitals. Each city has its own distinct appeal to prospective investment firms and their clients.

It was no surprise then that with the significant rise of private equity and hedge funds over the past two decades, these two cities would find themselves hosting so many of these firms. Perhaps what is surprising is the extent to which other financial centers of note, such as Frankfurt, Paris and Tokyo, did not see alternative fund managers flocking to their environs.

Boris Johnson, the erudite and refreshingly disheveled Mayor of London, made his support of the British financial sector clear in July 2012, when he urged his fellow politicians to stop banker-bashing. "It is time for British politicians to say it loud and clear and in unison: we need bankers, my friends! We need bankers who are not just cautious, owlish Polonious figures. We need bankers who are willing to take punts and put their necks on the line." Importantly, among the diverse and successful British banking community are a number of world-class private equity firms and hedge fund managers.

Two of the leading private equity firms in the United Kingdom are Permira and BC Partners. Founded in 1985 after the private equity team of Schroders was spun out, Permira is today one of the biggest private equity firms in Europe. Their investments include Genesys, a call center operator worth $1.5 billion; Natatim, an Israeli water irrigation company; Hugo Boss, the high-end clothier; and Telepizza, a Spanish restaurant chain. BC Partners has an equally diverse portfolio of investments, including

ComHem, a Swedish telecom company; Phones4U, a British retail mobile phone company; and GruppoCoin, an Italian fashion company.

British-based hedge fund firms are exceptionally diverse and vary greatly in size and structure. They include massive institutions such as Man Group, which is listed on the London Stock Exchange. Other well-known names include Brevan Howard Asset Management, CQS, Toscafund, Polygon Management, Ferox Capital Management, Boussard & Gavaudan, Caxton Associates, Cheyne Capital Management and Winton Capital, as well as large numbers of small- and medium-size managers based in lovely office buildings around St James's and Mayfair. London also has its fair share of colorful hedge fund characters. One who has received particular fame in recent years has been Anthony Ward of Armajaro Holdings. Ward earned the "Bond villain" nickname "Chocfinger" for his successful trading strategies involving cocoa, where at times he has reportedly bought up as much as 10 percent of the global supply.

In addition to being a location for fund managers to base their operations, the United Kingdom and Europe are also a prospective target for investing. Unfortunately, in recent years, with instability in the Euro and a macroeconomic crisis-of-confidence enveloping the EU, questions have been raised about the future prospects for Europe as an investment destination.

The financial crisis in Europe continued to rumble through 2012. In anticipation of a fire sale of deeply discounted loan and bond portfolios being unloaded by European banks in search of liquidity, leading private equity and hedge funds, such as Apollo, Avenue, Carlyle, Cerebus and Oaktree, raised billions of dollars in new capital to invest in distressed assets.

As David Rubenstein remarked in February 2012, "Europe is one of the world's greatest investment opportunities right now. There is no part of the world that will see so much assets sold at a discount as in Europe." At the same investing conference in Berlin, Leon Black noted, "The European credit situation is where we're spending a lot of time now." That same month, BC Partners announced that it had successfully launched a new fund with over $8 billion in investor commitments. Apax, Blackstone and Warburg Pincus were also in the market at this time raising new European funds. Unfortunately, choppiness in the market caused many investors to proceed with extra caution.

Sentiment turned again in regard to Europe's prospects in 2013. Reports circulated in February that Avenue Capital Group was raising a $500 million fund to invest in distressed European assets, demonstrating their apparent belief that the worst might be behind Europe and recovery is somewhere on the horizon.

Part of the reason that Britain has been so successful at maintaining its position as a center for financial services generally, and as a desirable home for private equity and hedge funds specifically, is that it has benefited from a highly effective regulatory system. However, the FCA (and its predecessor, the Financial Services Authority) has also been battling in recent years with its long-standing reputation as a "light-touch" regulator. Beginning in 2011, the tide began to turn within the British regulator. According to Tracey McDermott, the interim enforcement director, "Our view on enforcement has changed radically."

For example, it is estimated that the FCA now conducts about fifteen cases related to market abuse each year. In the United Kingdom and Europe, market abuse is a much broader offense than the simple insider trading crime as defined in the United States. High-profile investigations involving a number of City heavyweights, including David Einhorn of the hedge fund firm Greenlight Capital discussed earlier, have yielded great success. Einhorn was fined £7.3 million in connection with market abuse charges.

In November 2011, the UK regulator barred the compliance officer of a London-based hedge fund from working in financial services due to his failure to adequately supervise his firm's investing activities. After suffering huge losses in the volatile markets that followed Lehman's collapse, a senior trader at Dynamic Decision Capital Management entered into a fraudulent transaction involving deeply discounted bonds backed by diesel fuel from the autonomous Russian republic of Bashkortostan. Eventually, concerns were raised about the valuation of the bonds and whether they were simply being held to hide losses. The UK regulator ultimately determined that Sandradee Joseph did not fulfill her duties as Dynamic's compliance officer since she failed to investigate and act upon the information she received.

In 2012, a senior executive at JC Flowers, the private equity firm, was fined almost $4.5 million because of fraudulent invoices that he used. Ravi Sinha, chief executive officer of JC Flower's UK operations from 2005 to 2009, was fined by the FCA for misleading a portfolio company into paying falsified invoices issued by Sinha for his own personal benefit. The fine is one of the highest ever issued by the FCA (and its predecessor, the Financial Services Authority).

The UK regulator is also coming down hard on fund managers who lie to their investors. In May 2012, the FCA fined Alberto Micalizzi of Dynamic Decisions Capital Management, the hedge fund manager discussed above, $4.5 million in connection with allegations that Micalizzi lied to investors about the fund's performance. In an attempt to hide losses, Micalizzi purchased bonds at a deep discount and then recorded them at par on the fund's balance sheet.

Unfortunately, this change of heart has come too late for the prior Financial Services Authority as an institution. As noted above, during 2013, the Financial Services Authority was shut down, at least on paper. In its place, the Bank of England now has responsibility for overseeing British financial and investment firms, while the rebranded FCA can concentrate on investor protection and financial crime. Regardless of these high level changes, McDermott has made clear that this is not simply a short-term shift in enforcement priorities. "Maintaining credible deterrence is an important part of the regulator's going forward."

London must also adapt to the growing pile of new rules and regulations being promulgated by Brussels, the capital of EU bureaucracy. The latest salvo across the bow has been the Alternative Investment Fund Management Directive (AIFMD), discussed in earlier chapters.

Regulatory changes are a hot-button issue for Britain, since the financial sector based in London plays a crucial role in the country's current and future pursuit of economic prosperity. As its mayor, Boris Johnson, has made clear, "It is because Britain is so well placed – with the right time zone, language and legal system – to provide financial services that the sector employs hundreds of thousands of people, not all of whom are on stonking bonuses; indeed, most are on middling incomes. Collectively, they produce tens of billions – about 12 percent of government revenues – that go on schools, hospitals, welfare and roads."

AIFMD, like many EU directives, has lofty ambitions. It seeks to harmonize regulatory requirements for sponsors and managers of alternative investment funds (AIFs) across the European Union. AIFs are broadly defined to cover all non-retail investment funds not authorized for widespread distribution under the UCITS directive. As a result, hedge funds, private equity funds and a wide variety of other investment vehicles are AIFs and their management and administration fall within AIFMD. After over eighteen months of wrangling and back-room horse trading, AIFMD was finally passed in November 2010. AIFMD impacts managers and promoters of all AIFs and its reach extends to managers and advisers based outside as well as inside the European Union.

The road to AIFMD was not a straight one. Instead, it was filled with twists and turns due to the numerous power struggles that broke out along the way, both between the European Parliament and the European Commission, and between key member states. Criticisms of the legislative process that led to the final adopted text of AIFMD mounted up quickly. They included that the "one size fits all" approach failed to differentiate the unique risks posed by different types of funds, that the European Union's reaction was disproportionate to the industries' actual significance and that protectionist preference was the primary motivation behind the directive.

As Daniel Awrey of Oxford University has observed, "The EU has failed to mount a persuasive case for why the Directive represents an improvement over existing national regulatory regimes or prevailing market practices in several key areas. Furthermore, by attempting to shoehorn an economically, strategically and operationally diverse population of financial institutions into a single, artificial class of regulated actors, the EU has established what is in many respects a conceptually muddled regulatory regime."

Importantly, like its American cousin Dodd-Frank, AIFMD continues with the traditional regulatory approach followed on both sides of the Atlantic. The directive regulates the fund manager and not the fund itself. In addition to the expansive definition of AIFs, the geographic scope of AIFMD is also particularly broad, with all fund managers based in the European Union covered, as well as any non-EU managers who market their funds in the European Union. The AIFs themselves may be based either inside or outside the European Union.

The primary focus of AIFMD is on establishing consistent standards for the authorization and ongoing oversight of fund managers, including requirements related to conflicts of interest, risk management and liquidity. As a result of such harmonization, a new pan-European passporting regime will eventually be available, which serves as a "carrot" to complement the "stick" of further regulation.

However, AIFMD lacks any attempt to address the manner in which private equity and hedge funds are governed. This is a notable and unfortunate omission. No attempt was made as part of the AIFMD adoption process to better empower fund investors to effectively intervene in the management of the funds in which they invest, in order to address concerns which may have arisen or restrict the ability of the fund manager to act in a particular way under particular circumstances.

Additional layers of subordinate rules for AIFMD are being drafted and implemented during the course of 2013. As a result, a comprehensive assessment and appraisal of the directive is perhaps only possible in the years that follow. According to Awrey, "Perhaps not surprisingly given the broad nature of many of these requirements – to say nothing of the wide diversity of investment strategies, business models, conflicts of interest and other risks typically encountered in connection with different types of AIF – the Directive contemplates that the Commission will adopt level 2 implementing measures further specifying the precise substance of these requirements as they are intended to apply to each species of AIF. Accordingly, it is in many respects too early to evaluate the precise impact of these requirements in terms of the day-to-day conduct and practices of AIFMs."

Like most European legislation, AIFMD operates through harmonization of the laws of all member states of the European Union. Through common standards, like those applied to bananas, ladders and flashlights, AIFMD attempts to create a common rule book for all private equity managers from London to Athens, Lisbon to Tallinn.

As a general rule, the management of an AIF that is marketed within the European Union must be conducted by a manager authorized under AIFMD by the appropriate regulators in its home member state. EU managers managing EU funds could have the passport to market those funds in the European Union as early as 2013. No passports will likely be introduced for non-EU funds until 2015 at the earliest. As a result, onshore EU funds could have a significant marketing advantage over offshore funds for at least two years. This has led to accusations that, in fact, the directive is anti-competitive, and has as its primary motivation the establishment of a "Fortress Europe" protecting local managers.

When the passport eventually becomes generally available, allowing both EU and non-EU managers to market non-EU funds throughout Europe, those jurisdictions that have taken all the necessary steps to satisfy the AIFMD criteria to allow the fund to qualify for the passport will have a distinct advantage over those that do not. But the extent to which this will result in a change in the domicile of funds from one overseas jurisdiction to another is difficult to say. The main offshore jurisdictions (such as the Cayman Islands, Bermuda and the Channel Islands) appear confident that they are well-placed to benefit from the introduction of the AIFMD.

As mentioned above, non-EU managers, such as those based in the United States, for example, will not be able to obtain passports until 2015. Until then, they will need to market their funds by using the existing private placement regimes that operate in each individual EU member state. Although part of current market practice for many years, complying with dozens of different exemptions is a burdensome and repetitive process.

Once AIFMD is implemented by EU member states, US managers will be required to comply with certain "transparency" provisions of AIFMD. These relate to the production by the fund of an annual report, disclosure requirements to investors and periodic reporting to the local regulator covering such matters as the liquidity of the fund, risk management and leverage.

If the passport is made available to non-EU managers in 2015, a US manager will need to comply with all the provisions of AIFMD and then apply to an EU member state – the manager's "member state of reference" for the purposes of AIFMD – and the regulator in that state will, in effect, become the US manager's supervisor for compliance with AIFMD. The US manager will also need to appoint a legal representative in the member state of reference to act as its contact point with the local regulator.

Importantly, though, European managers benefit during the early years from the passport only with respect to European funds. For example, UK managers managing non-EU funds, such as Cayman funds, will also be excluded from using the marketing passport until 2015. Until then, UK managers must continue to market their non-EU funds in Europe through national private placement regimes. Once the passport becomes available for non-EU funds, the UK manager will need to comply with AIFMD in full.

Importantly, AIFMD defines "marketing" as offering of funds at the initiative of or on behalf of the fund manager. As a result, if an investor takes the initiative in approaching the fund manager and making an inquiry about the fund, then the fund manager will not be marketing its funds for the purposes of AIFMD. This distinction will be very important in practice. For example, a US fund manager will not be brought within the scope of AIFMD simply because he accepts investments from an EU pension fund manager. The fund manager would need to more actively market the fund to those investors in order for that to occur. Another related issue is internet presence. A US manager is likely to have a website that allows interested parties to access details of the funds. Although the manager will have taken the initiative by making the material on the website available, this should not be "marketing" for the purposes of AIFMD without some further overt act by the manager.

Fortunately, AIFMD provides exemptions if an EU manager has assets under management below certain thresholds. In general, AIFMD will not apply below either €100 million or, for unleveraged funds with no redemption rights for five years (such as private equity funds), €500 million. In such cases, however, registration with the local regulator, along with disclosure of investment strategies and trading information, will still be necessary, and AIFMD also allows the regulator to impose additional requirements.

By 2015, the European Securities and Markets Authority (ESMA) will also issue advice on whether the marketing passport conferred by the directive should be extended to non-EU AIFs, such as those formed in the Cayman Islands or the United States. The important question will ultimately be whether these non-EU funds can still be marketed under the private placement rules of each EU member state where marketing occurs, alongside the passporting regime described above. However, private placement rules in most countries are generally very restrictive and time-consuming.

The current private placement regimes are not likely to be available until at least mid-2018 when ESMA will decide whether national private placement regimes should be terminated. If terminated, then the passporting provisions will be the only option available for all private equity and hedge funds sold in Europe. In fact, in some European countries, such as Germany, the private placement regime may be discontinued in 2013. As a result, any private equity or hedge fund wishing to market itself to German investors will be required to be AIFMD-authorized.

Offshore financial centers – such as the Cayman Islands, Bermuda and the Channel Islands (Jersey and Guernsey) – are crucial to modern international finance, including private equity and hedge funds. Interestingly, the leading offshore financial centers all have strong historical and legal ties to the United Kingdom. British laws and traditions are still an important feature of daily life on these small islands.

It is important, however, to understand the precise role they play in order to evaluate their effectiveness, and their risks. Offshore financial centers exist as alternative legal and financial centers specifically because of the decisions by onshore financial centers to prohibit, either through regulation or taxation, certain structures or transactions. In essence, the needs that offshore financial centers seek to fulfill are created by the onshore financial centers. As the latter reconsider their attitudes toward alternative investment funds, the former will need to be proactive in finding other ways to facilitate innovation and flexibility.

Offshore financial centers share many common characteristics with one another. These include restricting access to the "offshore sector" to non-residents and limiting transactions to currencies other than the local currency. They often provide for the rapid formation of corporations and other entities with minimal taxation and ongoing reporting requirements.

As a result of initiatives launched by the Financial Action Task Force (FATF) and Organisation for Economic Cooperation and Development (OECD), offshore financial centers have moved away from simply offering bank secrecy to a wider focus on value-added services, such as investment funds, while maintaining their low tax regimes. These countries are expanding their regulatory power, fostering transparency and increasing disclosures requirements. With increased regulation come increased compliance costs and greater demands for the development of a "compliance culture."

Questions remain whether the OECD and the FATF are promoting "double standards," with offshore jurisdictions providing more transparency than many onshore jurisdictions are willing to do under similar circumstances. In some cases, onshore jurisdictions are looking to limit the outflow of capital due to "unfair tax competition," and are using the requirement to impose higher standards as a means to plug these leaks. Proponents of offshore jurisdictions continue to claim that these financial centers have a crucial role to play in enabling important financial participants to access the international capital markets.

As discussed in earlier chapters, many private equity and hedge funds make use of offshore companies and partnerships as part of their fund structure, in order to meet the needs of particular investors. A number of factors must be analyzed to determine the appropriate offshore jurisdiction for a particular fund. First and foremost, there must be no tax at the fund level. It is possible in some offshore jurisdictions to receive formal representations from the local fiscal authorities that the tax status of the fund will not be eligible for change for a predetermined number of years. Second, the local regulatory regime must be acceptable to investors while not proving unduly burdensome on the operation of the fund. Finally, there must be local service providers of sufficient calibre and experience to assist the fund effectively.

The process of establishing an offshore fund usually begins with preliminary answers to a number of related questions. What legal structures are available in the jurisdiction? What are the regulatory requirements (initial and ongoing)? How is the jurisdiction perceived by targeted investors? How will an interest in a vehicle established in this jurisdiction be taxed in the investor's home country? What are the costs and time requirements to launch a fund in this jurisdiction?

Typically, lawyers in the primary onshore jurisdiction where the manager is based (such as the United States or the United Kingdom) will draft the offering memorandum and oversee the formation of the offshore fund, the constituent documents for which will be prepared by the offshore lawyers. Because of the additional fees and regulatory regimes, both costs and timing requirements increase when offshore vehicles are used. Local regulators in an offshore jurisdiction will often require detailed information on the fund manager and any other sponsors. Further, there may be a requirement that certain activities relating to the fund (such as accounting or administration) occur within the jurisdiction, which could result in appointing service providers there rather than preferred partners elsewhere.

Interestingly, the market has developed a way to bring offshore vehicles onshore, so to speak, at least for the limited purpose of regulatory (or quasi-regulatory) oversight. The listing of offshore funds on onshore stock exchanges, such as the Irish Stock Exchange, has become an established feature of the hedge fund market. Principally, this is done not to facilitate trading in the fund's shares or units on a secondary market, but rather to meet the real or perceived needs of investors. For example, certain investors may be subject to external or internal prohibitions on the types of investments that they may make. Taking the shares of a Cayman hedge fund and listing them on the Irish Stock Exchange allows officials who work at the exchange to perform a quasi-regulatory oversight role with regard to the fund. As a result, investors with restrictions on what they own are now able to put their money into the hedge fund.

Simply put, the stock exchange is acting as a "regulator for hire." The would-be investors in the hedge fund take comfort in the independent, third-party staff of the exchange who review the various legal documents of the fund, as well as the periodic reports and notices that they are required to file under the exchange's rule book. Interestingly, the fund pays for the privilege of listing, demonstrating that there are other options to providing oversight and monitoring than simply tax-payer-funded government regulators. The exchange, therefore, operates as a commercial business that makes money from its reputation in the market, and is able to bridge the gap between "offshore" and "onshore" for all the parties involved.

Once funds are launched, they need to get their money invested quickly and profitably. For many private equity and hedge funds, the whole world is, indeed, their oyster.

For example, it is difficult to find a place on the map today where private equity is not active. The largest private equity firms today oversee business empires that span the entire globe. The private equity model has been successfully exported around the world and is being practiced in diverse regions, cultures and languages.

Since the global financial crisis began in 2008, private equity professionals have increasingly been looking East in search of the "next big thing" for private equity. At a time when Dodd-Frank is raising the compliance burden for operating funds in the United States, and the AIFMD attempts to create a "Fortress Europe," signs of optimism from elsewhere in the world are being well received. With both India and China producing annual growth rates of over 10 percent, while the United States languishes at under 3 percent, it is unsurprising these firms have begun looking at emerging and frontier markets. In India, Tata Capital has announced that it has signed up commitments of up to $800 million for its own private equity fund. KKR reportedly has $1 billion at work, despite the reluctance of family-owned Indian business to open up to international investors.

At the 2011 Milken Institute Global Conference in Beverly Hills, California, the biggest names in the private equity world, including the bosses of Carlyle, TPG and Apollo, championed China as an important market for private equity funds. More fearful souls might be put off by the risks that investors face in China, whether from arbitrary government bureaucrats or widespread graft and corruption. For the brave few, the opportunities are too good to resist. There may be as much as $50 billion raised for private equity investment in China, although it is difficult to identify sufficient targets that could put this much money to use effectively. Industry sources reported that in 2011 alone, over 100 China-focused funds were launched, having amassed a total of approximately $30 billion in commitments. By comparison, less than $7 billion was reportedly raised in 2009.

Hedge funds are also focusing on new international markets as well. 2012 was a record year for funds focusing on Asia, exceeding numbers previously seen at the last market peak in 2007. Importantly, an increasing share of these funds has managers actually based in Asia, including China, Japan and Australia. Some experts believe that China is now the fourth leading base for hedge fund managers, after the United States, the United Kingdom and Switzerland.

As a result, any decisions about how to regulate or react to private equity and hedge funds in the twenty-first century must take into account the international aspects of these industries and the declining ability of any one country to unilaterally dictate the terms on which those funds operate. In that respect, alternative investment funds have much in common with climate change!

David Rubinstein of Carlyle, who has long prioritized China as an investment destination, was fortunate enough to earn an invitation to the White House in January 2011 to meet Hu Jintao, China's president, in an exclusive session with President Obama. Rubinstein started his career in Jimmy Carter's White House, and once stated in 2010, "We cannot put enough money in China." He then made clear in April 2011 how he viewed the question of risk. "Political risk is as high in the United States as it is in emerging markets." For now, the opportunities in China are primarily for established Western private equity houses, but that advantage will not last forever. "At some point," Rubinstein reflected, "people in China or Brazil will say, 'Why can't we build a world-class private equity firm here?'"

Unsurprisingly, local firms are eagerly following Rubinstein's advice and are setting up private equity operations within these high growth emerging markets. The pursuit of high returns is no longer limited to the global heavyweights. In China, for example, the Fosun Group, a Chinese conglomerate with interests in mining, pharmaceuticals and real estate, announced in January 2011 that it would be forming its own private equity fund, with backing from Prudential Financial.

In the southern hemisphere, Patria, founded in Brazil by Luiz Otavio Magalhaes, has over $4 billion under management and produces 20 percent returns for investors. They recently sold a 40 percent equity stake in themselves to Blackstone. Notably, leverage has played little role to date in the success of private equity in Brazil, where interest rates can reach 20 percent a year. Instead, outsized returns are generated by operational improvements in the companies they buy, rather than simply relying on the dark arts of financial engineering. TPG head David Bonderman has remarked that "even Brazil is a China story."

There is also growing interest across Latin America generally for private equity. In March 2013, the Latin American Private Equity and Venture Capital Association announced that private equity and venture capital firms committed $7.9 billion to the region during the previous year. This number is over 20 percent higher than in 2011, with the total number of investments reaching 237, up almost 40 percent from 2011. Later that same month, Paul Capital, which traditionally focused on secondary private equity transactions, paid $40 million for an 18.2 percent stake in a publicly-traded fund managed by the Brazilian technology venture capital firm Ideiasnet.

There are even private equity firms in the Middle East. As the impact of the Arab Spring and its complex aftershocks continue to be felt across the region, there are still local and international private equity funds seeking to profit from restructuring and rescuing damaged businesses. For example, the female-owned Global Investment House in Kuwait, founded by Maha al-Ghunaim, is a diversified investment firm which oversees over $1.5 billion in private equity funds. There is also significant private equity activity in Turkey. Carlyle has a Middle East and North Africa fund, which launched in 2009, that does investments in Turkey. Saudi-based NCB Capital and Kuwait's Global Investment are also active.

Many of these funds operate on a traditional, Western basis. However, one of the most interesting developments in recent years has been the growth of Sharia-compliant private equity and hedge funds. Notably, Islamic finance is not confined to Muslim countries, but is spread over Europe, the United States and the Far East.

Simply put, Islamic finance is the application of the Sharia to the finance sector. Although it is most well known for its prohibition of interest, Sharia is, in fact, a wholly different "philosophy" from the conventional Western outlook of finance. The Sharia explains in detail the Islamic concepts of money and capital, the relationship between risk and profit, and the social responsibilities of financial institutions and individuals. Based on this philosophy, Sharia-compliant instruments and techniques have been developed and successfully used by Islamic finance units and customers worldwide in the funding of items such as property, ships, hotels and power plants.

The payment or receipt of all forms of usury (*riba*) is strictly forbidden by the Qur'an, as well as gambling and uncertainty. The purpose of this prohibition on interest is to prevent exploitation from the use of money by sharing in profit and loss. For Muslims, money should be used for a proper economic purpose and not treated as a commodity on which a return can be made by reference to time. Islamic scholars agree money is simply a means of exchange and not an asset, and should therefore not grow over time. However, capital can earn the returns derived from the productive use of capital.

There are a number of substantive prohibitions that also apply. In many ways, they are similar to the socially responsible investing parameters that have become fashionable in the last decade. For example, it is also forbidden for any Islamic institution or investment fund to deal in alcoholic drinks, pork, ham, bacon and related by-products, dead animals not slaughtered according to the rules of the Sharia, gambling machines, anti-social and immoral goods (such as tobacco, pornography and drugs), and armaments and destructive weapons.

Islamic investment funds operate by collecting investors' money and then investing it in Sharia-compliant trading activity companies. Complying with Sharia law is central to the value that these funds deliver. Therefore, all Sharia-compliant funds will have a Sharia committee or board comprised of Islamic scholars and practitioners who provide the Islamic financial institutions with guidance and supervision. The Sharia board members are independent of the Islamic finance institution and are not employees. Like an audit by an accounting firm, these boards often submit a Sharia audit for the annual report of the Islamic institution they represent and issue Sharia compliance certificates. The Sharia advisory board works closely with the bankers and lawyers to structure its investment activities so that they meet both Sharia and commercial requirements.

The ability of private equity and hedge funds, as well as a number of other types of alternative investment funds, to adapt themselves to Sharia law and operate under these constraints demonstrates how resilient their models actual are.

Islamic law, however, is not universally loved and admired. At least, not in the United States. In March 2011, the South Dakota state legislature debated several new bills that seek to limit the applicability of Sharia law by its courts, including in connection with financial transactions. Oklahoma previously adopted its own "Sharia ban," although implementation was delayed because of federal injunctions. Similar bills were being considered in other states at this time as well.

Much of the public discussion that has occurred so far has focused on the potential application of Sharia law in family law courts, or in connection with domestic disputes. The concern stems from a fear that local courts would seek to apply aspects of Sharia law when trying to reach difficult decisions between family members who are Muslim. However, the South Dakota bills were broader in their impact, expressly covering Sharia-compliant financial instruments, such as private equity and hedge funds, for example.

The growing importance of Sharia financing techniques in the global economy means that the adoption of such laws could potentially limit the ability of American firms and investors to actively participate in all aspects of the world economy, especially given the interconnectedness of the global economy in the twenty-first century and the increasing role played by private equity and hedge funds in contemporary financial markets.

The international expansion of private equity and hedge funds is good news for investors looking at where best to deploy capital in the coming years, but to what extent has recent regulatory and legal developments simply made the United States, the United Kingdom and Europe unappealing?

This is always going to be a very difficult question to try to answer. In the case of Dodd-Frank, limitations on proprietary investing under the Volker Rule discussed in earlier chapters may be influential at the margins when deciding how to allocate scarce investment capital or headcount. However, neither China nor India has the developed legal infrastructure, and ability to obtain certainty on important transactional questions, that the developed markets of the West can offer, although the significantly higher economic growth rates will continue to make them an attractive target for investment.

It is unclear what effect Europe's attempt to close its borders to private equity and hedge funds from third countries will have, but many seasoned and experienced investors based in the European Union will continue to know and prefer the best-of-breed when it comes to the fund managers with whom they are willing to entrust their money. So clearly a balancing of factors will eventually be required. The only question is how long it will take the bureaucrats in Brussels to let commercial reality trump regulatory fiefdom building.

Hopefully, legislators and regulators in the United States, the United Kingdom and Europe will acknowledge and accept that their writs are not without natural limitations. Market participants do value predictability and stability. But they also have options. As the private equity and hedge fund models continue to take root in more and more countries around the world, both champions and critics will need to recognize that more responsibility will need to be placed on the shoulders of the fund investors themselves, as national regulators will be increasingly focused on narrower and narrower bounds of malfeasance and frauds as they make do with lower headcounts and fewer resources.

11: FROM STRENGTH TO STRENGTH?

Private Equity and Hedge Funds, Their Investors and Life After the Global Financial Crisis

Venture capital is viewed as a creative industry, while the world considers private equity as finance, money men who do not create.
Steven Davidoff, *The New York Times*

Even before the recent financial market turmoil, regulators throughout the world were taking an increased interest in hedge fund activities. Fearful of such attention, the hedge fund sector on both sides of the Atlantic sought to head off further regulatory scrutiny by drafting self-regulatory codes of best practice.
Harry McVea, Bristol University

Despite the passing of years, and an unsatisfyingly limp reappearance in a 2010 sequel, the character Gordon Gekko from Oliver Stone's 1987 film *Wall Street* casts an awkward shadow across many private equity and hedge fund firms. The mantra of "greed is good" remains today a cultural touchstone by which various political or economic assertions are ironically judged.

But just as the greed on Wall Street is not only the greed felt within the investment banks, but also the greed felt by those bank's clients and counterparties trying to obtain an outsized profit from the trades they wish to execute, the greed that cuts across private equity and hedge funds is also found in the various institutional and individual investors who are eager to fund these capitalistic endeavors and pursue these promised profits. Greed, whether good or bad, is found everywhere in the financial markets, on both sides of each trade.

The greed in the hearts of the public pension fund seeking an 18 percent return on their money to fund the retirement obligations of their beneficiaries is not different in kind from the greed at the hearts of the private equity or hedge fund manager who agrees to help them earn the return. A moral philosopher might argue that the difference is, at most, simply one of degree.

Given the sustained resonance of the "greed is good" message, and the lambasting that, for example, the private equity industry received in 2012 during the US presidential elections, perhaps the time has come to take the public relations step that has served so many other down-and-out businesses in the past. Perhaps the time has come to "rebrand."

Stephen Schwarzman, chief executive of Blackstone, has even acknowledged that private equity is in need of a name change. When discussing private equity's public perception problems in January 2013, Schwarzman acknowledged that the 2012 election campaign seriously tarnished the industry's reputation. A branding exercise, therefore, might be in order. He noted how "corporate raiders" in the 1980s had successfully rebranded themselves as the "activist investors" of today.

The public's trust in private equity firms, what they do and how they do it is too important an issue to ignore anymore. The industry has previously survived an earlier rebranding exercise, when it shifted from "leveraged buyouts" in the 1980s to its current label, "private equity." Another change may be advisable.

When push-comes-to-shove, regardless of its current or future branding, private equity does work. Of course, not all the time, but much of the time and in a wide variety of circumstances.

Who saved Twinkies? Not the Occupy movement. Not "viewers like you" who support public broadcasting in America. Not the Obama administration.

When the world was close to losing their Twinkies, their Ding Dongs and their Ho-Hos, the private equity industry rode to the rescue, in the form of Apollo Global Management and C. Dean Metropoulos & Company. Future generations will have access to their snack cakes of choice because carried interest-earning private equity funds, staffed by current or aspiring members of the 1 percent, were willing to provide the lifeline that no one else could.

If this doesn't qualify for a Congressional Medal of Honor, then why are they even giving them out any more?

Hedge funds work, too – again, much of the time and in a wide variety of circumstances – which is why so much time is being spent now wringing our hands over their motives and impact on the larger financial systems. The fact that many funds do generate significant profits is what forces observers with strong moral compasses to contemplate whether those actions are ethical and justifiable.

For example, is it wrong for hedge funds to buy up deeply discounted Greek bonds in the hope of benefiting from an anticipated EU bailout?

Greek debt, initially in the hands of a small number of French and German banks, increasingly found its way during 2011 into the hands of hedge funds. The banks took the money on offer and walked away, while the hedge funds rolled up their sleeves and made themselves comfortable. By some estimates, €80 billion of Greek bonds were in the hands of independent investors, such as hedge funds, by the start of 2012.

How about food and farmland?

Fear moves prices, and as prices move, money can be quickly made or lost. Unsurprisingly, recent increases in the price of food on the global markets have meant that a number of investors, including hedge funds, have begun to look for outsized returns, or at least a hedge against runaway inflation, from farmland, water rights and agricultural businesses. Equally unsurprisingly, concerns soon arose of a "farm price bubble" driven by speculating hedge funds as the prices paid for arable land continued to increase year on year, just as fear over an uncertain future drove gold to all-time highs.

Any thoughts on usury?

As the global financial crisis lingered on, year after year, reports began to surface in the mainstream press of hedge funds acting as lenders-of-last-resort for various companies in distress. Unsurprisingly, these funds often required their borrowers to pay dearly for this money, especially when particularly complex funding structures were involved. With traditional sources of liquidity tapped out and shut down, many troubled companies had little choice than to take money wherever it was on offer. Unlike traditional bank loans, hedge funds need jaw-dropping rates of returns to keep their investors satisfied, and are willing to negotiate hard in order to get them. Stories eventually circulated of borrowers who ended up giving away significant shares of their revenue and equity to cover the costs of these loans.

According to Stephen Davidoff of *The New York Times*, "Hedge funds appear prepared to push for both the most aggressive terms and to be the actual one making the deal. They appear ready to risk public condemnation to do it."

Are there actually moral ways to invest that are superior to immoral investment strategies?

As discussed earlier, Sharia law makes these distinctions a central part of its financial philosophy. Certain moral decisions are made at a much earlier stage of the analysis of commerce and finance, and their consequences worked out through an analysis of the nature of money and the purpose of economic transactions. Even in the West, socially responsible investment has steadily gained in popularity over the last few decades. The Occupy movement had a unique opportunity to bring a similarly direct and critical analysis of the inner workings of Wall Street, but for its own reasons ultimately focused its attention elsewhere.

Underlying many of the criticisms lobbed at private equity and hedge funds is a suspicion that they are not playing by the rules, and that somehow the money they make for their ultimate investors is fatally tinged with corruption, illegality or immorality. Identifying and addressing these subjective concerns is, perhaps, the final, and in many ways the most troublesome, step that must be taken in the ongoing examination of alternative investment funds and their role in our lives today.

Several critical trends can be readily identified in today's private equity and hedge funds which, should they continue, will impact the structuring and marketing of these funds in the near future, including shifting investor composition, increasing intermediation and increasing concentration.

As discussed several times earlier, large pension funds are making increasing allocations to alternative investment funds. Due to the limited size of their investment staff, these sizeable sums of money must be invested in significant increments, so as a result only certain fund managers have the bulk and infrastructure in place to accept these checks. Questions have been raised about whether, in the absence of effective and appropriate regulatory enforcement, these investors have dedicated the appropriate resources to overseeing their investments, and the risks that arise from them. Rather than reflexively passing more and more regulations when the effectiveness of current rules are dubious, perhaps more thought should be given to how better to train and prepare investors to protect their own interests over the long term.

In addition, the rise of new entrants to alternative investment funds over the past decade, due to an insatiable demand from institutional and high net worth investors for stonkingly high returns, as well as the low barriers to entry for launching funds, has fuelled the growth of intermediaries providing advice, assistance and access. Placement agents and consultants, representing the interests of fund managers and investors, respectively, are becoming more influential, leading to more efficient fundraising efforts. Until the Madoff debacle cast aspirations on their value-added, funds of funds had also been showing steady growth recently as a percentage of funds raised. The need for intermediaries demonstrates quite clearly that investing in private equity and hedge funds requires additional expertise rather than simply the ability to effectuate a wire transfer of funds from one bank account to another.

Although the number of fund managers has again begun to increase, a general concentration of assets within the top tier is becoming evident. As discussed earlier, smaller fund managers appear increasingly vulnerable to competitive pressure from larger firms with more product-lines and more name-recognition. Consolidation among fund managers, within and across asset classes, looks to increase.

Despite initial concerns over the viability of some of the listed private equity and hedge fund managers that came to market both before and soon after the start of the global financial crisis, more recent indications are that their performance may have made a significant turn for the better. For many large publically listed alternative managers, 2012 ended well. Apollo, Blackstone, Fortress and KKR produced strong financial results in the fourth quarter, benefiting from stable financial markets and access to low-cost borrowings, which benefited both private equity and hedge funds.

Identifying new groups of potential investors will be crucial for the continued success of private equity and hedge funds in the next decade. Over-dependence on a single customer demographic is a high-risk proposition in any business. Retail investors, for example, are both numerous and under-allocated, although regulatory burdens and transaction costs are thought to make them impracticable in any significant numbers. On the other hand, the importance of large investors with frequent allocations has led a growing number of small- and medium-sized fund managers to sell equity in themselves in exchange for significant commitments to investors in future funds. The answer may be found in the continued globalization of the industry, as more investors around the world begin to make allocations to private equity and hedge funds the centerpiece of their portfolios.

As discussed in earlier chapters, the alternative investment fund industry is inherently international with both funds and fund managers structured and operating on a cross-border basis. Preferred vehicles vary significantly, however, from country to country as a result of widely divergent regulatory and fiscal regimes. As investors are approached in more and more countries, structures capable of accommodating their unique needs can rapidly become complex and expensive. Lack of tax transparency, permanent establishment risks, value-added taxes applicable to fund manager fees and withholding taxes on distributions to investors all impede the use of a single simplified fund structure across multiple jurisdictions.

But as they say, where there is a will, there is a way. For example, eliminating structural impediments within Europe and between the United States and leading developed countries would foster the efficient allocation of capital to private equity and hedge funds. Ultimately, these flows could benefit financial markets and investee companies globally, by increasing liquidity and offering further financing options to businesses in need of expansion or growth capital. Unfortunately, the trend since 2008 has generally been in the opposite direction.

The question for champions of alternative investment funds then becomes, simply put, how to get more people comfortable with the things that private equity and hedge funds want to do with their money once they have raised it from willing investors.

What should be done when securities in the public markets are mispriced?

Hedge funds methodically and systematically attempt to profit from trading opportunities in securities and other financial instruments. If estimates are correct that half of all trades on the New York Stock Exchange and London Stock Exchange are conducted by hedge funds, then the liquidity on which these markets depend is being provided by the hedge fund managers, and their willing investors. Were these funds to suddenly withdraw from the market, liquidity would rapidly dry up.

Much has been written over the years about what makes for a good investor. Analytical skills, memory and pattern recognition are believed by many to play a significant role. The pejorative "casino capitalism" is often lobbed at the modern financial markets, making the conduct of investment activities, and the detailed decision-making processes that support those activities, the moral equivalent of gambling. However, the question of whether the shares of Apple are fairly priced today is not the same as the question of whether the next roll of a pair of dice will add up to seven or not. They are fundamentally different questions, although to many, if not most, of us, the way we would answer each question is the same. We would simply guess. We would guess whether Apple shares will go up or down over the next month, and we would guess whether the next number rolled at a craps table would be seven.

Guessing leads to very poor investment returns. By contrast, those who possess the demonstrable skills that operate at the heart of effective investing can demonstrate sustained investing success. Not always, of course! No one wins in the market all the time, everyday.

Where can someone develop these skills away from the bright lights of a Bloomberg terminal and the loud noises of a trading floor? Some believe that skill and expertise in chess can be a good indicator of a successful investor. In fact, many hedge fund managers can be found who have had great success with this ancient and subtle game. Peter Thiel of Clarion Capital, Anna Hahn of DE Shaw and Boaz Weinstein of Saba Capital Management are a few of the well-reported examples.

Investing is about seeing patterns, in the markets and in the world around us. The person who sees the pattern clearer and earlier than others has the opportunity to profit from that knowledge. The person who fails to see that same pattern, or sees it later and only partially, stands to lose money.

The global financial crisis, and the volatility it unleashed in markets around the world, provided ample chances for fund managers to take a view and make a "bet." Often this took the form of "betting against" a company or even a country. As Greece, Italy and Portugal struggled, astute investors racked up big wins. Once those profits were booked, the funds went off in search of other big scores. Even Hungary, which is not in the Eurozone, eventually ended up in their cross-hairs during the autumn of 2011, due to its unfortunate trait of having one of the highest foreign currency debt to gross domestic product ratios in the world.

Often I have been asked, "Do you believe in hedge funds?" I answer that question with one of my own, "Do you believe in talent?" This more fundamental question is at the very heart of so much of our daily lives, as well as our philosophy, that it can prove a better entry point into a discussion on the proper role of alternative investment funds in contemporary finance than many other more politically slanted questions. Do you believe in Lionel Messi, the Argentinean superstar who plays soccer for Barcelona FC? Do you believe in any basketball, baseball or Olympic sporting legend who consistently outperformed his or her opponents on a regular basis? Do you believe that some authors, composers, musicians and painters are simply better than the rest? If so, then you believe in talent.

Although it would be politically expedient to deny that investment talent actually exists, in order to indulge in the allegations of "casino capitalism," the short answer is that, although never perfect, some investors are clearly better than others, and a small handful are better than most. Recognizing this is the first step toward a sensible and effective response to hedge funds.

What should be done with underperforming, undervalued companies?

Left to their own devices, some of these businesses will be allowed simply to stumble along for several more years, if luck is on their side. Many of them, however, will fail. Ultimately, their competitors will eat away at their market share and dwindling profits. A failing business is rarely a pretty sight to behold. The uncertainty builds over time. Bad decisions are followed by worse decisions. Some jobs may be preserved in the short term, but by failing to correctly diagnose and treat the illness that is killing the business, the fate of the business is sealed. No one benefits in the long term from ignoring these realities.

One pernicious myth surrounding private equity should be debunked once and for all. Private equity isn't looking for healthy, successful companies. Healthy, successful companies do not wake up one morning and find one or more private equity firms circling them. These companies are, in fact, generally fully priced in the markets by their investors, and any short-term inconsistencies in these views on value can be quickly smoothed out by the hedge funds discussed just above. By contrast, private equity firms seek their profits by focusing on companies that are in a steep or prolonged decline, but have still within them the seeds of potential future success.

If there are no serious problems in a business to solve, how will a private equity firm ever be able to conduct the extensive restructuring necessary to boost its value to the level needed for the high investment returns its investors demand? Put another way, the young couple in search of a "fixer-upper" home will not be attracted to a property already refurbished, or in mint condition. By definition, they will only be interested in a house that is in need of fixing up. They will be looking for a run-down house in an otherwise good neighborhood. They will be looking for the next up-and-coming part of town where properties can be repurposed and redesigned in order to fit the needs of new residents in the years to come. They are not looking for a model home on a new development that has just been completed.

By focusing on companies that are in the "danger zone," private equity is working with companies whose risk profiles are not the same as most other businesses. This important observation has significant repercussions to any attempt to analyze the long-term effect of private equity on the companies in which it invests.

Just like it is unfair to say that an emergency room doctor killed a quarter of his or her patients, since perhaps three-quarters of them would have died if he or she had not intervened, it is equally wrong to focus exclusively or disproportionately on those companies that are not ultimately saved by private equity firms. If the private equity industry can save four out of every five companies it tries to rescue, and as a result of restructuring and refinancing, most of the jobs at these surviving businesses are maintained, then private equity makes a significant contribution to the economy.

Paul Levy, co-founder of private equity firm JLL Partners, once put the purpose of private equity in very clear terms. "We want to build businesses. Nobody wants to fire people. We want to retain all of the value-added, high-quality people that work at these companies. But it's like any other endeavor. If there are more people there to make shoes than needed, you can't keep the people. It's not about wanting to get rid of people. It's about wanting to make the company operate on a size and scale that's commensurate with its opportunities and its revenues such that it can make profits and then build the business. It's as simple as that."

As has been discussed a number of times in earlier chapters, private equity funds have been subject to increased scrutiny since 2008. Two relatively distinct perceptions of private equity and what these actually do have developed. On the one hand, these funds seek to restructure and rebuild underperforming companies that desperately need expertise and capital to compete. On the other hand, these funds can be highly effective mechanisms for generating large amounts of wealth for a handful of senior professionals. In the twenty-first century, private equity funds operate in and around the intersection of these two perceptions.

Private equity clearly plays an important role in the wider financial markets. Often, these funds are willing to pay substantially more for a target company than another company in the same sector would. A series of acquisitions could see valuations for an entire industry segment, such as health care, substantially increase. To pay these prices, a private equity fund requires debt, and lots of it. When debt is cheap, it is easy for these funds to set their sights on larger and larger targets. Like the typical house purchase, examined earlier, a private equity firm will put up a relatively small amount of capital as equity and borrow the rest from a bank. As a result, another common term for private equity is leveraged buyouts. "Leverage" refers to this dependence on borrowed money.

Before the financial crisis, debt to earnings ratios exceeded six times in both the United States and Europe, but have fallen significantly since then. With interest rates so low in recent years, savvy investors seeking yield have put their money into so-called junk bonds. Private equity funds are increasingly using these high-yield bonds as an alternative to bank debt, which coincidently make them very good customers for Wall Street, generating large amounts of fees, and profits, for the major investment banks.

A frequently asked question, however, is what good (if any) does private equity actually do for the real economy? Critics have argued strongly in the negative for several years, and only recently has the industry attempted to provide its own answer. In April 2012, the Private Equity Growth Capital Council released a promotional video trumpeting the important contributions made by private equity firms to the larger economy, as part of the trade association's "Private Equity at Work" public relations campaign. The video focused on KKR's investment in battery maker Rockwood Holdings, and painted a very positive picture of one company's experience with private equity practitioners.

Of course, as mentioned earlier, companies that accept private equity money occasionally fail, and with failure inevitably comes an allocation of blame. However, far more companies take the money, expertise and management support that private equity provides them and successfully renew their companies' prospects for the future. There are real and tangible benefits provided by these turnarounds and rescues that cannot be dismissed as mere financial engineering or asset stripping.

Private equity's footprint in the real economy is much broader than most people realize. It is estimated that over 1,800 private equity firms currently operate across the United States, each with their own particular investment niche. There are approximately 14,200 companies in the Unites States alone that are financed by private equity funds. Clearly, each and every employee at these companies, together with their families and the various shops, stores and businesses they support, directly benefit from private equity in a real and tangible way.

In addition, another obvious social good that private equity accomplishes, and has been discussed several times above, is to provide high rates of return to the pension plans, endowments and other investors that entrust their beneficiaries' money to each new private equity fund. Retired teachers, police officers, firefighters and civil servants, who have spent their working lives providing essential services to their communities, directly benefit from private equity. World-class universities driving the boundaries of knowledge out further and further each year, while developing the talent needed to address the biggest challenges now facing us, directly benefit from private equity. According to Steve Klinsky of New Mountain Capital, "The returns delivered by private equity over the last decade far exceed the rate of return from the Standard & Poor's 500-stock index over the same period and are critically important to help pension plans and endowments achieve their own benefit goals."

Is that enough, though?

Clearly PE continues to wrestles with a genuine PR problem. In July 2011, Steven Davidoff, in his prestigious and widely read "Deal Professor" column in *The New York Times*, laid down the open indictment against private equity quite succinctly. "Venture capital is viewed as a creative industry, while the world considers private equity as finance, money men who do not create."

What about all that borrowed money, then?

As discussed above, a key contributor to private equity's success has traditionally been its ability to use borrowed money on top of the private money provided by large institutional investors to buy a target company and multiply the returns from restructuring and reselling that company in a few years' time. Of course, not all private equity funds are dependent on huge levels of borrowed money to generate their high returns. Golden Gate Capital, for example, closed its fourth fund in October 2011, with $3.5 billion in commitments, and uses only limited amounts of leverage when making its acquisitions.

Unfortunately, when it is used, leverage magnifies both gains and losses. So when a leveraged investment goes wrong, it tends to go very wrong. Using borrowed money as part of an investment strategy, regardless of whether you are a private equity fund, a hedge fund or just some guy at a casino in Atlantic City maxing out his credit cards and waiting for the dice on the craps table to fall a different way, increases risk by increasing the extremes to which the results will be magnified. The arithmetic is straightforward, but unforgiving and relentless.

Maybe it's the tax loopholes that they take advantage of?

Obama's re-election in November 2012 means that the shadow of carried interest tax hikes will remain over the industry for years to come. The administration estimates that it could raise $13 billion over ten years. Two Democratic representatives, Sander Levin and Charles Rangel, introduced the Carried Interest Fairness Act of 2012, which still sits in the House Ways and Means Committee awaiting next steps.

The uncomfortable truth about changing the tax treatment of carried interest is that it wouldn't make that much of a difference in terms of tax revenues. As Steve Judge, the president and chief executive of the Private Equity Growth Capital Council, observed in March 2013, the Joint Committee on Taxation, a nonpartisan committee of Congress, has estimated the additional tax revenue from carried interest at just $16.85 billion over ten years. Importantly, this estimate is based on some unproven assumptions. Even taking that amount as a given, Judge stressed this amounts to only 3.1 hours of government spending. When looking at the uncertain consequence of taking away this incentive for investing in troubled companies which can drive economic growth, it seems to be an unsatisfying trade-off.

The lack of overt concern and campaigning from the industry recently leads many observers to believe that private equity firms are either comfortable that they can pass the costs of a tax change on to investors, in terms of higher carried interest rates, or that there would be ways to structure around higher tax rates in the fund documentation. Tax planning involving the use of loan structures or offshore entities was quickly floated by different experts, although any eventual tax legislation could be updated readily to eliminate these work-arounds.

Of course, as the Obama administration prepares to raise taxes further on its highest earners, there are always other options. Perhaps this is the most important thing that wealth ultimately brings its recipients – options. Having choices means grudging acceptance is only one alternative, among others. For example, London, and its charismatic mayor Boris Johnson, has made it clear that he is ready and willing to welcome those super-wealthy financiers, including displaced private equity and hedge fund managers, who feel that the United Kingdom might actually be a better home for them.

As debate over private equity continues in many quarters, some of the biggest players in the industry are diversifying into other areas of high finance. Blackstone Group, for example, has now turned its attention to investment banking.

Some casual observers might be surprised that an alternative investment manager would become interested in underwriting securities offerings and earning commissions, rather than the more lucrative carried interest that has become the holy grail for many financial professionals. But with the highly accommodating tax treatment of carried interest increasingly under attack, and the future prospects for traditional "leveraged buyouts" still being questioned, it's not difficult to see the logic in diversifying revenue streams.

Schwarzman, it should not be forgotten, started his life on Wall Street as a highly successful investment banker. Competitors Apollo and KKR have already secured their own licenses to enter the underwriting business, and KKR has developed a very successful underwriting team that contributes $100 million each year in revenue. Large private equity firms are increasingly evolving away from their traditional business model, which allowed the general partners of these funds to wait patiently for the carried interest to start flowing. When it did arrive, the preferential tax treatment made it all worthwhile.

Public shareholders, however, are not known for their patience. Since listing their equity interests on stock exchanges, these private equity firms have had to become responsive to this new constituency. The public pensions funds and endowments and other institutional investors that entrust money with these firms are often taking the same long-term view on returns that the general partners have preferred. Public shareholders, by contrast, need returns delivered on a more regular basis.

Although the private equity model has survived the global financial crisis largely intact, its critics will allege that this broadening of the organizational chart demonstrates that these firms lack discipline, and are simply pursuing profit wherever they can find it in the market. Of course, the actions of the top tier of the private equity industry do not reflect the hundreds of firms who are still active in rescuing troubled companies and assisting them in securing their long-term prospects. Over-generalizing from the decisions of a handful of publicly listed firms would be a clear mistake.

Wall Street is still coming to grips with the consequences of the recent financial meltdown. It is unsurprising to see firms experimenting with different configurations and business models. Just as institutional investors drive much of Wall Street's profits from their activities in the public markets, they similarly drive most of the profit that private equity firms generate in the private markets.

Ultimately, it is these institutional investors, more so even than the public shareholders of Blackstone, Apollo and KKR, who sit in judgment on their effectiveness. Of course, questions over potential conflicts of interest will continue to swirl around any financial service firm that has more than one line of business. At this stage, there are no clearer answers on whether private equity firms can manage these conflicts than the answers provided by the investment banks. Monitoring, disclosure and oversight are still crucial.

Initial public offerings and other securities activities have a radically different risk profile than sophisticated buyers and sellers setting the price on a private company in a fully negotiated trans-action. Legitimate questions can and should be asked about how an underwriting business is best integrated within a larger alternative fund management business. However, traditional fund manage-ment business, focusing on both mutual funds for retail clients and segregated accounts for institutions, have been regularly integrated into underwriting and brokerage firms over the years.

The success of Blackstone's foray into underwriting work will ultimately be judged by their success at generating meaningful revenue while avoiding the higher risks. Perhaps the more important question, which like all questions most worth answering is at its heart a philosophical one, is at what point in time Blackstone (or Apollo or KKR) ceases to be a private equity firm at its heart, and becomes some other form of financial or investment enterprise.

We shouldn't forget that there was a time only a few decades ago when no one had heard of private equity.

Of course, neither private equity nor hedge funds are foolproof. This has been proven in the real world again and again, and recounted in detail in earlier chapters. The men and women who run these firms are, of course, only human. Some make eye-watering profits, others lose their shirts. Since the beginning of the global financial crisis, there has been a steady stream of stories in the press about the bigger losses.

For example, 2011 was a noticeably difficult year for the titans of private equity. Blackstone posted significant losses as did KKR and Apollo. Terra Firma, the UK private equity house headed by the charismatic Guy Hands, lost serious money on their short-lived venture into the music industry, through their acquisition of music giant EMI.

It is naive to think that these funds are all "one-way bets" and that the unforgiving laws of the market don't apply to them. All investors make mistakes, both large and small, on a frustratingly regular basis. Often though, when a fund loses money, it loses a spectacular amount of money.

Not every company that a private equity firm backs, therefore, is ultimately a success. Bad investments are a frustratingly regular occurrence. As discussed earlier, the two largest contributors to profit are carried interest payments when investments are finally realized and regular management fee revenue. If portfolio company sales dry up, or are far less than expected, the stream of carried interest will dry up. Similarly, if portfolio company values are written down, then the basis against which the management fee can be charged will also be lower.

For example, the biggest leveraged buyout in history was the acquisition of TXU (originally known as Texas Power and Light) in 2007 by KKR, TPG and Goldman Sachs. Even accomplished investor Warren Buffett managed to lose money on his investment in the company's bonds. Now renamed Energy Futures Holdings, the company has had a difficult time under its new owners. Low natural gas prices and significant customer losses have strained a balance sheet carrying $35 billion in debt. In a 2012 filing with the SEC, KKR reported that it held its TXU investment at a valuation of about 10 cents on the dollar.

In January 2012, *The New York Times* turned its attention to Marc Leder, a Romney fundraiser and co-founder of Sun Capital, a large private equity fund. In particular, the newspaper began to focus on the record of Sun's portfolio companies during the global financial crisis, and its claim that since 2008 one-fifth of its over 120 portfolio companies had filed for bankruptcy. Despite these setbacks for Sun Capital investors, Leder appeared to be still enjoying the benefits of success, with reports of his partying and socializing appearing in the tabloids. Labeled a "private equity party boy," Leder was keen to point out that this is not an accurate portrait of his life, or his lifestyle. In response to these stories, Leder observed that "rather than reporting on how I spend 340 days and nights of my year, the media likes to report on the other 25." Interestingly, despite Leder's impressive record for private equity investing, this experience and acumen didn't prevent him from investing with Bernard Madoff, and subsequently losing his money when the Ponzi scheme unraveled.

Fallibility is also found in ample supply among hedge fund managers. Contrary to the self-serving rumors and the occasional conspiracy theories that bubble up, hedge fund managers are neither omniscient nor diabolically lucky. They are simply men and women who have demonstrated investment ability and have been given the opportunity to set up their own firms and manage money with few limitations.

They can make mistakes and often do. Although some fraud has occurred over the years, most hedge funds operate without even the hint of fraud or wrongdoing. Some, surprisingly, are even victims of fraud themselves.

In May 2012, Alex Getelman, head of a general contracting firm called Aragon, pled guilty in a Manhattan court room to defrauding hedge fund giant Citadel Investment Group out of $1 million in connection with office space that Aragon was fitting out in the prestigious office building located at 601 Lexington Avenue. Citadel, led by founder Kenneth Griffin, recovered well in 2011, after having suffered serious losses in the market in 2008. Clearly, however, even astute investors can, on occasion, be swindled.

Another recurring feature of hedge fund managers is that, on occasion, some will realize that they can no longer read the market as well as they once could, and as a result, they will simply walk away. In recent years, a number of high-profile hedge fund managers eventually decided that it was better for them, and all concerned, to simply hand investors back their money, rather than try to figure out which way the market was heading – John Arnold of Centaurus (2012), George Soros (2011), Carl Icahn (2011), Chris Shumway (2011) and Stanley Druckenmiller (2010). Not all hedge fund managers, however, are so straightforward with their investors when they realize that they have lost their ability to beat the markets.

As a result of this reluctance to admit defeat, one lingering effect of the global financial crisis has been the proliferation of so-called "zombie funds." In a zombie fund, assets of formerly successful hedge funds remain locked up and out of reach from investors, despite no significant progress toward either renewed high returns or an orderly liquidation. Meanwhile, the fund manager and other service providers continue to earn their fees from the investors. At the height of uncertainty in the market in late 2008, it was estimated that as much as $175 billion in hedge fund assets was locked up and unavailable for redemptions. In mid-2012, some observers believed that as much as $50 billion could still be locked up.

As discussed earlier, hedge funds traditionally include lock-up provisions in the constitutional documents of the fund in order to give the manager a mechanism that allows them to avoid a disorderly liquidation of the fund akin to a "run on the bank." In that less-than-optimal scenario, early redeemers can enjoy disproportionate access to the more liquid (and therefore more valuable) assets of the fund. Investors who try to redeem subsequently can be left with less valuable assets to sell, causing a rapid collapse in net asset value.

To avoid this downward spiral, the fund manager is empowered to suspend redemptions from all investors in order to maximize returns for all investors. Some investors, however, eventually began to feel frustrated at not being allowed access to their money, and started to go to court to enforce their rights. Courts in the Cayman Islands and Delaware have honored these requests and forced the funds to return money. In anticipation of suing, or simply to apply pressure to reluctant fund managers, investors can also seek to enforce their rights to audit the books of a fund, or even attempt to compel the fund manager to make use of a third-party valuation firm.

Any prospective investor considering writing a check to a private equity or hedge fund must recognize that they are not in a "no lose" situation. In addition to the promised returns, they must be comfortable with the loss of some, or all, of their money. Bank accounts, backed by the government, pay the mediocre rates of interest that they do because the risks to investors are minimal. The high rates of return that can be earned from alternative funds are in a very real way the fair price that is being paid based on the risks the prospective investor is about to take on (whether they realize it or not).

Do private equity and hedge funds present systemic risks to the financial system?

This is a very important question that gets batted around on a regular basis, and raised its head yet again early in the global financial crisis. Their champions say "no" because they are not deeply interconnected with other significant financial and investment firms in such a way as to create a "domino effect" should a large private equity or hedge fund firm fail. Regardless of the lack of any hard evidence that private equity or hedge funds played any meaningful causal roll in the events leading up to the near-collapse of global financial markets, opponents have used it as a justification for throwing more government resources at these funds, regardless of other more pressing priorities that remain under-funded and unresolved.

Private equity funds were clearly impacted by the global financial crisis. The volatility and uncertainty lowered expectations for many private equity firms, at least in terms of deal size, for example. As mentioned earlier, in 2007, TXU was snapped up for over $40 billion by KKR, TPG and Goldman Sachs. In the years that followed, a ceiling of $5 billion seemed to be in effect, with mega deals relegated to the past. As Steven Davidoff of *The New York Times* remarked in March 2012, at the time of the Carlyle IPO, "Private equity is becoming a tougher business as the low-hanging fruit – inefficient companies – becomes harder to find." However, there has been no serious academic assertion that the failure of either a private equity investment or an entire private equity fund could have anything approaching the impact on the overall financial system as a run on a commercial bank.

Critics of hedge funds point to the strong ties that exist today between hedge funds and the rest of the investment banking superstructure. For example, many hedge funds use derivatives as a means to effectively and efficiently pursue their investment strategies. Warren Buffett once famously referred to derivatives as "financial weapons of mass destruction," although his own company, Berkshire Hathaway, has made hundreds of millions of dollars in profits from trading derivatives. The financial news website, thestreet.com, went so far as to publish an article in 2010 with the succinct headline, "Warren Buffett is a Hypocrite."

Questions are often raised about the reliability of hedging strategies employed by both hedge funds and the leading investment banks. The $2 billion loss suffered by JP Morgan Chase in May 2012 led many commentators to explicitly question the ability to measure and offset risk through arcane and complex trading strategies. Comparisons were swiftly made to the collapse of Long-Term Capital Management in 1998. No matter how "inevitable" a market movement or correction may be in the long term, short-term volatility is still highly unpredictable. When you throw leverage into the mix, it can be difficult to maintain positions into profit when margin calls and other factors pressure you to close out the trade and limit escalating losses.

In addition, critics point to the important personal linkages between hedge funds and investment banks as well. Vikram Pandit, who eventually became chief executive officer of Citibank, first joined the bank when it bought his hedge fund business, known as Old Lane Capital. But these connections are decreasing, instead of increasing. In addition to prohibiting proprietary trading, the Volker Rule also limits the stake any bank can have in a private equity or hedge fund managers to 3 percent. This has driven the exodus of hedge fund teams from leading investment banks in the last few years. The effect that this diaspora on the industry remains to be seen, but the case in which these business units have shifted out of banks and transitioned to independent existence seems to undermine the assertions that these links were somehow dangerous.

It is important to always remember that there are many participants in the public and private markets at any one time. For all of the money they might earn when they are successful and all the publicity they have garnered in recent years, the simple truth remains that private equity and hedge funds only make up a small portion of the total international financial system.

As a result, with general rules concerning transactions and overall operations in place to regulate the markets, and all the parties transacting in these markets at any one time, attention can turn now to the more specific concern of investor protection.

The global financial crisis is serving as an important catalyst for recognizing and prioritizing concerns about how private equity and hedge funds are structured and operated. These concerns warrant a vibrant debate by academics and practitioners, as well as investors and savers.

Raising new funds has become more difficult, and fund managers face more demanding investors. Vivid memories still remain of how many fund managers made free use of their broad powers in the fund documentation to their own advantage. As discussed earlier, investors today are increasingly willing to use whatever contractual and other rights are available to them in order to protect their interests. Threatening and pursuing litigation against fund managers is now a ready tool for the disgruntled investor. This is a very positive development that has not garnered the general recognition and support that it deserves.

Investors in private equity and hedge funds can address many of the challenges that they currently face when they are adequately empowered with both the information necessary to monitor the ongoing compliance of the fund manager with its duties and obligations to the fund and the effective means through the legal documentation of the fund to ensure that any breaches that may occur are remedied. Such well-armed investors do a good service not only for themselves, but also for their fellow investors and other participants in the financial markets generally.

Prospective fund investors, however, must overcome any remaining inertia or apathy, and acknowledge their obligation to themselves and their ultimate beneficiaries to fully negotiate, and adequately oversee, their investments in these funds. Accepting terms offered on a "take-it-or-leave-it" basis, or failing to engage with the fund manager on an ongoing basis, will leave the real problems facing many private equity and hedge funds unsolved. Fund investors must also realize that the traditional mechanism for voicing displeasure toward a fund manager – refusal to participate in the next fund or to put more money in the current fund – is often an inadequate solution. Concrete and immediate action is often the only effective way to address the problems that arise in these funds.

Alternative investment funds clearly serve an essential role in the global financial markets. Regardless of any short-term concerns, they will remain a feature of these markets for years to come. Simply wishing them away, together with the talented men and women who run them, is not a meaningful strategy. Neither is ignoring them. As a result, issues surrounding their operation and governance must be addressed. The question is simply by whom? The government or by the private actors who participate in them?

The very aspect of alternative investment funds that raises so many concerns with certain commentators and regulators – their "private" nature – can actually provide adequate scope for the parties to construct through negotiations mechanisms to address the challenges that they face. These vehicles are "private" precisely because neither party desires to conduct their business through public-regulated vehicles. This is a choice which both parties elect as optimal to them and their long-term commercial interests.

It is reasonable to look at the "private" nature of the organization for solutions to the unique challenges posed by private equity and hedge funds.

Simply put, the most pressing public policy question concerning alternative funds is, who is the best placed to oversee them? Clearly, certain actions by these funds or their managers will be of such public concern that regulators will need to directly intervene. But what about their other activities? Who should be responsible for the rest of the monitoring?

Just as no regulatory regime is complete and final, no regulatory reform can be expected to totally eliminate the prior shortcomings or gaps. As Saule Omarova of the University of North Carolina has observed, "[F]inancial regulation reform in an era of rapid technology-driven innovation is an inherently dynamic phenomenon. Conceptually, it should be viewed as an ongoing intellectual enterprise, a process of continuous collective deliberation and exchange of ideas, rather than a static set of rules enacted into law at any particular point."

Although alternative investment funds have opted out of many aspects of the financial regulatory regime, their managers, promoters and counterparties are within the regulated sphere. Most instances of fraud and governance failures that have been discussed in earlier chapters have occurred in the context of a fund manager who is registered with the SEC or authorized by the FCA. These entities were well known to their regulators and subject to supervision and periodic review. Importantly, as noted repeatedly in the case of Madoff, accusations and allegations had been frequently filed with the SEC, and the SEC failed to take meaningful steps to investigate this registered investment adviser.

Unfortunately, there will always necessarily be a gap between the number of professionals in a financial regulator with the requisite level of skills, experience and sophistication, and the number of private equity and hedge funds active in the markets and soliciting prospective investors. Absent an attempt to prohibit such vehicles outright, this inability to have sufficient "cops-on-the-beat," especially in light of other investment protection failures involving mortgage lenders, banks and mutual funds, which potentially impact a vastly greater number of citizens, we must recognize that individuals contemplating investing in these funds are both best placed and most motivated to ensure that the vehicles comply with desired standards of governance and investor protection.

The risk of "regulation for regulation's sake" is ultimately that it will lure investors into a false belief that it is the regulator, rather than the investor him or herself, who has ultimate responsibility for the initial and ongoing oversight of a fund and its manager. Rules without adequate staffing and continuous policing will be inadequate to ensure that investors' rights are properly protected. As discussed earlier, the information required to be provided as part of Form ADV used to register investment advisers in the United States, even as expanded and updated under Dodd-Frank, is rudimentary and subject to material gaps. Investors who conduct even a basic due diligence exercise on the fund manager will often obtain much more relevant information than Form ADV provides.

So what should be the appropriate role for "investor protection" in the context of alternative investment funds, especially in light of other competing regulatory priorities? As Niamh Moloney of the London School of Economics has noted, "Investor protection has traditionally been concerned with the defensive protection of the vulnerable investor against unscrupulous market participants."

Importantly, prospective investors who are permitted by marketing regulation to participate in private equity and hedge funds must demonstrate certain objective or subjective characteristics sufficient to distinguish them from the wider class of retail investors. This is not to say, though, that those non-retail investors will necessarily always have negotiating parity with each fund manager. To require such parity as a condition of being exempted would leave few perfectly balanced counterparties to actually do business.

Therefore, it is important to acknowledge that informed investors who can effectively use the legal rights and governance mechanisms already built into the alternative investment fund vehicles themselves can be better positioned in many instances to operate as an effective limitation on fund managers than bureaucratic regulators who may lack the specialist expertise to correctly identify problems and shortcomings, and who must allocate their limited resources and headcount among numerous competing priorities. This realization can then play a larger role in the widening public debate about how private equity and hedge funds should fit within the financial markets, the economy and society as a whole.

All attempts to solve a newly identifiable problem in the financial markets with new regulation immediately re-opens the difficult discussion on the cumulative effect of all of that regulation on the market itself. Simply passing more and more rules does not, in itself, make the underlying problems simply vanish.

On the one hand, additional regulations will often increase the cost of doing business for any affected firms. As a result, such firms may be placed at a material disadvantage either to other categories of firms in that country that are unaffected by the new rules, or to similar firms in other countries that are less regulated. As discussed earlier, private equity and hedge funds are now a global phenomenon that are active across the global financial landscape. Regulating actions in one country (e.g. the United States) will quickly become moot if other key countries (e.g. the United Kingdom, Switzerland or China) do not take similar steps. On the other hand, unresolved problems that exist in a regulatory gap can harm firms by making them less appealing to counterparties.

In either case, however, the outside reach of regulation exists, and cannot be eliminated or ignored. Each new rule extends the scope of regulation incrementally, but does not eliminate the fact that certain parties, instruments and transactions inevitably remain beyond that outside reach. Every regulatory system necessarily

315

has a frontier. And along that frontier, both government oversight and self-regulation are necessary components of the overall regulatory regime.

Although financial regulation continues to evolve and adapt over time, significant extensions of regulation tend to occur in cycles, linked often to the rise of perceived abuses or shortcomings, that are revealed as part of market crashes, whether large or small. The changes to the frontier between alternative investment funds and the US and EU regulatory regimes embodied in Dodd-Frank and AIFMD in all likelihood represent the high water mark of significant reform for some time to come. Other regulatory concerns, more directly related to the causes of, and continuing ramifications from, the recent global financial crisis will rightly take priority in the near term.

Debates about financial regulation ultimately involve complex questions on how best to protect investors from new waves of financial innovation that inevitably lead to further complexities in the financial markets. Judgments on the effectiveness of regulatory regimes, and the individual regulators who police them, must be based on a realistic assessment of what they can accomplish in the real world. Since the trend toward ever-increasing complexity sees no signs of abating in the foreseeable future, financial market participants, from the largest financial conglomerate to the single individual investor, must acknowledge that there can often be a lag or gap between a new innovation in the market and the identification, deconstruction and categorization of that development by the particular regulators with responsibility for that area.

The report ultimately produced by the Inspector General of the SEC documenting the pattern of failure within the financial regulator in connection with the Madoff debacle still makes for sobering reading, especially in light of the number of investigations conducted which failed to uncover the massive fraud. Perhaps the most disconcerting aspect was not the SEC's failure to uncover the fraudulent activities of Madoff itself, by way of its reporting requirements and periodic on-site inspections, but rather the simple fact that when the SEC was provided with detailed evidence of the crime that Madoff was committing, its personnel was unable to perceive and understand that a crime was even being committed.

As occurs with all government agencies, the SEC is also now facing the challenge of staff turnovers. In November 2012, as Chairman Mary Schapiro announced her departure from the SEC, a shadow was cast over the lagging implementation of the signature financial reform effort in recent years: Dodd-Frank. Questions quickly began to circulate within the Beltway over who will be picked by President Obama to replace her, as well as how long it will take a closely divided Senate to conduct a formal confirmation. With a history of missed Dodd-Frank deadlines well established for the agency, the SEC still had considerable work to do. The appointment of Mary Jo White to lead the beleaguered agency is a strong statement of intent by the White House. It remains to be seen whether White will be able to reinvigorate the SEC and continue the push toward greater effectiveness.

The politics of Capitol Hill during the second Obama administration could also significantly impact the speed of further Dodd-Frank implementation, as well as whether any of the more controversial portions of the law are reopened for further negotiations. The adoption of the JOBS Act earlier in 2012, to the surprise of many long-term staffers within the SEC, demonstrated that sentiments about Wall Street have clearly changed from the early years of the financial crisis, at least in the minds of some in Congress.

In his appointments to the SEC and other key financial regulators, President Obama has the ability to shape the direction of the agency in the years to come. He also has an opportunity here to send a clear message to the markets generally, and to investors and savers specifically, about his priorities regarding Wall Street during his second term. Obama must either drive Dodd-Frank to its full implementation or openly acknowledge that the pendulum has begun to swing away from over-regulation and toward a more balanced approach.

A regulatory regime only half-implemented, overseen by a gridlocked agency, is not what the financial markets need right now.

Given the extensive responsibility that national financial regulators have, and the numerous priorities that have been set for them by their governments, it is unsurprising that attempts to regulate alternative investment funds have been largely limited to indirect regulation by way of their fund manager. Additional requirements addressing private fund concerns can be added, albeit indirectly and often incompletely, by existing requirements applicable to fund managers.

Even with the changes effected in recent years by the passage of Dodd-Frank and the adoption of AIFMD, which were discussed in the previous chapters, many important questions concerning their structure and governance remain unanswered by the top-down financial regulatory regime. Realistically, if the global financial crisis was insufficient to compel governments to consider and address all concerns they had about private funds, then it is unlikely that any further extension of regulation will be forthcoming in either the near or medium term.

Accordingly, our attention must necessarily turn to the private actors themselves. Fortunately, where state-based regulation ends, fund managers and investors have developed detailed and elaborate rules among themselves that govern the organization, remuneration, risk management and reporting activities of these funds by means of voluntary, contractual arrangements.

The first decade of the twenty-first century witnessed a steady accretion of self-regulatory initiatives in the alternative investment funds industries. In the hedge fund arena, trade associations promulgated their own best practice standards. In the private equity industry, guidance was regularly issued on a variety of topics that included valuation, transparency and ethics.

Critics contend that these developments were motivated primarily by a desire to avoid top-down regulation by national regulatory agencies. According to Harry McVea of Bristol University, "Even before the recent financial market turmoil, regulators throughout the world were taking an increased interest in hedge fund activities. Fearful of such attention, the hedge fund sector on both sides of the Atlantic sought to head off further regulatory scrutiny by drafting self-regulatory codes of best practice." However, given the narrow and incomplete regulatory changes embodied in Dodd-Frank and AIFMD, the ability to utilize market discipline and private actors to obtain identifiable regulatory goals remains an important means to address those issues involving alternative investment funds which remain unresolved.

As discussed in earlier chapters, private equity and hedge funds evolved largely outside the financial regulatory regime, although often in ways directly related to how and where the regime had chosen to draw various lines of demarcation. The evolution continues to this day, spurred by the desire of fund managers and investors to innovate and pursue new opportunities in the financial markets. As such innovations continue and new approaches are adopted by fund investors, unique concerns will arise as a result, leading to new questions about how these vehicles should be best structured and operated.

In practice, regulation extends beyond the mere issuance of new rules and longer rule books. To the extent that financial regulators, such as the SEC and the FCA, continue to assess the managers of private equity and hedge funds as "low impact" relative to the other supervised entities for which they are responsible, such managers will be the subject of only limited or thematic reviews. In 2011 and 2012, much prominence was given by financial regulators across the world to their increased focus on alternative investment funds and the risks they posed to their investors. What remains to be seen today, of course, is the extent to which headcount and resources are permanently reallocated to the alternative investments space, as well as whether the loss of headcount and resources in other areas results in unforeseen consequences.

The idea of self-regulation in the financial sector has been, and remains, controversial. Self-regulation has been championed by its supporters as responsive, flexible and informed, while at the same time being criticized by sceptics as self-serving, self-interested and ultimately a sham. Some critics have gone so far as to argue that governments and financial regulators who seek to utilize self-regulation as a complement to other regulatory tools are abdicating their responsibility and creating a democratic gap in the exercise of their obligations to citizens. In practice, however, there are a wide variety of arrangements and approaches that can be referred to as self-regulation, and which undermine the traditional dichotomy between top-down regulation on the one hand and self-regulation (in essence, deregulation) on the other.

As mentioned above, industry guidelines and statements of best practice, promulgated either by specific trade associations or by financial regulators (or groups of regulators) themselves, are increasingly being voluntarily adopted by private equity and hedge funds. Their managers want to demonstrate to concerned investors, whether prospective or existing, that their policies and procedures are in line with recognized standards. These guidelines both serve as an educational effect on fund investors and counterparties and establish a consistent baseline for analyzing the operational and structural elements of a fund manager and their fund.

Due to the nature of alternative investment funds as historically unregulated financial arrangements between knowledgeable and sophisticated parties, guidelines can be particularly effective in assisting the industry to continue to develop and respond to issues of common concern without the rigidity and delay (and cost) associated with formal regulation.

There will always be a frontier at which the mandate of top-down, centralized financial regulation ends. It is not feasible in the real world for any financial regulatory system to anticipate all potential outcomes. Further, any claims that additional rules and regulations can in themselves serve as an adequate deterrent to the repeat of such incidents must be thoroughly and soberly reflected upon in light of the systemic failure of SEC personnel to take heed of any one of the early indicators it received of Madoff's pyramid scheme.

To be lulled into the belief that a particular financial reform or oversight agency once and for all rights all the wrongs and secures investors against any foreseeable or unforeseeable risks is dangerous and ultimately counter-productive. Inevitably, top-down systems will apply more detailed prescription to products and transactions involving retail investors, and less detailed perceptions to larger, more sophisticated institutions. To attempt a one-size-fits-all approach could either expose retail investors to unacceptable risks or suffocate the wholesale markets in red tape and unnecessary paperwork.

For those sophisticated investors who wish to participate in private equity and hedge funds, they will need to develop their own framework in which to have their pre-investment and post-investment due diligence conducted. In the absence of public disclosure requirements imposed by the national regulator, it is ultimately left to the private actors themselves (in other words, fund investors and fund managers) to establish such a framework.

Investors, therefore, are left to fend for themselves, supported by whatever rights they can pursue on their own behalf in the courts. The central question that arises in connection with recent enforcement actions and legal cases involving alternative investment funds is to what extent investors had access to adequate information, both initially and on an ongoing basis, to monitor the actions of the fund manager and its key personnel, in order to detect and prevent the occurrence of fraudulent misconduct. Investors in private equity and hedge funds who want to ensure that they have access to the necessary information will need to take steps when negotiating with the fund manager that they obtain those rights prior to writing their first check.

Frauds and other malfeasances involving private equity and hedge funds, whether structured as partnerships or offshore companies, may occasionally occur because a fund was originally established with the intention of defrauding investors. More likely, these bad acts occur where the fund was initially launched with the intention of being a successful venture, but due to unexpected poor performance, engages in fraud to preserve an illusion of success. In either case, underlying these incidents is the need to implement more effective governance and oversight mechanisms within the fund in order to better protect investors over time.

There are clearly limits to the extent which investors can protect themselves from outright fraud simply through reviewing and negotiating legal documentation. If those who are purporting to be independently verifying the documentation are in on the fraud themselves, then there will be little hope for investors. However, at the very least, investors need information that they could have independently reviewed and verified in order to make an initial investment decision and to review investment performance over the course of the relationship.

In the case of the Madoff scheme, it appears unfortunately clear that many investors conducted little or no due diligence prior to handing over significant sums of money. According to Felicia Smith of Mississippi College, "Investors or their professional money managers may not have adequately scrutinized Madoff's investment program for any number of reasons. Madoff's prominence on Wall Street may have obviated the need to conduct customary diligence. Years of steady (but mythical) 'investment returns' may have dulled investors into disregarding potentially troubling signs."

Importantly, as noted in earlier chapters, several prospective investors who conducted due diligence on Madoff ultimately decided not to invest. The importance of this fact cannot be ignored or under-estimated. This strengthens the argument that sophisticated investors who choose not to perform due diligence, but *still* invest in an alternative fund, should be left to suffer the consequence of their actions or inactions.

The question of what constitutes sufficient due diligence is an important one. Such due diligence will often necessarily involve a review by lawyers of the constitutional documents and material legal agreements entered into by the fund, and a review by accountants of financial statements and trading records, as well as good old-fashioned detective work. Often, key personnel within the fund manager will be interviewed, including the portfolio managers and the chief compliance officer, as well as those persons within the fund's administration who are responsible for the valuation of the fund's assets. Current and former investors may also be approached in order to see if any concerns exist. On an ongoing basis, investors should have access (directly or indirectly) to sufficient information to determine whether or not the factors that led them to invest initially in the fund are still correct.

Investors who make a sustained effort to understand and negotiate the key fund documentation in order to provide themselves with adequate information and legally enforceable conduct standards can in effect operate as "deputized regulators" for their own benefit by seeking to better ensure that the fund manager is complying with its various obligations. Since in the real world regulatory, prosecutorial and law enforcement personnel are not unlimited in number, time or attention, there will always be a counter-argument to regulatory expansion that unsophisticated and inexperienced investors should be the primary focus of such resources.

Although the "victims list" of the Madoff affair still to this day makes for solemn reading, those individuals and institutions repeatedly fall into the category of prospective investors who financial regulators have consistently expected to be able to understand the risks they face and make the simple decision of whether or not to invest in a particular fund. The approach of both the SEC and the FCA has been, and remains, that their resources are focused on those elements of the financial system that pose the most risk to the most people.

Many would argue that wealthy citizens should not receive a greater allocation of scarce police personnel and resources to protect their homes and belongings. If they believe they need increased protection, then they should consider hiring their own private security personnel as needed, who can drive patrols down the streets of their affluent neighborhoods as often as they feel necessary. Other neighborhoods should not be expected to suffer.

And some could contend that the exact same analysis should apply to the regulation of private equity and hedge funds.

How can private equity and hedge funds gain the public trust? The question is not as absurd as it might appear at first reading.

Rebranding will need to play a part, almost certainly. Schwarzman's observations concerning the label "private equity" are convincing, and "hedge fund" is a term that has failed to accurately describe its constituency for the last few decades. By explaining more clearly what it is that they are trying to accomplish, the wider world will be able to replace broad-brush caricatures with more nuanced and true-to-life representations.

This, however, is only a first step. A better understanding of how Wall Street and the City of London operate, and why it is needed to overcome the increasing financial illiteracy of this generation, and the next. Without a practical understanding of the basic building blocks of stock and bond markets, there is little hope that most individual savers and investors will be able to follow either the rapid evolutions underway across the financial system, or the debates over the risks they pose to the wider society.

As it stands now, when private equity and hedge funds hit the headlines, they rarely do so for the "right" reasons. A number of hedge fund blow-ups over the past decade have raised concerns over the consequences for the so-called "real economy." Names of now-defunct firms such as Long-Term Capital Management and Amaranth Advisors have become bywords for the possible systemic risks that we could face if a hedge fund is big enough and its bets are wrong enough. Indeed, hedge fund managers (and stories about them) occasionally turn up in the least likely places. In December 2011, three fund managers in Connecticut won the state lottery draw, earning them $254 million off of a ticket purchased at a gas station. Much of the media coverage seemed to infer that the money they won through gambling was somehow more "legitimate" than the sums they earned on their day jobs.

Meanwhile, private equity continues its rescue activities, among companies who are stumbling toward collapse. When a business finally calls it quits and shuts its doors, it is an incredibly painful experience for all concerned, from the employees who may have worked for that company most or all of their lives, to the other businesses that act as suppliers to, or clients of, the bankrupt firm who may now need to scramble to fill the gap created by this failed business. According to Mark Florman, head of the British Venture Capital Association (BVCA), "As key funders of entrepreneurs, as well as established SMEs, private equity and venture capital must not be dissuaded from investing in ... businesses." Sometimes, only private equity money stands between a wounded business and oblivion. Remember the fate of Twinkies!

Private equity and birthday parties apparently go together in a deeply symbolic and important way. For reasons not readily apparent, the big birthday celebrations of leading private equity figures regularly make their way into the news and features sections of the newspapers. Days after Obama's re-election in November 2012, David Bonderman, founder of TPG, celebrated his seventieth birthday at the Wynn Resort in Las Vegas with a party featuring a Paul McCartney concert. The former Beatle was joined by funnyman Robin Williams and rocker John Fogerty. A decade ago, Bonderman had the Rolling Stones and John Mellencamp help him celebrate his sixtieth birthday. Guests in 2012 included Michael Eisner, the former Disney boss, and Hamilton James, the president of Blackstone.

Comparisons to Stephen Schwarzman's 2007 party and Leon Black's 2010 party were unavoidable. Perhaps the industry had finally come full circle.

Private equity and hedge funds do what they do in order to earn high investment returns for their investors. Granted, these funds are not suitable investments for everyone, but those with the means and inclination to research fund managers and their performance numbers seem convinced that there is real talent at work here.

For example, in 2008–09, many hedge funds were forced to close their doors due to a landslide of investor withdrawals and concerns over the safety of investors' money in the short term. Regardless of the dip in performance across the industry in 2011, $67 billion flowed into hedge funds in 2012, with the overall industry thought to exceed $1.7 trillion. According to the analysis firm Hedge Fund Research, the average hedge fund earned about 5.2 percent in 2012. While hedge funds did worse than the leading equities index, the S&P 500, many individual hedge funds did phenomenally well.

Equally noticeable, despite a tough fundraising environment, there was a steady flow of new private equity funds launched in 2012 with over $1 billion in commitments. One of the largest was Coller International Partners VI, which raised approximately $5.5 billion dedicated to secondary fund investments.

With all this good news coming in, sentiment in some quarters in Washington shifted quietly in favor of Wall Street, generally, and alternative investment funds, specifically.

As noted earlier, in 2012, the JOBS Act signalled President Obama's willingness to open the door for more wealthy, experienced investors to put their money to work with private equity and hedge funds at capitalism's "very pointy end." Obviously, chest-pounding concern about these "vampires" only went so far. Some of the investors who take up Obama's offer and put their savings into these funds will be rewarded, while others may lose significant sums. But that pointy end of capitalism is a necessary component that allows the rest of the economy to operate effectively and efficiently.

As has been demonstrated again and again in earlier chapters, there is no need either to demonize or romanticize private equity and hedge funds. Capitalism's pointy end is where they must operate in order to uncover those lucrative returns for their investors. US public pension plans and university endowments continue to depend on these high returns in order to balance their budgets. Post-JOBS Act, Congress has clearly placed responsibility for these investment decisions squarely in the hands of the interested investors themselves.

As a result, these investors must dedicate the necessary time and attention before they invest in order to ensure that they do not end up sticking this pointy end into their own eye.

Epilogue

There will be another financial crisis.

To say otherwise would be dangerous and wrong. Whether it occurs in five years, or in twenty-five years, inevitably gaps in the regulatory regime will be found, and financial firms will again lead the markets, the economy and the world to the brink of disaster. Or perhaps beyond.

Could private equity and hedge funds cause the next financial crisis?

Since no one has a crystal ball, it would be counterproductive to spend too much time tilting at a series of theoretical windmills. The real issue is to be as prepared for a range of potential crises and risks as we can be, while at the same time recognizing that shutting down global finance, as we now know it, is not possible. As private equity and hedge funds will continue to be key components of the global financial infrastructure for many years to come, it is right that they be regularly examined and thoroughly understood in order to ensure that their regulation is appropriate and effective.

In the meantime, the investment management industry as a whole is continually evolving in response to client demands. Private equity and hedge funds are not standing still while we figure out what to do with them.

The underlying rationale of funds remains solid and compelling. As the numbers of both traditional mutual funds and alternative investment vehicles rose over the last decade, one would presume that these managers are sufficiently compensated for their efforts and that their investors believed that they were receiving an added level of performance, net of such fees and other expenses, than they could achieve on their own. What is being bought and sold in the investment management arena is advice and discretion to act on that advice unilaterally.

Unregulated products are generally believed to present more risks to investors than regulated products. However, the implementation of substantive restrictions on, for example, investment policy and concentration would, in effect, eliminate the product. Sophisticated investors, whether individual or institutional, would then be denied access to potentially innovative investment products. Due to the global nature of modern finance, where a particular country decides to put in place impediments, whether tax-related or otherwise, motivated investors and incentivized managers will simply seek out new ways to pursue their particular investment strategies in a more suitable commercial and regulatory environment.

Importantly, the traditional and alternative investment management industries are increasingly interconnected today in ways that were not imaginable a decade ago. In similar fashion, the distinction between production and distribution of investment products is becoming more evident as different segments of the industry attempt to reinforce their competitive advantages. Concurrently with the drive to include alternative investment funds within the product lines of traditional investment managers, the industry is also witnessing the expansion of successful alternative fund managers into other alternative asset classes. As discussed earlier, private equity houses have expanded into real estate and hedge funds, and vice versa. Further, alternative managers continue to expand their geographic scope, both on the management side and the investor side.

These commercial forces are operating to continually reshape both the financial markets, and the Wall Street firms operating with agility and dexterity to profit as much as possible along the way. We must learn the lesson that eluded the Occupy movement. We must broaden financial literacy extensively across society. The failure to do this is having ramifications at the personal level, as well as at the level of public discourse around the future of financial markets and a government's responsibility to protect its citizens from excessive risks.

Many savers today are buying into a vision of the financial markets as a potentially magical source of investment returns. Strangely, the cult of personal finance seems to redouble each time the markets enter turbulent periods. Despite the regular occurrence of catastrophic losses, and prolonged periods of ambivalent returns, self-proclaimed gurus regularly appear on the scene to convince would-be armchair investors that they actually have what it takes to make large sums of money.

We want to believe that simply by saving, we can materially improve our station in life and the future prospects for our children. We want to believe that there are rules to investing that, once learned, can deliver us the answers to the wide variety of problems and challenges we are currently facing. Of course, there are many "experts" who are willing, for a small fee, to expound on the inner-workings of stocks, bonds, commodities and real estate for the sufficiently motivated student. Every few years, new trends and terminologies replace old ones, but the dream still lives on.

Optimism can have a very powerful effect on our evaluation of opportunities and risks. When we need to believe in an ability to pick winning stocks, and outperform the markets, and deliver the investment returns that we need to make up for the numerous obstacles we are facing in modern life, we find it very easy to believe in the advice being sold by experts that purports to do exactly that.

Obviously, there is a role for financial advice in all of our lives. However, much of the best advice is neither new nor innovative. Charles Dickens outlined some in colorful detail in his novel *David Copperfield* many, many years ago:

"My other piece of advice, Copperfield," said Mr. Micawber, "you know. Annual income twenty pounds, annual expenditure nineteen nineteen and six, result happiness. Annual income twenty pounds, annual expenditure twenty pounds ought and six, result misery. The blossom is blighted, the leaf is withered, the god of day goes down upon the dreary scene, and – and, in short you are forever floored. As I am!"

Basic decisions about incomings and outgoings can have a great impact on someone's personal financial standing. Bad decisions about the cost of borrowing, as well as a society that indulges debt as the solution to any budgeting shortfalls (either at the personal level or at the national level) plague large segments of the country.

A certain level of financial literacy, meaning simply an ability to budget effectively and understand the consequences of important choices, is essential. Unfortunately, this term is becoming increasingly debased by attempts to commercialize "financial literacy" into yet another profitable industry. The modern saver must sail between a Scylla of apathy and a Charybdis of faddish trends. Despite the genuine need for informed and appropriate advice, the charismatic gurus who populate the media landscapes are often shown not to be up for the task. With their seminars, books and audiotapes, these men and women are wrapping up in brightly colored foil paper an "American dream" that is becoming harder and harder to obtain, and attempting to resell it at a substantial markup to families often buckling under the monetary challenges they are facing in their day-to-day lives.

Who doesn't want to get rich? Who doesn't want to be empowered? Who doesn't want to learn the simple secrets that will open the door to social mobility?

The global financial crisis that erupted in 2008, and the prolonged recession that has lingered on afterwards, are only the latest in an ongoing series of market events that have eroded many families' 401K retirement accounts. More importantly, perhaps, the collapse of the US housing market further destroyed working-class savings. An asset class previous viewed by many as a "one-way bet," immune to the volatility of the stock market, quickly unravelled with devastating consequences for many families.

Interestingly, when a high-profile pundit's prior recommendations are disproven by current events, further recommendations are promptly offered up and the past mistakes are quietly ignored. Savers, desperate to continue believing in the dream, seem willing to put that bad advice behind them in favor of new advice, however equally unproven. For an example, we need to look no further than two of the most prominent gurus gracing American television screens today – Suze Orman and Jim Cramer.

Orman has built a successful media career around a willingness to reach out to the common man and woman, demonstrating with her Midwestern accent and relaxed manner that she is, in fact, just like them. By contrast, Cramer's show on CNBC, *Mad Money*, comes at you fast and furious, full of testosterone. With his talk radio presentation style, Cramer grabs his viewers' attention and maintains it, while glamorizing the thrills and spills associated with active stock trading.

Salesmen (and saleswomen) have updated their pitches and delivery models to adapt to changes in technology and society, but their central message of the unlimited potential of astute investing has remained surprisingly constant. Orman and Cramer are simply the latest in a long series of media-savvy and camera-friendly gurus sincerely selling their stock-picking versions of the American dream. The rhetoric they use can be very seductive. Saying that you can simply "refuse to participate in the recession" that is dragging down the economy around you is both an intoxicating image of self-empowerment and a seemingly legitimate basis for judging your friends and neighbors who have failed to keep their heads above water.

No matter how you dress it up – whether with late-night talk show pranks or self-help infused, philosophical meanderings – the investment decisions that we make in our lives are very important, and mistakes made along the way can have serious repercussions. However, what savvy investing cannot reliably do for men and women who are not trained financial professionals is magically transform their situation in life. Such transformation requires more than simply investing the money saved from a single grande latte from Starbucks each day, as would-be guru David Bach has suggested in his female-friendly book, *Smart Women Finish Rich*. No Horatio Alger's rags-to-riches story ever stretched its credibility with readers that much.

Unfortunately, there are no easy answers to the numerous problems facing the modern American economy, which are combining to put middle-class families under huge pressure. It is a grave mistake for anyone to believe that there is some panacea readily available for the cost of a $29.99 hardcover book, or a $199.99 seminar held in the conference room of a large hotel chain.

When things unexpectedly go wrong and we are suddenly faced with the loss of a job, or unforeseen expenses, or a serious illness, the solution to these problems will more often than not involve a combination of family members, networks of friends and colleagues, community support organizations and government services.

Budgeting and savings will be crucial. Consistently good decision-making will be essential. But the siren song of gurus and cheer-leaders in the personal finance industry, seeking to profit from the dream of financial security that is escaping more and more Americans, will do little to actually improve the situation.

In the midst of this personal financial uncertainty, wrestling with the particularities of esoteric investment strategies and complex financing structures becomes particularly trying. Acknowledging that private equity and hedge funds, like the global financial markets in which they operate, have a necessary and legitimate purpose does not mean that the real and pressing economic problems faced by millions around the world are any less important. That acknowledgement is simply the start of a larger discussion of the most appropriate government policies to put in place to address these concerns.

In hindsight, it can be seen that many in the Occupy movement had sincere concerns over the real world implications of contemporary capitalism. The mounting concerns and frustrations described above that affect a wide variety of individuals and families should be the subject of critical analysis and debate. Unfortunately, it was also foreseeable that it wouldn't take long for the Occupy protests to become grist for the humor mill of late-night talkshow hosts. Unable to bear the weight of growing expectations and unwilling to commit itself to definitive demands, the Occupy movement soon began to crumble as more and more media attention was focused on it. By Christmas, the movement had retreated from public view, and as 2012 began, its remnants hid from view as the campaign for the White House began in earnest.

The one-year anniversary of the Occupy movement that occurred on September 17, 2012 in lower Manhattan was too great an opportunity to let pass uncelebrated. For one day only the Occupiers returned to reclaim their place in the sun. The celebration had all the traits that we have come to expect from them, for better or worse effect. An umbrella organization acting as a collective for numerous smaller groups with their own agenda? Check. Lots and lots of hand-painted signs? Check. People dressed in polar bear costumes? Check.

With several hundred protesters staging sit-ins and obstructions in various locations around Wall Street, the police on hand were quite busy. It is estimated that well over 100 individuals were ultimately arrested for various acts of public disorder. The media was in attendance and dutifully reported back the efforts by Occupiers to reignite their movement after several months of inaction. Unfortunately, though, the demonstration failed to garner anywhere near the national and international attention that the early protests in the autumn of 2011 were able to muster.

In the greatly reduced number that took part in the anniversary celebration, it was evident that the base of the movement had substantially dwindled. Equally important, it is clear that those who are left to set and pursue the Occupy agenda are the most extreme in the anarchical wing of the original Occupiers.

Where were the tens and hundreds of thousands of sympathetic members of the so-called "99 percent" who were motivated by the early protests to take to the street and join in? Where was the wider coalition of progressives and moderates who formed the overwhelming number of demonstrations when they were at their peak in October and November 2011? Unfortunately, the exceptionally modest turnout on such a symbolic anniversary for the movement forces us to draw some uncomfortable conclusions about the legacy of Occupy. Hopefully, these conclusions will help avoid similar issues when considering difficult questions involving finance and society in the future.

At some point in the historical reckoning, the actual effectiveness of the Occupy protests that first began in September 2011 at Zuccotti Park, in the heart of the Wall Street financial district, will ultimately be what matters most. Much of what has been written and said about these demonstrations has been content to avoid awkward questions and indulge in a much less rigorous analysis. This cannot and should not continue any longer.

The euphoria that built up as the Occupy movement spread out from New York was intoxicating. Austin, Boston, Buffalo and Chicago. Denver, Des Moines, Hartford and Miami. Philadelphia, Sacramento, San Francisco and Seattle. Many Americans concerned about the challenges facing their country, and the escalating pressuring being placed on working families, began to believe that a popular movement was coalescing in front of their eyes which would seek to emulate, at least in part, the Arab Spring protests that had been a recurring feature of news reports for the prior six months.

"We are the 99 percent" became the slogan that galvanized Occupiers from coast to coast, as well as sympathetic protesters in the United Kingdom and across Europe.

As the demonstrations grew, expectations about what would eventually be accomplished by the movement rightfully grew alongside them. The earlier Tea Party movement had a direct and meaningful impact on the structure and operation of the Republican Party, as demonstrated in both the 2010 mid-term elections and the 2012 primaries. It was reasonable to envision that in short order the Occupiers would be able to exert a similar impact on the Democratic Party, its policies and its political machinery.

Except they didn't.

Senior Democratic politicians, as well as high-profile supporters of the Obama administration, went out of their way to provide sound bites of support for the protesters. After an initial period of mass media indifference, the Occupiers eventually began to earn coverage in newspapers and on television. Their message was spreading. People were ready to listen. Social media was buzzing with encouragement for those who had taken to the streets.

Unfortunately, as Christmas and cold weather approached, the carnival atmosphere that had become the dominant theme in many Occupy camps ceased to be enough to keep the movement moving forward. Reclaiming public space was not enough. Establishing free libraries and kitchens was not enough. Providing a real-time experimental case study in communitarian living alternatives was not enough.

During November 2011, the Occupiers held in their hands an opportunity to provide their wider audience, and their elected representatives in government, with concise and clearly fashioned demands that could influence policymaking priorities in the short- and medium-term. It was clear even then that the elections in twelve months time would be frustratingly close. The Obama administration, as well as the Democratic Party as a whole, would need all the support it could muster in order to maintain its hold on the White House and the Senate, and limit Republican gains in the House of Representatives. Occupiers could demand a high price for their crucial support.

Like the Tea Party groups that sprung up after the Obama stimulus plan was adopted in 2009, Occupiers could have pushed their loose confederation of assemblies and gatherings into a structure that would persevere through the cold days of winter and influence the upcoming Democratic primaries in a way that served to embed their demands directly into the mainstream political discourse.

Except they didn't.

The frustrating lack of an Occupy legacy was clearly displayed a few weeks before its one-year anniversary celebration fizzled out in Lower Manhattan. In Charlotte, North Carolina, on the penultimate night of the Democratic National Convention, crowds of Democratic Party faithful erupted in rapturous applause to a speech given by none other than the Great Triangulator, Bill Clinton. What was soon being called the "political speech of the year" roused people to their feet not with progressive critiques of the global economic system or the structural impediments that limit social and economic mobility, but with policy wonkery and focus group-tested charm that was more designed to reaffirm the historical position of 1990s' moderation than to promote a contemporary desire for genuine progressivism.

At that moment, the Occupy movement seemed in hindsight reduced to little more than a particularly transgressive camping trip, open to all ages. It is clear now, even if it wasn't at the time, that you can indeed be too inclusive and too indefinite to actually have an impact on subsequent events. Where were the Occupy candidates in the 2012 Democratic primaries? Where were the policy pledges that could force incumbent politicians onto the record as either supporting or opposing key Occupy demands? Where was the sustained pressure on Wall Street to explain itself and its methods of operation?

Numbers were a correct priority in the early days of Occupy, when it was necessary to get the attention of national and inter-national media. In that initial phase, the name of the game was turnout. As the numbers built, however, it was not enough to let old-school unionists and hope-and-change Obama volunteers and roaming anarchists simply mill about together waiting for a natural consensus to emerge organically and holistically. Unlike in Tahrir

Square, for example, a cohesive agenda never solidified around the Occupiers, uniting the diverse groups and cliques. Without the pragmatism necessary to capture and direct the exceptional enthusiasm that was on display last autumn, the numbers wouldn't be enough in and of themselves.

Many vocal champions of the Occupiers argued persuasively at the time that direct impact on the political process in the current election cycle shouldn't be the end-goal of the protests. The legacy of Occupy in their eyes would be symbols, slogans and processes, rather than actual change. Two years on, it seems as if this view of the protests as an abstract expression of dissent was victorious.

When the Occupiers eventually receded back into their former lives, an awkward silence replaced them in the unfolding electoral discussions and debates. A cynic might say that despite constant avowals that the protests were spontaneous, participatory and separate from everyday partisan politics, at some point when the winter began to set in and some semblance of future priorities had to be agreed, the ad hoc leaders of the movement ultimately balked.

Did these leaders tacitly, if not explicitly, fear an Obama defeat in November 2012 so much that they refused to run the risk of another "Nader surprise" like they witnessed with open-mouthed disbelief in 2000?

Would images of ongoing demonstrations, implicitly undermining Obama's presidency, drive votes away, thereby gifting the White House to the Republicans for four (or perhaps eight) more years?

Just like the Stop the War movement that has studiously kept its head down since Obama's crucial victory in 2008, despite escalating drone attacks under the direction of the CIA which have snowballed so much during the first administration that European newspapers began to refer to America's "secret wars," the Occupiers appear to have been reluctant to risk inadvertently playing the role of Ralph Nader in the 2012 elections.

Without a clear and definitive purpose, the movement quickly ground to a halt as the winter turned into spring. The General Assembly of the principal Occupy group in New York formally disbanded in April. Its idealistic quest for consensus was eventually undone by infighting and fatigue. In the meantime, further banking scandals of breathtaking scale have unfolded in the press, with inconclusive Congressional hearings and frequent hand-wringing by mainstream commentators. The need for a vigorous debate on the scope and purpose of global financial markets has never been more pressing.

Occupy, however, is nowhere to be seen.

Learning to set up a tent or operate a portable chemical toilet can be important life skills that enable an individual to take more direct control over their immediate life, at least for a few days. Having recently begun camping with my school-age children, I appreciate as much as anyone indulging in the myth of self-sufficiency and self-reliance that this experience brings.

Unfortunately, as the fallout from the recent global financial crisis continues to pile up around us, it is becoming more and more clear that in order to effect meaningful changes to how Wall Street operates, a number of precisely crafted changes must be made. Simple rhetoric will do little to realign the allocation of risks and rewards within the global financial system. Regardless of what you happen to think about the Dodd-Frank reform act, it remains only partially implemented, and the much-vaunted Volker Rule remains subject to seemingly endless revisions and concurrent horse-trading between regulators and the large financial institutions that they are seeking to regulate.

The sincerity of many (if not all) of the Occupier protesters is not in question. By participating in the demonstrations and advocating for alternative approaches, these men and women went on record, which is the first step toward genuine political action. As they say, to win the fight, first you have to be in the fight.

Over those three months in late 2011, millions of people across the country and around the world heard their slogans: "Please don't feed the bankers." "Greed is bad." "My kid deserves a future." "The rich can't have everything." "People over profits." "We are not overthrowing a democracy. We are restoring one." Their message came across live video feeds on the internet, as well as Twitter and Facebook. YouTube quickly filled with images of speeches, assemblies, marches and confrontations.

The Occupy movement deserves to be rigorously evaluated and critiqued and where mistakes were made they should be identified and analyzed. I find it difficult to believe that many of those new faces that flooded into Zuccotti Park in mid-October and populated the other Occupy camps across the country and around the world in the weeks that followed had in mind that two years later there would be little to show for their efforts. Expectations were high then, and even if you don't agree with all their contentions and proposals, it seems to do them a disservice to simply explain away their lack of legacy with post-modern theorizing and empty propaganda. They didn't join the demonstrations to be part of a conceptual process-art piece or an extended flash mob. They joined the demonstrations to try to fix things.

When the small remnants of the 2011 Occupiers tried to disrupt traffic at their one-year anniversary, the sense of missed opportunity was palpable. Given the philosophical "big game" that they were hunting at the peak of the demonstrations, questioning the very nature of protesting and attempting to construct an elaborate process that fostered consensus and prioritized inclusion over decisiveness, blocking a few intersections during rush hour seems an excessively modest goal.

Looking back five decades to the sit-ins and direct action campaigns that took place during that time of great social upheaval, it is not particularly difficult to draw lines directly from those protests to actual changes in law and government policy that benefited millions of people in need. The effectiveness of these actions can be measured and assessed. As we continue to sift through the wreckage of the global financial crisis, it is clear that some people acted unethically, other people acted self-servingly and many people acted irresponsibly. In order to correct the systemic problems that underpinned many of the excesses that led up to the crisis and to establish a more solid foundation on which to build sustained prosperity in the future, much intellectual heavy lifting is still required to improve the financial infrastructure. The Occupiers could have made a unique and meaningful contribution to this process.

Except they didn't.

Perhaps now that the final votes have been tallied in the November 2012 campaign and the second Obama administration is well under way, the Occupy movement will have the courage to continue the conversation that it began in 2011. By choosing not to risk being accused of repeating the damage caused by Ralph Nader in 2000, however, Occupy forfeited invaluable momentum that will be difficult, if not impossible, to restore.

With so many of our problems still unsolved and questions unanswered, it seems today a frivolous waste.

Does capitalism need a moral defense? This question was implicitly raised by the global financial crisis and its aftermath, and explicitly by the Occupy movement and its many sympathisers. Private equity and hedge funds, as essential elements of modern finance, are necessarily swept into this query. In an attempt to answer this question, it is useful to look back three decades to another time when capitalism seemed on the defensive, weak and lacking higher justification.

When George Gilder published his seminal book, *Wealth and Poverty*, in 1981, the world was much different from the one we encounter today. The threat of Soviet and Chinese communism loomed large. Japan seemed to be doing capitalism much better than America. Europe was wrestling with the consequences of excessive statism. At the dawning of the Reagan era, Gilder laid out a comprehensive detail-rich series of arguments that attempted to provide a rousing defense of pure capitalism, of the sort that had been lost under decades of government expansion in the United States.

Wealth and Poverty was a highly influential book in its day, studied intensely by those wishing to mount a vigorous defense of the free market, but when its second edition reached bookstore shelves in late 2012, the world had changed considerably.

Technology has fundamentally reinvented the way information and data moves from point to point, both in our day-to-day lives and in the business and financial world. Perhaps more importantly, the last twenty-five years have also seen belief in the discipline of market forces surpass its more obvious philosophical rivals. After decades of stalled growth and the accumulating by-products of repression, a long list of totalitarian states that professed Marxist ideas, but ultimately made do with militarized garrison states, set aside their past mistakes and began taking steps toward open markets. Some even argue that capitalism no longer needs defending, having been adopted as the reigning economic approach by policy makers in all parts of the globe.

But the global financial crisis that erupted in 2008 has given free marketeers a number of awkward questions to answer – questions about how markets operate in the real world, especially when governments and too-big-to-fail financial institutions begin to act in ways that shift losses away from those who have incurred them and onto the backs of others.

Gilder, a moral philosopher at his core, returned in 2012 to revise *Wealth and Poverty* at a time when the "golden years" of the Reagan administration had receded far enough into the background to have obtained an ivory-carved sense of inevitability. The "new normal" that was established during those eight years has not yet been systematically rejected despite two turns in the White House by notionally populist Democratic successors.

Importantly to Gilder, capitalism is much, much more than simply the "least bad" system available to us. Capitalism is something more moral and more effective than the alternatives. The 1981 edition of this book was a key component in the Reagan revolution that was about to unfold. As such, *Wealth and Poverty* will always hold a position of historic importance, which is why it remains such an important touchstone when contemplating how free market economics should best be defended.

Interestingly, Gilders' original opening sentence was stunningly prescient. "The most important event in the recent history of ideas is the demise of the socialist dream." Many readers in 1981 could be forgiven for believing that socialism in the Soviet bloc and across the Far East was alive and, if not actually well, at least stable and evolving at its own internal pace. Today, the sentence needs little in the way of elaboration or explanation. The bipolar philosophical standoff of the second half of the twentieth century is now consigned to history. But the assertion that follows continues to strike an uncomfortably awkward note. "The second most important event of the recent era is the failure of capitalism to win a corresponding triumph."

The fact that the market economy works is not enough for Gilder. As billions of people have turned away from the socialist dream in the past three decades, Gilder wants more than a reluctant acceptance of capitalism. In the face of the Obamacare and the Occupy movement, the Enron collapse and the Madoff debacle, Gilder today believes that he and his supply-side comrades were ultimately too timid in their arguments and their aspirations. "All these years later," he now writes, "it has become clear that we were not radical enough."

To Gilder, the free markets and government operate at the expense of each other. As government grows, the market is stifled and suffers. By expanding the power of the markets, governments will be beaten back to their smaller, more limited size.

The Tea Party, representing millions of Americans disenchanted with "Big Government," seems to agree.

Critics of capitalism are quick to blame free markets for the current global financial crisis, which we are slowly and tentatively coming to grips with. The Occupy movement was able to capture the world's imagination, if only for a short time, in order to make the case that the current economic approach was flawed. Unfortunately, the Occupiers failed to provide any direct or memorable message that viewers at home could take away and actually use in their daily life. As a result, Occupy became distracted and introverted and ultimately ineffective.

Establishing the morality of capitalism, which is Gilder's larger goal, provides an added buttress to the defense of the free market system, which is especially useful when evidence contraindicates belief in the inevitable success of markets. Although many "market failures" can be readily explained away as actually being "government intervention failures," there is an obvious appeal for free marketeers in having a general defense on philosophic grounds, one that provides a foundation for their assertions in these debates.

The report published by the Financial Crisis Inquiry Commission in 2011 laid the blame for the meltdown squarely at the feet of people, not the system as a whole, noting that, "The crisis was the result of human action and inaction." People made certain decisions, or went to great lengths to avoid making certain decisions. These people worked in the investment banks and commercial banks, and in the regulatory institutions. They created arcane investment structures or they entrusted their saving to sellers of arcane investment structures. People made mistakes and now people are paying for those mistakes.

The 2010 Dodd-Frank Act sought to plug holes in a regulatory system that suffered a series of stinging criticisms for the manner in which it failed to limit, or even adequately acknowledge, the scale of the problems that became evident beginning in 2008. Unfortunately, important portions of Dodd-Frank remain unimplemented, or under-implemented, and the SEC continues to fall behind on its Congressionally-imposed timetable for adopting the required rules and procedures.

Making promises in legislation that regulators can't fulfill on the ground, on a day-to-day basis, is perhaps the worst thing that can be done to insure investors are protected. An investor who thinks that a regulator is watching out for his or her best interest, who naively believes that someone "up there" is actually reviewing filings and processing whistleblower tips and following up on red flags that arose in inspections will be deeply disappointed, and potentially grievously harmed, when the truth is later revealed that staff at the regulator were in fact doing nothing like that at all.

When Dodd-Frank was first passed, even some of its most ardent champions warned that delegating so much of the details to existing regulators was potentially a grave mistake. Today, we continue to wait and see what the new regime will actually look like.

When the next financial crisis occurs, as it inevitably must, will it be seen by the next generation of commentators, pundits and think tanks as a failure of market participants to comply with the rules of the road, or as a failure of the last round of government intervention to accomplish what was promised?

One wonders what Ayn Rand, that stalwart advocate of objectivist theory, would have made of private equity funds and hedge funds if she were writing her thick novels today.

Would she portray these champions of hyper-capitalism in glowing terms, as turnaround experts who rescue companies from the brink of collapse and save many jobs at the cost of some painful restructuring, or as financial rocket scientists who are able to identify temporary inefficiencies in the market and take profits from their ability to locate and monitor these brief glitches? Perhaps Rand would now set her book in Greenwich, Connecticut, or Geneva, Switzerland or the fashionable streets of Mayfair and St James's in London.

Importantly, Gilder immediately recognizes private equity and hedge fund managers as new species of entrepreneurs, who have risen up to do battle with oligarchic banks, smothered in government regulations. These funds were among the first to realize that the AAA ratings being hung around the necks of mortgage-backed securities were undeserved. Contrasted with the ignorance that he associates with the large financial conglomerates (ultimately bailed out by the government), these financial innovators look simply heroic.

Of course, not all of capitalism's various faces look equally appealing at first glance. Unfortunately, moving the debate toward larger issues, such as the morality of capitalism and the proper role of government in a free society rarely makes an impact on the next day's news cycle. Ad hominem attacks and inflammatory accusations riddled with words such as "greed" and "tax dodger" are much more effective.

To Gilder, however, capitalism is about optimism.

For those inclined to believe in the primacy of the economic over the political (or the cultural), Gilder has attempted valiantly during his life to turn belief in an economic theory into a wider philosophical system, one that can sustain adherents across a broad array of life experiences. But some observers will find that making secular saints of entrepreneurs and financiers populates a relatively sparse celestial display. In 2013, the goal lines are not quite where they were in 1981, and the force of Gilder's renewed arguments, which were so powerful three decades ago, don't compel the same sort of ground-shaking effect today.

Even someone as repeatedly amazed by the power of the market to allocate scare resources, drive innovation to unimagined heights, and ensure the continued production and distribution of increasing varieties of goods and services, as indeed I am, does not necessarily need to look to capitalism for a philosophy that can be applied across the range of all human endeavors.

The market doesn't explain why I love my three mischievous and exhausting children so much. It doesn't explain why I find bonfires at the beach after sunset so aesthetically fulfilling. And most importantly, it doesn't explain why the best comedy to ever run on American broadcast television – namely *Arrested Development* – was unceremoniously cancelled after just three seasons.[1]

For these important issues (and countless more), we simply must look elsewhere.

---

[1] Special thanks are obviously due to the men and women at Netflix, Inc, the on-demand video streaming company headquartered in Los Gatos, California, responsible for commissioning and broadcasting in May 2013 the new fourth series of *Arrested Development* to an eager and thankful audience.

About the Author

Timothy Spangler is a commentator, lawyer and academic who divides his time between the United States and the United Kingdom. The two decades he has spent working on Wall Street and in the City of London has given him unlimited access to the inner workings of the global financial markets, and the economic trends that that are driving international affairs in the twenty-first century.

Timothy has appeared on CNN, CNBC, BBC and Sky News, and has been featured in *The New York Times*, *The Wall Street Journal*, *The Washington Post*, the *Financial Times* and *The Economist*.

He also writes the award winning blog, "Law of the Market," dedicated to covering the politics of Wall Street regulation and the regulation of Wall Street politics (www.lawofthemarket.com and @lawofthemarket).

When not contemplating the ridiculous and absurd aspects of finance and politics around the world, Timothy follows the rising and falling fortunes of Fulham Football Club in the English Premier League, and beyond.

INDEX